TREASURE

TREA

MAN'S 25 GREATEST QUESTS FOR ELDORADO

Edited by B. A. Tompkins

Designed by Ken Kendrick

Produced by Jean-Claude Suarès

Photo research by Robert Rodriguez

Times BOOKS

SURE

Published by TIMES BOOKS, a division
of Quadrangle/The New York Times Book Co., Inc.
Three Park Avenue, New York, N.Y. 10016

Published simultaneously in Canada by
Fitzhenry & Whiteside, Ltd., Toronto.

Library of Congress Cataloging in Publication Data

Main entry under title:

Treasure.

  "A New York Times book."
  1. Treasure-trove.   I. Tompkins, B.A.
G525.T67   1979   910'.453   78-20676
ISBN 0-8129-0810-4

Manufactured in the United States of America.

To the treasure hunters
who have risked their fortunes,
their respectability and their
lives to look for ElDorado

CONTENTS

1

COSTA RICA'S TREASURE ISLAND

Cocos Island's enigmatic history can serve as a quintessential example of the lure and frustration of the treasure story. Associated with pirate Henry Morgan and a vast store of gold supposedly hidden somewhere on the island by aristocrats fleeing Bolivar's siege of Lima in 1820, Cocos may well have served as the model for Stevenson's *Treasure Island*. None of the rumors of treasure caches on Cocos Island have ever been entirely disproved, and estimates of the prize to be claimed by the lucky treasure hunter (and the Costa Rican Government) range between $8 million and $125 million in gold, jewels and plate . . . if there is anything there at all.

2

THE MYSTERY OF THE SPANISH PAYROLL

After the defeat of the Spanish Armada in 1588, the legend goes, a solitary galleon limped into Tobermory Bay, Scotland, escaping from the British fleet. The *Florencia* is said to have been carrying the payroll of the entire Armada, some $68 million in ducats. Her captain approached local Highlanders for food and took an unlucky hostage, the son of the Chieftain of Clan MacLean. That fiery fellow managed to blow up the ship's powder magazine and sink the fabulous payroll—or did he? A Duke of Argyll nearly bankrupted himself in the 1950s trying to find out.

3

THE LEGEND OF THE "LOST LOUISIANA"

Somewhere in Arkansas, lost among the quartz ledges beyond the conflux of the Arkansas and Big Mulberry Rivers, lies an Indian gold mine. Spanish conquistadores discovered it and worked it with Indian slaves, until U. S. troops entered the area following the Louisiana Purchase. After stuffing the mine shafts with gold ore and the hoard of plunder they had brought with them from Mexico, the Spaniards killed the Indians and vanished. People still talk about the "Lost Louisiana" in the Arkansas Hills. But no one has gotten lucky yet.

4

THE KING AND THE CONQUISTADOR

When Pizarro looted the Inca capital at Cuzco and captured King Atahuelpa, the monarch offered two rooms full of gold and silver for his ransom. Pizarro took the loot and killed the King anyway. He was after bigger game, namely the legendary treasure of the Temple of Pachacamac, and the locations of the mines which supplied the Incas with treasure. Searchers in 1929 found an Inca idol surrounded by skeletons in a mountain pass on the border of Ecuador, perhaps the only clues to the fortune which eluded Pizarro.

5

THE TEXAS TREASURE

A hurricane in 1553 sent the Spaniards' first sizable haul of looted Aztec treasure to the bottom off Padre Island. Unlike other fabulous galleon wrecks, this one has been largely salvaged. But bringing up the gold, in 1969 and 1970, was in a way the easiest part of the salvage. A multipartied court battle over rightful possession of the treasure ensued, involving everyone from the U. S. Customs Department to the Texas Land Commissioner, who protested that while the lawsuits were flying, modern-day pirates were busily looting the treasure site.

6 7 8 9 10 11 12

SAMUEL PEPYS, TREASURE HUNTER

The famous seventeenth-century diarist created a Tower of London legend which has persisted to this day, when he initiated a dig in the Tower's cellars for a golden treasure supposedly extorted by Oliver Cromwell's Lieutenant of the Tower from captured Royalists. The "Barkestead Hoard" may still be there, but the Beefeaters aren't telling.

THE TREASURE TROVE OF VIGO BAY

An epic sea battle begins the story of the largest single Spanish lost treasure on record. British Admiral Sir George Rooke and his fleet penned up a convoy of 17 galleons in Vigo Bay, Spain, in 1702. The galleons reputedly bore pearls and plate valued at $70 million. They were scuttled by their commander after Sir George defeated a French frigate force defending the entrance to the Bay. By 1955 close to $2 million worth of plate and jewelry had been recovered. But if the original estimates are correct, the vast majority of the treasure still lies on the bottom.

THE TREASURE COAST OF FLORIDA

The Atlantic Coast of Florida between Cape Canaveral and West Palm Beach harbors more than launch pads and luxury yachts. A Spanish treasure fleet went down off present-day Ft. Pierce in a 1715 hurricane. Salvage attempts in the early 1960s, spearheaded by the famous Kip Wagner and his Real Eight Company, netted an estimated $3 million in gold and silver coins and artifacts. The salvage brought a hornet's nest of legal battles over permits and rights to treasure trove, but meanwhile chains, crosses, and other *objets d'art* from the find went on sale at Parke-Bernet in New York, one of the most important auctions of Spanish treasure on record.

THE SECRET OF THE BLACK CITY

Half-buried in the sands of the Gobi Desert lies the thirteenth-century city of Kharo-Khoto ("Black City"), once an outpost of Genghis Khan's empire. Its last ruler made an unsuccessful attempt to conquer China, and during the siege of his city which followed, he was supposed to have buried 80 carloads of silver in a dry well. Russian expeditions in the 1920s made valuable artistic and archaeological finds, but the Black City's silver secret remains undisclosed to this day.

THE GOLD OF NEW YORK HARBOR

The British frigate HMS *Hussar* was carrying an estimated $4 million in gold bullion when she went down in the East River during the Revolutionary War. The wreck lies only fifty yards off the Bronx shoreline, between present-day East 130th and East 140th Streets. Although an anchor inscribed with the vessel's name has been brought up, numerous salvors, including the flamboyant Simon Lake, submarine expert of the 1930s, have been defeated in their search for the gold by the East River's notorious currents. Still, it is tantalizing to think that the river bottom may yet yield more than beer cans and the remains of cement sneakered gangsters.

THE BALLAD OF CAPTAIN KIDD

Never convicted of piracy, the raider of the Spanish Main is reputed to have left hoards of pieces of eight at various spots along the entire Eastern Seaboard of the U. S. and Canada. Favorite locations for supposed Kidd treasure include Oak Island, Nova Scotia; Casco Bay, Maine; Thimble Island off New Haven; and Cold Spring in the Cape May peninsula of New Jersey. A road crew building a highway in the 1930s hoped to strike it rich when they learned that the proposed route would take them through "Money Hill" in Westchester County, New York, a rise persistently associated with the Kidd legend. But the wily pirate left no clues, and "dead men tell no tales."

KING JOHN'S LAST CAMPAIGN

Bad King John was forced to sign the Magna Carta at Runnymede in 1215, but that was not the last of him. The following year he set off on a punitive campaign against some of his weaker barons, carrying an immense baggage train loaded with gold and treasure. Somewhere in the marshes of Warwickshire the gold bogged down. The treasure of King John may be only a legend, but it was attractive enough in 1934 to cause a nasty altercation between an American treasure-hunter and his British agent.

13 | 14 | 15 | 16 | 17 | 18

JEAN LAFITTE, PIRATE PATRIOT

The romantic Lafitte managed at different points in his career to obtain privateer's papers from both the American and the French governments, and he grew rich on them. His finest hour occurred at the Battle of New Orleans at the end of the War of 1812, where he fought on the American side in return for a pardon from Andrew Jackson. After that he promptly set himself up as the governor of his own private colony on Galveston Island, Texas. That island remains the most probable site of his fabled loot.

BLACK-BEARD'S BOOTY

Edward Teach may not have been the most efficient pirate of all time, but he was certainly the bloodiest. Swarming aboard the ships of his victims with his beard tied up in red ribbons and the smoking fuses for his matchlock pistols stuck in a circle around the brim of his hat, he terrorized shipping from the Carolinas to the Spanish Main in the late 1600s and early 1700s. His hoard, supposedly guarded by the headless skeleton of the hapless crew member who helped bury it, has been sought from New Hampshire to Florida.

THE NOBLE BUCCANEER

Sir Henry Morgan's life is an object lesson in successful buccaneering. Beginning as a loyal servant of the British Crown in the seventeenth-century wars with Spain, Morgan helped capture Old Providence Island and the town of Puerto Principe in Cuba, culminating his exploits with the famous sack of Panama in 1671. Unlike most of his fellow high-sea raiders, however, Morgan ended his days peacefully as Lieutenant-Governor of Jamaica. The whereabouts of his immense treasure, comprising the golden hoard of Panama City as well as loot acquired during his privateer days, has never been firmly established.

TORY TREASURE

When the Revolution began to turn against the British, numerous Tory sympathizers, whose ranks included the richest families in the Colonies, such as the Dewitts of New York, began to hide money and household valuables to safeguard it from the Continental Armies until after the war. They never got a chance to recover their goods, and there are rumored caches of Tory treasure all over New Jersey, the Hudson basin, Long Island and Upper New York State.

WORLD WAR II: NAZI LOOT AND JAPANESE SPOILS

Immense treasure was piled up by the Japanese and the Germans over the course of World War II, and although much of it was recovered after the conflict, enough remains hidden to justify continued searching. A geisha's tip led to a hunt for the Japanese "war chest" of $2 billion in gold, sunk in Tokyo Bay. Some $30 million worth of plunder from the Nazi death camps was recovered after the war, including the bizarre hoard of Hermann Goering: a vast art collection and a set of "crown jewels." A German fighter, supposedly crammed with "Hitler gold" crashed in an Austrian lake and led to the disclosure of a Nazi counterfeiting scheme.

THE TRUTH BEHIND *TOBACCO ROAD*

When Jeeter Lester dug up his yard hunting for a pot of gold, he was acting out of a persistent Southern tradition that Rebel families buried their valuables all over the South to protect them from Sherman's invading army. Money has been found from time to time, but the chief source of Civil War treasure remains the sea bottom off the Southern coast, where Confederate blockade runners carrying British gold and supplies for the Secessionist armies ran afoul of the guns of the Union Navy.

19 20 21 22 23 24 25

THE STORY OF THE *LUTINE BELL*

At Lloyd's of London, the famous insurance company, a ship's bell hangs in the Committee Room, and has long served as a signal to agents and investors awaiting news of overdue ships. Two strokes announce the safe arrival of a ship feared lost, and three signal that hope has been abandoned. The bell is from HMS *Lutine*, a British frigate carrying an estimated $10 million in gold and silver bullion, bound for Hamburg to shore up a bank panic during the Napoleonic Wars. The *Lutine* went down in the Zuider Zee, Netherlands, and salvagers have been at work on the wreck since the year after she sank.

PAGE 168

THE SALVAGE OF THE *EGYPT*

When the P&O liner *Egypt* collided with a French steamer in 1922, salvage firms at once set out to recover her cargo of £2 million worth of gold and silver bullion, from the waters of the Bay of Biscay. Efforts were unsuccessful until the early 1930s, when an Italian firm took on the job. The salvage of the *Egypt's* treasure, in the course of which the Italians pioneered a full battery of modern salvage equipment, including explosives which lost them their first work-shipis a heroic story of professional treasure-hunting, covered in daily dispatches from The New York Times correspondent aboard the Italians' second vessel.

PAGE 174

RAISE THE *LUSITANIA!*

There have been many schemes for bringing up the famous liner since she was torpedoed by the Germans in 1915, all based on the supposition that she was carrying bullion. No one has completely disproved the existence of a Lusitania treasure, but recent evidence suggests her cargo was more sinister: munitions bound for the British Army. If the story is true, then the Germans, far from being the ruthless destroyers of an innocent passenger liner, as they were painted in the American and British press at the time, had a legitimate wartime reason for sinking the ship.

PAGE 198

FAKES, FOOLS, AND FRAUDS

Three stories exemplify the wiliness of the treasure-bilkers and the greed of their victims. The first involves a laborer who claimed to have found part of the fortune buried by a World War I draft dodger. The second traces the career of a shifty American, Edward Emile Jochen, who gulled a British bullion merchant into investing in a scheme to recover a "Spanish treasure galleon" supposedly lost off the English coast. The third story emerges, appropriately enough, from the depth of the Depression, and it involves mysterious dynamite blasting in Palisades Park, Spanish silver, and a band of "little men" resembling the gnomes of Washington Irving's *Rip Van Winkle*.

PAGE 210

THE QUEST FOR THE *MERIDA*

Several attempts had already been made to salvage the Ward Liner *Merida*, which went down off Virginia in 1911, by the time Anthony Drexell Biddle, Jr. and a crew of New York bluebloods decided to extend the aristocratic passion for clue-and-joke "treasure hunts," then the rage in London and New York, to a quest for a real treasure estimated at $3 million. The fancy yachtsmen's expedition failed, as did a more serious venture in the 1930s, in which rival salvors nearly engaged in a sea-battle over the wreck. Socialites aboard a four-masted windjammer tried again in 1937, but the *Merida* to date has kept her secrets.

PAGE 224

THE CONTROVERSY OF THE KEYS

Two rich treasure finds made off the Florida Keys in the late 1960s and early 1970s revived the battle over rights to treasure trove which had begun with Kip Wagner's discoveries off Fort Pierce ten years before. The principal salvor involved in the new controversy, Melvin Fisher, is a successor to Kip Wagner as president of the same company which made the "Treasure Coast" find in the mid-1960s. As of October, 1978, Florida had failed to make good its claim to Fisher's treasure. But the continuing squabble illustrates clearly, finding the fabled galleon is only the first step in a "salvage" effort in which lawyers descend to the treasure through fathoms of legal documents.

PAGE 232

THE "CONCEPCION:" A TREASURE DREAM COME TRUE

The current story of Burt B. Webber, Jr.'s discovery of the Spanish galleon *Concepcion*, lost off the Dominican Republic in 1641, is squarely in the romantic tradition of treasure hunting. But Webber's long search was nothing if not methodical. Solidly based upon research into authentic documents from the period, Webber's four-year hunt for the *Concepcion* relied at last on a highly sophisticated piece of equipment which pinpointed the galleon.

The technical advances which gave Burt Webber the right tool for his job are revolutionizing the salvage and marine exploration businesses.

PAGE 244

1

Cocos Island, a tiny Costa Rican possession off the Pacific coast of Central America, has been a favorite hunting ground for treasure seekers for over a hundred years. Lying well away from the major Pacific trade routes, and for years visited only by occasional whalers putting in for water, the island seems a logical cache for the old pirates who raided Spanish shipping and ports along the Pacific coast from the sixteenth through the eighteeth centuries. And in fact Cocos is associated with no less than six different treasures, ranging from the paltry $72,000 supposedly hidden by the crew of a privateer-slaveship in the 1830s, to the vast store of loot, valued at $125 million, which may or may not have been carried off by the buccaneer Sir Henry Morgan after his sacks of Panama City in 1671. Treasure expeditions to the island have ranged from the highly organized (and expensive) venture of an Anglo-Irish nobleman, to the hapless voyage of three teenagers in a leaky ketch. The Cocos legend, nourished by tales of old maps and bits of gold and jewelry making their way to the mainland, continues to captivate the modern imagination. Even thrill-killer Perry Smith, as reported by Truman Capote in his book *In Cold Blood*, nourished a dream of using the loot from his own crime to finance an expedition to Cocos. But contemporary treasure-hunters should keep in mind that as of 1932, according to *The New York Times*, an estimated $75 million had already been spent over the years in various efforts to find a treasure most sensibly estimated at $60 million. And, as several expeditions have discovered to their cost, the Costa Rican government maintains a lively interest in its enigmatic possession. Attempts to explore the island without the requisite permit and an agreement to turn over the lion's share of any treasure found there to the mainland authorities, run the risk of, at best, seizure of all equipment and forcible deportation, and at worst an unpleasant sojourn in a Costa Rican jail.

January 31, 1932:
New York Times
Magazine

COCOS ISLAND A PLACE OF FABLED TREASURE

Cocos Island lies in the Pacific Ocean in Lat. 5 degrees 32 minutes 57 seconds N. and Long. 88 degrees 2 minutes 10 seconds W., some 400 miles southwest of Costa Rica, to which it belongs, and more than 500 miles from Balboa, the Pacific terminus of the Panama Canal. It is crowned by twin peaks and walled by ramparts of unscalable rock. Mount Iglesias soars 2,800 feet into the blue while behind it another peak rises 1,580 feet. The rest of the island is 200 to 600 feet above sea level.

Cocos Island is about six nautical miles long and a little less that in width. Its abundant streams and pools of fresh, pure water have been the subject of comment by many brine-drenched, salt-weary mariners. Rain is abundant, and except for escarpments of bald rock the island is verdant and overgrown with creepers and dense jungle. Lime, lemon, orange and coffee trees exist, but the principal food supply is cocoanuts. Wild pigs, descendants of domestic hogs set free on the island by early mariners, are fairly plentiful, but there are no carnivorous animals and no snakes.

Facing Page:
Lonely Cocos Island
in the Pacific has
been a target for
treasure hunters for
more than a century.

AN ISLE OF MYSTERY

Captain William Dampier, privateer turned pirate, may have left part of his loot on Cocos.

Various dates, 1871-1940

THE SOURCES OF THE COCOS TREASURE

Cocos has always defied men who have attempted to break down its secret fastnesses, or maintain themselves for long on its shores. One of the best descriptions of it is by naturalist William Beebe.

"The only passable paths were up the center of the rocky streams which leaped and swirled down from the high interior. Four-fifths of the island is on end, with slopes so steep that the trees are set in at most acute angles. The rain which falls heavily for many months of the year keeps the island as saturated as a sponge, and the squashy yellow clay and dripping vegetation seem seldom to become even approximately dry.

"I walked along shore beneath groves of giant tree ferns whose lacy foliage fretted the sky overhead. Every now and then a silver column of water would appear, falling from high up on the mountains, to spend itself in spray and a trickle over the pebbly beach. The sun came out and the whole island glistened like a jewel with myriad facets."

Into the history of Cocos Island is woven a tale of treasure trove—ingots, doubloons, gold and silver images, jeweled swords and crucifixes—for which many adventurous men have sought in vain, following their charts, maps and clues into the tropical undergrowth. Cocos is jealous of its secret. It refuses to give up that which man seeks.

There are no known records of the island's discovery. It first appears on maps of 1541, and was probably visited by early Spanish navigators who might have been becalmed and drifted thither. Small and easily missed, often veiled in thick mist, Cocos suffered from misrepresentation and was moved about on early maps in a most reckless manner. At times the geographers placed it above the Equator, at other times south of the line; while there seemed to be no limit to its sideslips. For awhile it appeared as twins, the one called Cocos, the other Santa Cruz. The first, and until recently the only chart of its shores was an incomplete map made by Sir Edward Belcher, RN, in 1838.

Despite the geographers' confusion, Cocos is famous, because of its reputation as a treasure island. Conflicting and contradictory reports of various treasures reputedly buried on the island have surfaced over the years, ranging from the prosaic to the luridly romantic, and the interwoven skeins of rumor, half-truth, and downright impossibility which make up the Cocos legend offer an insight into the process by which old sailors' yarns and exaggerations become accepted as fact by otherwise sensible people, simply because they have to do with the alluring will-o'-the-wisp of hidden gold.

It used to be generally believed that the Franco-Spanish pirate Dampier had stocked Cocos with loot taken from the Pacific "treasure coast" of Spanish America. Operating in the brig *Relampago* in 1822, Dampier was supposed to have captured a number of Spanish ships and then set sail for Cocos, where at various locations he excavated sandstone caves, leaving in them a collection of jewels, gold-hilted swords, church plate and gold bars valued at more than $60 million.

Dampier's hoard, which is almost certainly confused with the treasure of Lima and Callao (of which more later), gave way to the tale which credited the bringing of the loot to the privateer and slave-ship *Lark* in the 1830s. One Charles Henderson of Weuseon, Ohio, broke the news, but it was a plain, unvarnished tale with much too moderate an amount of treasure, for only $72,000 was mentioned.

Henderson is said to have been one of the *Lark's* crew. The vessel was chased by a British man-of-war, ran upon a rock, and sank in shallow water off Cocos. The Captain had the $72,000, and he took it ashore with him in a boat containing seven other men, burying it somewhere on the island. Believing all hands of the *Lark's* crew to be drowned, the man-of-war stood away and left the eight men to their fate. All died but Henderson, who was rescued by a passing ship. He made several attempts to charter an expedition to recover the treasure, but took his secret with him to the grave.

The next tale, far more glamorous, is at once the most convoluted, and least improbable one of the Cocos store of treasure lore. It concerns the schooner *Mary Dear* (variously spelled *Deer*, *Deare*, and in one instance, *Read*), a vessel out of St. John's, Newfoundland. This ship, sailing under the British flag, was hired by certain Spanish aristocrats of Lima, Peru, to transport themselves and their treasure of plate, gold and jewelry to a safe port during Simon Bolivar's 1820 revolution in that country.

The story immediately begins to branch out into conflicting accounts. According to one, the Limans first intended to leave their treasure in the Peruvian coastal fort of Callao. But when that redoubt proved less than impregnable, the nervous grandees decided to place their treasure aboard the *Mary Dear*, then at anchor in the roadstead. The Anglo-Canadian crew proved to be villains. They clubbed the Peruvians, slipped the cable and put to sea with a cargo valued at £12 million (1820 value: close to $100 million today).

The *Mary Dear*, fleeing from vengeful Peruvian ships, made for Cocos Island, where her crew had decided to bury the treasure. Boatloads of precious metals and stones were ferried ashore and concealed in a cave with a "natural door." Then the *Mary Dear* tried to run for the mainland and the safety of a neutral port. But a Peruvian frigate, the *Espeigle*, intercepted her, and all but two of the crew were killed.

The names and ranks of the two survivors vary through the accounts. In 1893 a Mrs. Richard Young of Boston told the following story concerning them and the subsequent history of the treasure:

"My father was John Keating, a native of St. John's, Newfoundland, and one of the crew of the *Mary Deer* (sic). After burying the treasure the schooner was captured by a Peruvian man-of-war and all the crew but two were shot. The survivors were my father and William Thompson, who jumped overboard and were picked up by an American whaler. For three years they cruised for whales.

"Then they went to England and secured a vessel, the *Edgecomb*, Captain Boag, and went to Cocos Island and got some of the treasure. Returning, they were shipwrecked near Panama, and Capt. Boag was eaten by a shark. Then Thompson died of fever, leaving my father the sole survivor. My father

reached Newfoundland with $7,500 in gold. Merchants of Newfoundland built a vessel, the *Gauntlet*, and he sailed again for Cocos Island. Putting in at Panama, he was arrested, and he would have been executed but for the intervention of the British Consul. Then he gave up and returned home.

"On his deathbed he gave my husband a chart and directions for finding the place of burial of the gold. Mr. Young went to the island and he found it inhabited by fifty-five Spanish convicts, and he dared not dig. Mrs. Eliza Knight, a wealthy resident of Brooklyn, bought charts and papers of the widow of Mr. Keating, but we have the only correct ones."

Curiously enough, the Chief of the New York City Police during the 1890s, a man named Byrnes, wrote a book on famous American criminals of the time, in which a certain Mrs. E.E. Peck is described as one of the most ingenious swindlers he had ever known. "Mrs. Eliza Knight" was her chief alias, according to Chief Byrnes.

Later accounts promoted Thompson from cabin-boy to Captain of the *Mary Dear*, and maintained that Keating was never aboard the ship, but met Thompson in 1844, while the latter was a passenger aboard another ship. When the pair reached St. John's, the story goes, Thompson went to board at Keating's house. He confided his name and the secret of the Cocos treasure to his new friend, and abruptly disappeared.

Keating then contacted Boag, by now a Newfoundlander who spelled his named "Bogue", and interested a firm of local merchants in the project of recovering the treasure. Using the rough chart Thompson gave Keating before he vanished, they outfitted a ship and sailed for Cocos.

In this version the crew, learning of the voyage's mission, mutinied upon reaching the island, and insisted that all hands should share alike in the proceeds, despite Keating's protests that the outfitters of the expedition were entitled to the greater part. In fear of their lives, Keating and Bogue pretended to consent. But after dark, having supplied the sailors with plenty of rum, they slipped away in a whaleboat. Somehow, ashore in the darkness and in spite of dense jungles and slippery hillsides, the cache of treasure was located, and as much was brought away as the two men could stagger under.

Keating was picked up at sea and said that Bogue had drowned attempting to carry too heavy a load of ingots from shore to the whaleboat. A more gruesome story was circulated later, said to have been based on Keating's deathbed confession, to the effect that the two men had returned to the cave, and while Bogue was inside, Keating, mastered by avarice, had closed the "natural door" on him and wedged it shut with rocks. The story is a good thriller. Believe it or not.

In any case there was a half-hearted attempt to try Keating for murder, but in the absense of a corpse, the case came to nothing.

Keating, however, despite his daughter's rather mild portrait of him, seems to have been a marked man. When he was not shunned as a murderer he was fawned upon by those who regarded him as the possessor of a clue to wealth. A man named Fitzgerald, who won his confidence shortly before he died, received verbal directions for finding the treasure cave, complete with bearings, the number of paces from certain landmarks, and a fanciful description

Facing Page: Though the island boasts a cozy anchorage, its rocky shores afford no sandy beaches for careening ships.

of the "natural door": a cliff that revolved, to reveal the treasure.

By 1926 Fitzgerald's verbal information had metamorphosed into a map, handed by him to British Commodore Curzon Howe and by the latter to his son. This son reportedly gave the map to an expedition headed by Sir Malcolm Campbell, the British "speed king", and his partner Lee Guinness. But the pair returned treasureless from their 1926 expedition to Cocos, and the *Mary Dear* story stops there.

Still other treasures are associated with Cocos Island. The seventeenth century English seadog and buccaneer Edward Davis was supposed to have captured a 36-gun Danish vessel, happily renamed by him the *Bachelor's Delight*, and in the course of spreading the gospel of the black flag, landed at Cocos's Chatham Bay for fresh food and water. He is supposed to have careened his ship there to remove barnacles, taking time off from the task to bury some of his Spanish loot nearby. But the story is doubtful, since there are no beaches on Cocos suitable for such careening activities.

Another knight of the jolly roger, the renegade British commander of the warship *Devonshire*, an officer named Graham who tired of naval discipline and turned pirate, was supposed to have left treasure on Cocos about 1710.

Finally, one of the most persistent treasure hunters of Cocos, a German named Gisler or Giessler, who spent several years living on the island as a hermit, always maintained that the object of his quest was the fabulous wealth of Panama City, hidden on Cocos by the buccaneer Sir Henry Morgan after his raid on that city in 1671. (MARGIN NOTE: SEE *THE NOBLE BUCCANEER*) But he never produced so much as a doubloon in evidence.

Cocos Island still basks in the sun in the blue remoteness of the Pacific. The Costa Rican Government is beginning to develop it as a fishing resort, and it is gradually being drawn into the twentieth century. Presumably the treasure is still there for anyone who wants it. All he has to do is to find it in some thirty square miles of unpenetrated and all but unpenetrable mountains and jungle.

Abundant streams of fresh water from the island's highlands attracted salt-weary whalers in the nineteenth century.

March 26, 1871
RETURN OF UNSUCCESSFUL TREASURE-SEEKERS

The schooner *Fanny* with the last party of pirate treasure-seekers has returned from Cocos Island. They report that no treasure was found. Ludwig Anderson, the second mate, was shot dead while hunting wild hogs on the island, by Jacob Burgi, a passenger. Burgi maintains he mistook Anderson for a hog.

November 23, 1871
THE COCOS ISLAND TREASURE

San Francisco papers announce that a new joint stock association has been organized in that city by one Captain Welch. Its shares have been fixed at $200 each. In the event of success the sum of $750,000 will fall to each shareholder. The Captain stated that he is the only person living who knows the whereabouts of the treasure, and it is not hard to believe that at all events no one else knows of it. He naturally declined to entrust the secret to

his interlocutor, but he hinted that it was in the South Pacific Ocean, and expressed the firmest confidence in the success of his enterprise.

Not a few sharp-eyed Yankee sailors and Californian travelers have roamed over Cocos Island, probable goal of the Welch expedition, but we have never heard of their finding anything but a few rusty pots and pans that might have belonged either to a departed Chilean penal colony or to Alexander Selkirk, the mate of an American whaler who jumped ship some years ago and lived on the island for a long time. Whether he had any eye for hidden treasure or not, he would have had a good chance, living in so small a space for a term of years, to stumble on such a thing if it were there.

November 8, 1879
ANOTHER COCOS EXPEDITION COMES TO GRIEF

The schooner *Vanderbilt*, which sailed from San Francisco on the 12th of April, has been heard from, having arrived at Santa Barbara a week ago with a discouraged, goldless crew. For three months the adventurers toiled under the tropic sun of Cocos Island, running tunnels and drifts, and digging pits and ditches. But their labor was in vain, and as their supplies ran low they were compelled to leave. Once at sea, with provisions very short, it became necessary to seek some port where fresh supplies could be laid in. It was at first proposed to go to Punta Arenas, the nearest mainland port, about 400 miles northeast of Cocos Island, lay in supplies and at the same time try to secure a cargo of sugar cane for San Francisco. But as a strong current sets steadily down the coast, it was resolved to stand out to sea and make as direct a course as possible for home. Calms and light head winds retarded their progress, and everything on board in the way of provisions was consumed except flour and tea, on which the company subsisted for the last twelve days. A storm was encountered, which blew away both the schooner's topmasts and came near disabling her. The voyage to Santa Barbara took 66 days.

Various dates, 1892-1902
THE GIESSLER EXPEDITIONS

Captain Giessler (also known as Gisler), a German-American seaman from Stockton, California, was convinced that the loot of Sir Henry Morgan, amounting to some $60 million in gold, jewels and plate, was concealed somewhere on Cocos Island. He lived for four years on the island in the 1880s, having thrown up his job as commander of several vessels of the Pacific Mail Steamship Company, but returned to the mainland treasureless in 1890. Undaunted, he organized an expedition in 1892, aboard the yacht *Hayseed*, attracting support with a tale of having found, and reburied, a cache of emeralds, diamonds, rubies and pearls. This trip was unsuccessful, and the Captain next appears in an 1895 report, having conceived the grandiose scheme of obtaining a permit from the Costa Rican Government to colonize Cocos. This time he had received information from the Chief Officer of the steamship *Acapulco*, a vessel which had thoroughly explored the island's waters. The *Acapulco's* crew had also performed extensive excavations ashore, using heavy machinery, and Giessler presumably thought they might have turned up something he himself had missed during his long so-

journ on the island.

Armed with the *Acapulco's* information, and dangling before his prospective investors another tale he claimed to have heard from an old woman in Panama who said she was a descendant of the intrepid Morgan, he succeeded in obtaining his colonization permit from the President of Costa Rica. He set sail in the steamer *Costa Rica* with a party of Germans and Americans, which included three women and two children. But the treasure colony quickly grew disgusted with the wild-goose chase the Captain had led them on, and returned to the mainland penniless. Giessler vanishes from the reports after 1902, having contributed to the Cocos legend the history of a man who was either a blindly dedicated believer in the island's golden secret, or one of treasure-hunting's greatest con-men.

Various dates, 1897-1903
THREE MORE FAILURES

Treasure buffs in December, 1897, were electrified by a report that $15 million in gold coin and jewelry, found on Cocos by the crew of the British Navy flagship *Imperieuse*, acting under the personal command of Admiral Palliser, had been safely loaded onto a second ship, the cruiser *Amphion*. But the tale, replete with enigmatic details such as the discovery of a buried slab of granite that had once borne some sort of inscription, proved wishful thinking on Admiral Palliser's part, and he was roundly reprimanded by his Government for using the crew of Britannia's Pacific Fleet flagship for a private treasure hunt, while supposedly on an official naval patrol.

The next attempt to uncover the secret of Cocos was mounted by a team of Canadians operating in the brigantine *Blakely*, out of Victoria, British Columbia. This expedition was elaborately outfitted and carried with it a mysterious "gold-finding instrument", which did not perform as expected. After a day's initial reconnaissance on the island, the instrument was brought out, and the men started working at the spot it indicated. A twenty-foot shaft was sunk in vain, and the instrument was given another trial. It pointed in a completely different direction, and in fact every time it was used thereafter it changed its mind. The *Blakely's* crew returned to Canada somewhat chagrined.

In 1903 a steamer, the *Mariposa*, investigated Cocos in the course of a treasure-hunting grand tour of the Pacific. Acting on the advice of a Captain James Brown, a rumor-mongering seadog in the Giessler tradition, the steamer's party ransacked Cocos looking for the 1820 treasure of the Lima grandees. They found nothing.

Various dates, 1905-1912
THE EARL'S TREASURE HUNT

Earl Fitzwilliam, a wealthy British peer, set sail for Cocos in 1904 in the yacht *Veronique*, the largest private yacht in England. The Yorkshire nobleman, whose estates in England and Ireland gave him a revenue of more than $500,000 a year, was accompanied by Admiral Palliser, who had retired from the British Navy in order to devote himself fulltime to treasure-hunting. The Earl's expedition seems to have been rather loosely organized: his Captain, E. W. Morrison, stated later that the whole affair had been "a merry lark engi-

neered by his Lordship." It did not end very merrily, however. The Earl was determined to use dynamite to uncover the treasure, and workmen were landed to set off a heavy charge at the base of a certain high shelving cliff. The blast went off, and the cliff collapsed on top of the party, burying twenty of them. Four were seriously injured and no one, including the Earl himself, escaped unhurt. The incident threw a damper on the Earl's treasure hunt, and he and his party returned immediately to Southampton.

Mrs. Roswell Hitchcock, socialite widow of a U.S. naval officer and moving spirit of New York's Entertainment Club, whose chairman at the time was the uncle of President Theodore Roosevelt, set out for Cocos in 1906 with a party which included society people, professors of botany, and the intrepid team of Earl Fitzwilliam and Admiral Palliser. Acting on a tip allegedly received from a Klondike miner, Mrs. Hitchcock announced that she was convinced there were three separate treasures on Cocos Island, amounting to some $33 million all told. A Boston merchant backed the venture, and seems to have had a difference of opinion with Admiral Palliser concerning the choice of crew. The Admiral felt that there was grave danger of mutiny unless an all-Chinese crew was chosen; the Boston backer on the other hand was wary of Orientals and put his trust in the sailor men of Gloucester. Only the party's botanists brought back anything of interest, in the form of field observations of Cocos Island's profuse vegetation, which includes rare orchids.

Society treasure-hunting continued to be the rage in 1912, when two British socialites, Miss Baritelly and Miss Davis, outfitted an expedition for Cocos in search of the treasure of a Portuguese pirate variously known as Bombosa and Benito Bonito, who ravaged the Pacific Coast from Peru to Mexico in the 1820s. Bombosa's name has been linked with that of Thompson, the surviving cabin boy of the famous *Mary Dear*, and the Baritelly-Davis voyage hoped to find some evidence of the treasure of the Lima grandees, as well as the loot of the Portuguese pirate. The Costa Rican Government was interested enough in the expedition to send along a company of soldiers, to protect the ladies from possible interference and to make sure that if anything was found, Costa Rica would get its share. But the trip was as fruitless as its predecessors.

Expeditions of varying degrees of seriousness continued to put out for Cocos in the second and third decades of the present century. A mysterious adventurer named Steele who claimed to have unearthed a portion of treasure on a previous visit, sailed for the island in 1916 with a party of four, and was never heard from again. In 1922 Professor Homer R. Dill of the University of Iowa took a leave of absence to hunt for "museum artifacts" on Cocos, armed with the usual mysterious treasure map. This one reportedly came from the widow of a retired seacaptain, James Brown, who claimed before he died that he had helped transfer the Lima treasure from another island to Co-

March, 1906-July 1912
SOCIETY WOMEN ON TREASURE HUNT

Various dates, 1916-1932
THE SEARCH CONTINUES

TREASURE HUNTERS TIRE OF WILD PIG DIET

Representatives of Costa Rica Ask to Be Relieved in Search for Cocos Island Gold.

Special Correspondence, THE NEW YORK TIMES.

SAN JOSE, Costa Rica, Dec. 20.—The legendary Cocos Island treasure, if it ever was buried there by the pirates of the days of the Conquistadores, is still undiscovered, according to the reports of representatives of the government, recently returned from the island and also members of the Cocos Island Treasure, Inc., who had been engaged in the search for six months.

President Jimenez has received a report from the representatives of his government who were sent to the island to reserve a proper share in accordance with the concession if the golden doubloons, silver pieces of eight, jewels and tons of gold and silver plate should be discovered. The representatives of the Costa Rican Government do not feel optimistic and have asked to be relieved of their task, explaining that they were tired of a diet of fat wild pork.

The treasure hunters have killed more than 200 wild pigs, but they have not found any treasure. They have opened seven or eight huge tunnels in Waffer and Chatham Bays where their treasure-finding instrument, the "metalaphone," is supposed to have indicated the presence of metals. So far $75,000,000 has been spent in the work of fruitless exploration, and it was reported that the work would be stopped until the end of the present rainy season, but instructions have been received from the home office at Vancouver to carry on for at least two months.

It also was reported that if exhaustive search convinced the seekers that the treasure never was buried on Cocos Island or had been removed, they would continue searching on Canas Island where they have reason to suspect that treasure has been hidden. Canas is a small island about twenty miles off the coast of Costa Rica at the head of the Bear Peninsula.

COCOS ISLAND GOLD TO BE SOUGHT AGAIN

Another Company Being Formed to Delve for Treasure With Diving Apparatus.

ALL HAVE FAILED SO FAR

Many Expeditions Have Hunted for Reputed Pirate Wealth—Speed King Heads Present One.

By C. H. CALHOUN.

Special Correspondence, THE NEW YORK TIMES.

PANAMA, R. P., April 13.—The long-sought treasure buried on Cocos Island, according to a legend that has grown with the years, is again the object of an expedition that is claimed to be certain of success and includes Sir Malcolm Campbell, automobile speed king; Colonel Leckie, C. M. G., D. S. O. F. R. G. S., and W. S inventor of the Clayto which is to locat the treasure h

The ship just a b John galla land. on th port o Dennis Campbell civilized when this twenty-four mined men a ist in his part. hunting. Sir the prospectus o ure, Ltd., as sayi ure-searching as a legitimate pursuit.'

To one who has se ing expeditions go to Cocos Island for twe that statement suggest of "especially in times and unemployment." It that the ship Riverdale British auspices, set out t the plate, doubloons, rare pieces of eight, patacones an have you of Cocos Island.

COCOS ISLA
A Tiny Tropi
By Ma

COCOS ISLA
ing to the
Now, as
very n
myster
has been
the days
when, le
from
there

WOMAN TO HEAD SEARCH FOR $33,000,000 TREASURE

Mrs. Roswell Hitchcock Will Sail to Cocos Island.

MANY FAILED BEFORE HER

A Boston Merchant Backing the Expedition—Search to be Directed by a Miner.

Mrs. Roswell D. Hitchcock said yesterday afternoon at the Hotel Cambridge that she expects in the early Summer to head an expedition to the Island of Cocos, which lies about 600 miles southwest of Panama, and where it has been lieved for many years that a vast ure is buried. She believes it $33,000,000. There have be ditions in search of t' but nobody has Even the Cost said to be c sentative raiso

---

Cocos Treasure Hunters Reported Near Mutiny

Special Cable to THE NEW YORK TIMES.

PUNTARENAS, Costa Rica, Sept. 19.—The treasure ship Veracity sailed for Cocos Island today carrying a contingent of Costa Rican police to rel' he guard that has be there for six m ported that s ers on C verge n

---

British Treasure Hunter To Be Sued by Costa Rica

Special Cable to THE NEW YORK TIMES.

SAN JOSE, Costa Rica, May 29.—The Government of Costa Rica has instructed its Consul neral at London to bring suit Treasure Recovery, Ltd., stock company, for hire and other in evacuating ters from of

---

A PLACE OF FABLED TREASURE
aradise in the Pacific Which Has Been Scoured
Search of the Loot of the Old Buccaneers

rain call-
re hunters.
ries past, its
sts adven-
remoteness. It
Eldorado since
Conquistadores,
it, the rich loot
thedral was hidden
buccaneer. Many
d seekers of gold who
its green jungle in
undaunted by past disap-
three more expeditions
Vancouver, B. C.,
xpected to voy-
to search
eru, of

the blue while behind it another
peak rises 1,580 feet. The rest of
the island is 200 to 600 feet above
sea level.

Cocos Island is about six nautical
miles long and a little less than that
in width. Its abundant streams and
pools of fresh, pure water have
been the subject of comment by
many mariners. Rain is abundant,
except for escarpments of bald rock
the island is verdant, and overgrown with creepers and dense
jungle. Officers of the United States
gunboat Sacramento, on their recent visit, report having seen lime,
lemon, orange and coffee trees, but
the principal food supply is cocoanuts. Wild pigs, descendants of
gentle hogs set free on the island
mariners, are fairly plenti-
Malcolm

vious career of Thompson that they
should have known, for he put to
sea, and at night, while his passengers were asleep, he and his crew
murdered them all, tossed the bodies
overboard, cleaned ship and then
headed for Cocos Island. He hid
his precious cargo there, according
to the story which has survived,
in a cave with a natural door,
then sailed south, but had the bad
luck to run afoul of the frigate
Espiegle. Thompson and one other
member of the crew were spared
upon their promise to reveal the
hiding place of the loot. The rest
of the men were executed.

The frigate went to Cocos Island,
but before landing its crew to the
precious cave Thompson and his
companion managed to escape into
the jungle. Without any clue to
the treasure, the frigate sailed away.
Weeks
later a whaler, putting in at
the island for water, re
cued the two fugitives
an emaciated condit
Thompson's compa
died at sea soon aft
the old reprobate
lved to reach N

cos in 1850, aboard his schooner *Sea Foam*. The story, and the map, proved to be fakes.

Nothing daunted, a party of sixty British scientists in 1924 were diverted from their serious scientific investigations of the South Pacific to hunt for Morgan's treasure on Cocos. One of their scientific colleagues, the Balboa Heights correspondent of the *Medical Journal and Record*, rapped them soundly for "believing in fairies." And for all the treasure they found, they might have been hunting for fairy gold indeed.

A list of "treasure-seeking vessels" discovered by the naturalist William Beebe while on Cocos as the head of a New York Zoological Society scientific expedition to the Pacific, was put into perspective by the curator of the New Bedford Whaling Museum, Arthur C. Watson. In a letter to The New York Times written in July, 1926, he stated:

"As a matter of fact the names (Beebe) copied so industriously are mostly those of whaleships well known in the records of the Whaling Museum . . . The whalers all went to Cocos for water, which was usually unobtainable at the Galapagos (Islands), about which much of their whaling was done. They were not wasting their time digging holes. Their treasure was all about them in blowing, spouting sperm whales, and there were nearly 700 vessels in the fleet during the period under consideration."

Expeditions continued to set out for the island, despite the record of total failure, and in 1931 the Costa Rican Government granted the exclusive privilege of searching for treasure on Cocos and in the adjacent waters, to the Clayton Metalphone Company, Ltd., of Vancouver, British Columbia. The company, which had allegedly used its Metalphone to locate metals buried in forty feet of earth and rock, lent the device to the Cocos Island Treasure Company, Ltd., also of Canada, in return for a share in any treasure found. For the first time a scientific approach and the methodology of professional, heavily capitalized salvage were to be brought to bear upon the enigma of Cocos Island.

February 22, 1932-
March 1, 1933
LECKIE AND THE "SILVER WAVE"

Colonel J. E. Leckie, the Canadian leader of the Clayton Metalphone-Cocos Island Treasure Company expedition, sailed from Vancouver on February 22nd, 1932, on board the small motor vessel *Silver Wave*, a United States ship which had seen service in the Arctic before being chartered for the treasure hunt. Although two rival expeditions were reported to be on the same search, one from New York and the other from Liverpool, Leckie claimed absolute right to the property by virtue of his concession from the Costa Rican Government. Leckie was accompanied by W. S. Clayton, the inventor of the Clayton Metalphone which was supposed to locate the treasure, and Sir Malcolm Campbell, holder of the world land speed record at the time. Sir Malcolm had made a trip to Cocos himself in 1926, guided by a mysterious map supposedly handed down to him from John Keating, who may or may not have been a member of the crew of the *Mary Dear* (see above). Sir Malcolm's first trip ended in failure, and he was eager to try again, this time substituting an impressive-looking scientific instrument for

his romantic old parchment charts. He was quoted in the prospectus of Cocos Island Treasure, Ltd., as saying "I regard treasure-searching as a praiseworthy and legitimate pursuit." To which may be added, considering the year of the expedition, "especially in times of depression and unemployment."

Cocos Island Treasure, Ltd. offered to the public 40,000 shares at $2 each. Its prospectus explained that if only (sic) $100 million was found, there would be $600 for every $2 share, after the Costa Rican Government had been paid its share. It carefully covered itself against charges of fraud by the following statement: "The treasure hunt . . . will be under the direction of men of honesty, men of integrity, men who will play the game. But it is all a speculation or venture, and Cocos Island Treasure, Ltd. shares are not offered or recommended by us as an investment."

An initial report from the expedition, made in July, suggested that Captain Graham's *Devonshire* treasure (see above) had been located by the Metalphone, at a spot eighteen by twelve feet in the bed of Wafer Creek on the island. This report was quickly denied by Leckie, whose wireless operator added, in the course of a conversation with the radio operator of the United States Naval Reserve Station at Balboa, Canal Zone, "How did anybody ever get the notion we would ever find anything on this god-forsaken island?"

By the end of July the expedition was running short of supplies, and were subsisting on a diet of wild pig and cocoanuts. A member of the expedition, Lieutenant Denis Rooke, abandoned the hunt and returned to Costa Rica with reports of dissension among the ranks of the treasure-seekers. Officials of the Costa Rican Government, sent along to guarantee Costa Rica's intersts, were openly grumbling about their diet of wild pig, and although eight huge tunnels had been opened up along Wafer Creek and Chatham Bay, the hunters had found nothing, despite promising readings from the Metalphone.

One of the expedition's supply vessels, the yawl *Vigilante*, sent to Balboa in October for supplies, had to be rescued at sea on the return voyage. Leaking badly and out of fuel oil, unable to make progress against head winds, the *Vigilante* was rescued by the steamer *Susan Luckenback* and later towed to Frailes Island off Balboa by a United States Navy ship, the *Nokomis*.

The loss of the *Vigilante* was the last straw for the Leckie expedition, and he and the Cocos Island Treasure Company abandoned the search, leaving behind them a vast network of excavations as a testimony to the most thorough treasure hunt to date on Cocos Island. What happened to the maddening Metalphone is not recorded.

Members of another Cocos Island expedition arrived in Balboa, Canal Zone, today in the schooner *Franklyn Bennett* with the owner and leader, E. U. Valentine, New York writer, aboard. The party spent a month on the island. All were reticent about the object of the visit. They found traces of work by the Cocos Island Treasure, Ltd. expedition which abandoned the island several months ago after a fruitless search. Mr. Valentine's son,

June 12, 1933
NEW YORK MEN LEFT TO LIVE ON WILD HOGS

Ronald, a scientist, and Stanley Lewers, an engineer, were left behind on the island.

The schooner may remain in Balboa and return to the island or the pair may be left there to await the arrival of a yacht or tuna fishers to take them off.

"We have planted beans and other vegetables and they have guns and ammunition," said Mr. Valentine. "Wild pigs still are numerous on the island. They will not starve."

*September 16-
November 14,
1934*

THE CRUISE OF THE "QUEEN OF SCOTS"

A British expedition organized by S. MacFarlane Arthur and financed by Treasure Recovery, Ltd., which claimed to have taken over the treasure-seeking rights on Cocos from the defunct Cocos Island Treasure Company, Ltd., set sail for the island in the 600-ton vessel *Queen of Scots* on September 16th, 1934.

"This is the first scientific treasure hunt," said Mr. Arthur, who had already spent ten months on Cocos. "Our experts will tackle it as an engineering problem. We are using an airplane for survey purposes."

Stratford D. Jolly, one of the organizers, further stated, "There are about five separate treasures on the island, buried by pirates who robbed the Spanish Main. They may be worth anything up to £25 million." The fact that the Spanish Main lies in the Caribbean and Jolly's hypothetical pirates would have had to round Cape Horn in order to hide their treasure on Cocos does not seem to have occurred to the organizers of the expedition.

In any case, the expedition set out, capitalized at $375,000. Jolly's original estimate quickly dropped to a conservative $30 million, and the treasure party swore an oath of secrecy by which the discovery, if made, would not be revealed until the group reached England.

Unfortunately, Treasure Recovery, Ltd. based its title to treasure-seeking rights on Cocos on a dispute concerning Costa Rica's ownership of the island. In its prospectus the company maintained that according to a 1900 boundary commission, Costa Rica had no claim on any territory lying seaward of its Coiba Island, which is located immediately off the Costa Rican coast.

Costa Rica disagreed. In October, 1934 a Costa Rican military force landed on Cocos and took the 18 members of the Jolly expedition into custody without a fight. The Costa Rican Foreign Minister later stated that the party had been warned before leaving London that its venture was unauthorized and illegal. The Costa Rican Government's policy was, and is, that although it is skeptical of the Cocos treasure legend, anything found on the island must be shared with Costa Rica according to the terms of a permit or lease agreed upon between the nation and the treasure-seeking party before the latter lands on what is, despite Treasure Recovery, Ltd.'s feelings to the contrary, Costa Rican territory.

The eighteen British treasure hunters were deported after a trial for smuggling and illegal invasion. Their valuable equipment, including a radio station, an electric plant, a refrigerator and firearms, were confiscated. Al-

Cocos Island is a lonely dot in the Pacific Ocean some 400 miles southwest of Costa Rica.

though leaders of the expedition threatened to lodge a suit against the Costa Rican Government for the confiscation, which left the party with only their clothes and personal effects, by November 14th the party was on the way back to England, restricted to the *Queen of Scots* by immigration authorities.

TREASURE RECOVERY, LTD. TRIES AGAIN

The diehard British concern mounted a fresh expedition in 1935. This time it was headed by Commander Frank Worsley, who had accompanied the Shackleton expedition to the Antarctic. Worsley commanded a small (45-ton) converted fishing boat, the ingenuously-named *Veracity*. Eric Hankey, Treasure Recovery Ltd.'s new chairman, boosted the estimate of treasure on Cocos to $125 million, an all-time high for the legend. Shares were sold in the company all over England, based on the representation of one Bergmans, a mysterious Belgian who claimed to know the exact location of the hoard.

The *Veracity*, crammed to the scuppers with experts and equipment, set sail. A geologist, two "electrical prospecting engineers" (shades of the Clayton Metalphone!), a drill operator and a motion picture crew accompanied the party. To prevent a recurrence of the *contretemps* with the Costa Ricans which had resulted in the deportation of the first expedition, Hankey claimed he had made an agreement with that government, by which the latter agreed to return the confiscated equipment and grant Treasure Recovery, Ltd. a limited treasure-hunting permit, in return for a payment of $5,000 to cover the cost of ousting the first party from Cocos, plus one third of whatever the second might find. The expedition was also accompanied by a band of armed Costa Rican police and a government radio operator, to keep everything aboveboard.

Upon arrival at Cocos in June, 1935, the expedition found four American treasure-hunters from San Diego, who had been marooned when their sloop the *Skukum*, burned the previous April. Several tuna fishermen who had stopped at the island in the interim had offered to take the castaways off, but they were infected with treasure fever and refused to leave, despite their semi-starved condition. The Costa Rican police contingent arrested them and sent them back to the mainland for deportation.

Meanwhile Treasure Recovery, Ltd.'s search proceeded. But in Costa Rica a Congressman charged that the concern was using the name of the Costa Rican Government illegally to sell shares in the venture in England. He alleged that the company's operations in London were fraudulent, and he urged the President of Costa Rica to cancel its concession.

As time went by the Costa Rican police assigned to the island began to complain about lack of supplies. Hired members of the *Veracity*'s crew grumbled about their pay, by now four months overdue. Finally, word came from the expedition's chief backer in London that the *Veracity*'s charter had been cancelled, because the balance of £500 was overdue. The ship was duly sailed back to the mainland, leaving the hungry policemen and only two British members of the expedition on Cocos Island.

Wilier heads than the hapless treasure-hunters left on the island had remained behind in Costa Rica. S. M. Arthur, one of the organizers of the

FDR successfully brought home "treasure", in the form of marlin, mako and other game fish, from the waters off Cocos in the 1930s.

President Roosevelt aboard his "fishing skiff": the cruiser U.S.S. *Lang*.

first Treasure Recovery, Ltd. expedition (see above), and a certain Hardy MacMahon, admitted to increasingly suspicious Costa Rican authorities that of the £40,000 subscribed by the British public for the venture, only one-tenth had been spent on the voyage, the remainder going for "administration" in London.

Costa Rica had had enough. The hungry policemen were rescued and the two remaining Britons, abandoned by their promoters, were repatriated to England as "destitute British subjects." The enigmatic Bergmans, whose so-called exact information had refueled Treasure Recovery, Ltd. for a second try, disappeared in Jamaica.

The slippery operators of the scheme were last reported, in May 1936, to be facing a suit for $2,000 brought against them by Costa Rica for launch hire and other expenses involved in evacuating the remnants of the expedition from the island. Thus ended the last major Cocos treasure hunt. Minor efforts, mostly amateur, to recover the legendary loot persisted, but Treasure Recovery, Ltd.'s two schemes stand as the high water mark of treasure fever associated with the island.

Admiral Claude C. Bloch, Commander-in-Chief of the United States Fleet, instructed all navy craft along the Pacific Coast today to keep watch for the ketch *Tira*, believed to be carrying three Santa Cruz, California youths. The youths were said to be bound for Cocos Island on a pirate treasure hunt. The $20,000 ketch, owned by Lew K. Foote, disappeared with the boys last Thursday.

May 30, 1938
SEEK YOUTHS ON TREASURE HUNT

Unreported for two days since its radio became silent, the sixty-seven foot ketch *Spindrift*, carrying a treasure-hunting crew of eight men and one woman, was the object of an appeal today by the United States Hydrographic Office to ships between Southern California and Panama. Sidney Field, Costa Rican consul, announced on January 5th that the *Spindrift* expedition had sent word that it had found on Cocos Island the $60 million "loot of Lima." An air-mail letter to Mr. Field late in December stated that the ketch was returning to Newport Beach for power equipment with which to dig up the treasure.

Mr. Field said it was "rather early to become alarmed."

January 10, 1940
FEAR FOR TREASURE SHIP

President Roosevelt, aboard the *U. S. S. Lang*, explored the fishing grounds off Cocos Island today, combining trolling with reviews of stories about the famous Costa Rican treasure island. From a whale boat, where he fished for sailfish, the President could see the hills where expeditions have sought to unearth treasure believed to have been buried in past centuries and estimated to be worth $20 million to $40 million (sic).

Although a Californian named Davenport recently searched for treasure

February 24, 1940
PRESIDENT ROOSEVELT SPINS YARN OF TREASURE

27

with permission of the Costa Rican Government and was reported without confirmation to have discovered evidences of its existence, the island was uninhabited when the President arrived.

The President's visit here was his fourth. He fished these waters in 1934, 1935-1936 and 1937. He stressed that although the cruise is in the nature of a vacation, it also included the business of investgating long-range defense sites for the Pacific approaches to the Panama Canal.

February 24, 1949
"LOST LOOT OF LIMA" REPORTED

Ellis Patterson, who sailed from Los Angeles on January 21st with the 444th expedition to search for Cocos Island treasure, returned by plane last night. He said that James A. Forbes 4th, leader of the expedition, claimed that with the aid of metal detectors, he had located the fabled "Lost Loot of

Landfall at Cocos, taken from the *Bolivar*, which carried American treasure-hunters on the 445th expedition to the island in 1949. The ship was named for the great South American liberator whose revolution in the 1820s caused frightened Spanish grandees to flee Lima with their precious plate and gems.

"Lima", estimated to be worth $50 million (sic), or, at least, "a deposit of metal underground."

Mr. Patterson, a former Lieutenant Governor of California, said 150 tons of excavating equipment, now aboard a remodeled landing craft, was to be unloaded on Cocos by next weekend, and soon afterwards the digging should start.

No further reports reached *The New York Times* from the expedition. If Forbes found anything, he kept it to himself. In all probability, however, this venture, like its 443 predecessors, came to nothing. Cocos Island keeps its secrets. It is possible that when the Costa Rican Government begins developing the island as a fishing resort, a new wave of treasure fever will strike. But until that time the island will continue wrapped in its mysteries, the quintessential object of man's most persistent quest for Eldorado.

Tobermory Bay on Scotland's west coast may be the grave of the richest treasure galleon of Spain's 1588 Armada.

Various dates, 1912-present

THE FATE OF THE "FLORENCIA"

Facing Page: Stores of gunpowder and "Greek fire" carried in the holds of the wooden ships of the period made them floating tinder boxes.

One of the most famous authentic treasure wrecks in history lies deep in silt at the bottom of Tobermory Bay, off the Island of Mull on the west coast of Scotland. The vessel, a Spanish galleon variously identified as the *Duque de Florencia* and the *San Juan Bautista*, went down in the aftermath of Sir Francis Drake's victory over the Spanish Armada in 1588. Surviving ships of the Armada, fleeing south along the Scottish coast, were battered by a severe storm, and more than sixty of them piled up on the rocks. Scots highlanders killed most of the crews. According to tradition, the *Florencia*, carrying the fleet's payroll, enough to pay the Armada's entire complement of 30,000 soldiers, was sunk "by treacherie" in the course of an altercation between her Captain and the Chief of Clan MacLean, who at that time claimed Mull and the land around Tobermory Bay as part of his domains.

Since salvage attempts began in 1661, various artifacts, including Spanish silver medallions and a bronze cannon signed by Benvenuto Cellini, have been brought up. But despite the best efforts of the Duke of Argyll, whose family has hereditary title to the wreck and its cargo, and who sponsored an expensive Royal Navy salvage operation in the 1950s, the legendary payroll, estimated at between $68 million and $84 million in gold ducats, has yet to be found.

After Drake's rout of the Armada, the fleet attempted to escape by rounding the northern coast of Scotland and sailing south for the Irish Sea and St. George's Channel. But a succession of violent storms struck the fleeing vessels and scattered their wreckage all along the shores of Scotland and Ireland. Of the 129 large ships that left Spain, only 54 reached home again.

One ship, the 1,400-ton Florentine galleon *Duque de Florencia*, part of a contingent contributed to the Armada by that Italian city's ruler, was rumored to have been carrying the Armada's entire payroll, plus (an ironic touch) a jewelled crown sent by the Pope, with which Philip II of Spain was to be crowned King of England. The ship, named in Armada commander Medina-Sidonia's roster as "El Galeon del Gran Duque de Florencia de Nombre San Francisco", was under the command of a captain named Andres Pereira. Escaping the storms which had decimated the rest of the fleet, she sought shelter in Tobermory Bay, in the lee of the Isle of Mull, then part of the domains of the MacLeans of Morven.

According to one account, the tempestuous Chieftain of Clan MacLean was by no means sympathetic to the English cause at the time. Hoping to take advantage of the disorganization of English authority brought about by the Spanish wars, he made a deal with Pereira. In return for enough stores and provisions for the *Florencia's* long voyage home, the Spanish captain agreed to lend his vessel, his guns and his crew to MacLean, who wished to settle some old scores with rival clans in the area, and extend his personal holdings. With Pereira's help MacLean laid waste the Isles of Rhum and Eigg to the north of Mull. Then the Spaniard called for his payment.

MacLean, his eyes on another target, Ardnamurchan, insisted that the campaign be continued. Pereira refused, and, furious, strode to his ship.

The Ninth Duke of Argyll, who continued his grandfather's search for the *Florencia* in the late seventeenth century, employing divers with rudimentary breathing helmets for undersea work.

MacLean's son Donald, arguing hotly, followed him aboard. The enraged Spaniard pulled up anchor and sailed away.

But Donald MacLean would serve as no man's hostage. He rushed below, threw a lighted torch into the powder magazine, and blew the ship, the crew and himself to kingdom come.

Thus much the legend. Scholars in recent times have objected to it, stating that there is no proof that the wrecked galleon is in fact the *Florencia*. It seems more probable, according to some opinions, that the vessel was one of seven smaller ships, all named *San Juan Bautista*, which sailed in the Duke of Medina-Sidonia's squadron and never reported back to Spain. Some historians doubt that the Spanish payroll amounted to as much as the 30 million gold ducats cited in the treasure legend. Further, say the skeptics, even if the payroll was as valuable as believed, it is unreasonable to suppose that the Spanish would have entrusted the entire hoard to a single lumbering galleon, in view of the disastrous demonstration they had just been given of the superior speed and maneuverability of Drake's warships.

Evidence that the wreck in Tobermory Bay is indeed the fabulous payroll ship rests on two stories exhaustively researched by the Duke of Argyll, who mounted the last major salvage effort in the 1950s. The first, from the archives of the Argyll family, relates that in 1611 the Seventh Earl of Argyll was traveling in Spain and met Andres Pereira himself, the Captain having miraculously escaped the destruction of his ship and returned home. Pereira gave the Earl some advice:

"Buy the sunken ship lying off the Scottish coast. Her belly holds an unimaginable fortune."

The second story comes from a man named Archibald Miller, who claimed to have made several dives onto the wreck in a primitive diving bell, from 1661 to 1680. In 1683 he wrote a letter asking James, Duke of York, for funds to continue the diving effort. The letter, now in the Bodleian Library in Oxford, states:

"I saw one paper of Lattin extracted out of the Spanish records that there was thirty millions of cash on Board the said shippe." The cash, Miller added, "is under ye sell of the Gunroome."

Based on this evidence, the Argyll family has been searching for the treasure since the seventeenth century. King Charles I gave the Earl of Argyll a grant to the vessel in 1641, reserving 1% of anything recovered for the Crown. In 1950 the British Admiralty upped the Government cut to 11%. But even at that, the bulk of the treasure would fall to the Argylls, and since dives on the wreck have indeed yielded authentic Spanish artifacts of the Armada period, the family has gone on searching. That there is indeed a wreck in the silt of Tobermory Bay, and that she is of the right vintage to have been a galleon of the Armada, has been established beyond reasonable doubt. That she is the legendary *Florencia* is still moot, and the answer will have to wait for the next salvage attempt. If the current generation of Argylls remain faithful to their family's three-hundred-year-old treasure tradition, the attempt will be an Argyll effort, despite the vast sums the Duke spent fruitlessly twenty-five years ago.

One of the most romantic of present-day adventures in search of treasure is the attempt to recover the great amount of gold that is known to lie in the wreck of a large Spanish galleon, one of the vessels of the Great Armada, that was sunk off Tobermory, Scotland.

This is the fourth season that a treasure-trove syndicate has brought modern salvage skill and appliances to bear on these operations. Many of the descendants of families connected with the Court of Queen Elizabeth I, including several members of the Argyll family and of the Clan MacLean, are shareholders in the salvage adventure now being determinedly carried on in the stormy bay in the northern part of the Isle of Mull, in the Scottish Western Highlands.

Bright hopes are held of the success of this salvage venture. The latest suction pumping plant is being used; apparently dynamite is not the most satisfactory agent for clearing the mud and accumulations of centuries away from the sunken ship. But a spiral steel cutter at the lower end of the suction pipe slices up the material, and the great indrawing power of the steam pumps brings the mud, sand, clay, small stones and shells in a constant stream to a large sievelike apparatus on the deck of the salvage ship, where everything is examined before being cast away. Already various objects of value—coins, plates, and arms—have been recovered.

An ambitious scheme is projected. The aim is to raise the galleon bodily, repair it, and tow it to London. It is said that the plan is quite possible. The ship was one of the stoutest of the Armada, built of oak, clamped with tons of copper bolts, and sheathed in lead. Imbedded in the mud at Tobermory Bay the warship would be protected from harm, and oak is a wood that endures.

In any case the treasure on board—chests full of gold and silver Spanish coins—will, it is hoped, be brought to the surface.

Encouraging results reached London yesterday from the salvage party at work on the sunken galleon in Tobermory Bay. Among the finds was a metal plate, of considerable brightness when relieved of its lime incrustation, weighing 20 pounds 2 ounces, and with a diameter of 10 inches. A stone cannon ball was also recovered, and two pieces of African oak.

The next day another plate of the same description was found, as well as the lid of a hammered copper kettle.

Four charges of dynamite were exploded in order to loosen the masses of hard crust overlying the vessel. This material has been found to be much tougher than the silt underneath it. As soon as the surface mass had been broken up the suction pump was put back to work, much sand, mud and shells being removed from the sandbank where the Galleon lies.

As a relief from the output of stone cannonballs and metal plates from the sea bed where the supposed Spanish Armada treasure ship lies, there have now been recovered thirty-two copper coins. Twenty-four of them came up

March 17-May 8, 1912
PLAN TO RAISE SHIP OF THE SPANISH ARMADA

Salvors using suction pipes similar to those used by a modern Duke of Argyll's divers in a hunt for Armada loot in the 1950s.

April 7, 1912
PIECES OF PLATE RECOVERED FROM SUNKEN GALLEON

May 8, 1912
GOLD SHIP YIELDS COPPER

in a cluster. Two are dated 1579 and 1582 respectively, and are clearly marked "Philippus", the Latin form of Philip II, King of Spain at the time of the Armada.

These are the first Spanish copper coins of the period of which there is any record. It had been believed that Spain, then by far the richest kingdom in the world, handled money imperially and did not deal in small copper coins.

The coins came up shining like burnished gold, and the staff of the salvage ship was sure that the long-expected treasure had been reached at last. They greeted the glittering coins with cheers. But all is not gold that glitters, and the coins turned green under the acid test.

August-December 1919

NEW EFFORTS TO SALVAGE GALLEON: DIVERS TO SEEK TREASURE

This massive access tube and diving bell was designed by the Dutch to give divers a safe pipeline to the bottom of Tobermory Bay in the 1930s, but it was never used.

Active operations are going on again in Tobermory, where a Sykes digger, using a hose working at a pressure of 100 pounds per square inch, is cutting up and clearing away the clay and mud between the trenches cut by the digger in the tumulus containing the Armada galleon, revealing any solid material, which is immediately raised in the care of a diver. Already quite a number of relics have been recovered, including a silver peso. It was the finding of a gold doubloon caught on the fluke of the ship's anchor that started this search for treasure in 1903.

The finding of many rounded stones of three and four inches in diameter in the clay surrounding the hulk helps to authenticate the Tobermory wreck as a ship belonging to the Spanish Armada, and pieces of lead sheathing further establish the ship's identity. Extracts from Spanish State papers in the Castle of Simancas explain:

"General orders for the Armada by the Duke of Medina-Sidonia, May 1, 1588, page 298: Every ship will carry on board loads of casting stones to be used during the fight. These stones are to be divided between the deck, the poop, and the fighting tops."

A further order on the same page contains a cautionary note concerning the handling of the "artificial fire", probably the pitch-like inflammable also known as "Greek fire", which the Armada carried into battle. The ships of the Armada were heavily sheathed in copper and lead to prevent being set afire by their English enemies, who also used "artificial fire" extensively in naval battles. It is possible that some of the galleon's store of "artificial fire" was still left on board at the time of her destruction at the hands of a member of Clan MacLean after she had fled from the battle. This, plus the residue of her powder magazine, would explain the violence of the explosion, which scattered the *Florencia* and her contents over a wide area of sea bed. Early plans to raise the vessel whole and restore her are thus impracticable, but quite a number of relics have been brought up in the last ten weeks, including calcarous accretions containing rusted muskets, daggers, swords, and axes. Lead piping, pewter, and quantities of black African oak much perforated by worms have also been raised. The *Florencia's* treasure of gold ducats, however, has not been located, nor has the crown which was allegedly on board the galleon, a present from the Pope to King Philip of Spain, intended for use when that monarch assumed the English throne.

Miss Margaret Naylor, described as the first woman deep sea diver, has arrived here to assist in the search for millions of gold doubloons on the Spanish treasure ship *Duque de Florencia*. Miss Naylor, especially trained by Colonel Fox, who was in charge of a similar treasure hunt in 1919, has made several descents, adding information as to the position of the wreck. Nothing has been recovered since the 1919 expedition, which yielded pewter dishes, copper coins and cannonballs.

April 14, 1924
WOMAN TO DIVE FOR GOLD

Another treasure hunt, in which two women have an interest, is about to begin in the waters of Tobermory Bay. One of the women is Lady Edith Fox-Pitt, daughter of the eighth Marquess of Queensbury. The other is Mrs. Leask of Dymchurch, Kent, who before her marriage was a diver (see above) and has actually walked on the deck of the sunken *Florencia*. The two are co-operating financially with a private syndicate headed by Colonel K. M. Foss of London in this effort to recover some of the ten to fifteen million dollars' worth (sic) of jewels, plate and ducats with which the chests of this Spanish vessel are said to bulge.

Divers who succeeded in reaching the wreck as long ago as 1661 found part of the deck blown away, apparently confirming the old story that the *Florencia* was sent to the bottom by an irate member of Clan MacLean who ignited her powder magazine. The hunters of 1661 thought themselves near success. The vessel was not so deeply imbedded in the clay as it is now, and they reached the poop, which housed the "gunroome" under which the treasure was supposed to lie. Unfortunately for them, their operations did not meet with the approval of the local clan, and they were driven away.

Since then divers have brought up a number of objects, including a piece of silver and gold plate, beautifully worked, which might have been worth $15,000 if it had been recovered undamaged.

In this latest attempt divers are using a three-ton diving bell fitted with plate-glass windows and powerful electric lights. The two women added that the work was in expert hands, the head diver being a man who has been at work at Scapa Flow helping to raise German battleships sunk in the famous naval battle of the Great War.

Mrs. Leask had a narrow escape from death when, as a diver, she descended to the wreck. She found a leak in her diving suit, and when, in response to her signals, she was brought to the surface, her suit was nearly full of water.

November 18, 1928
ARMADA TREASURE SOUGHT BY WOMEN

The *Florencia* may soon yield her secrets to twentieth century ingenuity, Simon Lake, famous submarine builder and inventor (MARGIN NOTE: SEE *RAISE THE LUSITANIA!*) said last night at a dinner at the Hotel Madison, New York.

Mr. Lake, who is co-sponsor with Captain H. H. Railey of the Lake-Railey *Lusitania* Expedition, which is expected to start work on February 1st on the wreck of that vessel, stated that if the *Lusitania* effort proves to be "as easy as going down in an elevator," the steel tube which is expected to be the principal means of effecting the salvage operations may be used to assist in the ex-

December 1, 1931
SUBMARINER SIMON LAKE TO WREST THE SECRET OF THE "FLORENCIA" FROM THE DEEP

ploration of the *Florencia.*

In explaining the operation of his steel tube, Mr. Lake revealed that he has already received communications from the representative of the Duke of Argyll, whose family has owned the wreck of the *Florencia* for centuries. Many diving operations have been attempted on the old flagship in the past, and although the hulk lies only about eighty feet from shore, none of the salvage expeditions have proved successful because of the silt with which the galleon is covered. Since ordinary diving operations have proved unsuccessful, the Duke is apparently anxious to see what Mr. Lake's tube can do, the inventor said last night.

March 3, 1950-
October 20, 1954
THE SEARCH OF THE DUKE OF ARGYLL

In 1950, Ian Douglas Campbell, eleventh Duke of Argyll, who evidently decided against using Simon Lake's steel "elevator" when the flamboyant inventor's *Lusitania* attempt came to nothing (MARGIN NOTE: SEE *RAISE THE LUSITANIA*), engaged the services of the Royal Navy in an all-out effort to find his private galleon's treasure, by that time estimated at between $68 million and $84 million in gold ducats and *reales de oro.* The Royal Navy, with divers and the latest in military salvage equipment, went to work on March 3rd, 1950. The Duke contracted to pay for the use of two naval diving vessels and the team of twelve divers, hoping to recoup his expenses either by finding the treasure or, at worst, syndicating the film and publicity rights to the search in the United States.

By April a dozen divers, working in sixty-minute relays eight hours a day, were beginning to blast the silt and clay away from the hulk. Using 28-foot long brass probes, they were able to retrieve bits of the ancient oak of the ship's timbers, ascertaining that the North African oak used to build the vessel was still in a state of good preservation after three and a half centuries underwater.

The Duke conducted extensive research on the vessel in Spain as well as in his own family records. As one of his most striking pieces of evidence that the sunken hulk was indeed the fabled *Florencia,* he cited the eleven-foot long bronze cannon recovered from the bottom of Tobermory Bay in the eighteenth century, which is now in Argyll Castle at Inverary. The gun bears at its touchhole the device of its maker, Benvenuto Cellini, and the *fleurs de lys,* salamanders, and capital "F" of Francois, Premier of France, for whom it was made. The cannon was lost to Florentine armies at the battle of Pavia in 1525. Since the famous payroll galleon was a Florentine ship, named for the Duke of Florence and presented by him to Philip of Spain for the Spanish war effort against the English, the Cellini cannon clue is provocative indeed.

In May, 1950, *The New York Times* reporter Benjamin Welles went aboard one of the Royal Navy diving ships, and made a dive himself. Descending with Royal Navy salvage divers on the wreck, he filed the following report:

"In a diving suit eighty feet below the surface of this historic cove, a reporter quickly learns how jealously nature is guarding a Spanish treasure galleon that legend says is buried here with 30 million reales of gold.

"Wind and waves, treacherous tides and the deceptively gentle mantle of silt accumulated over centuries have locked fast in the bay's bottom whatever

treasure remains from the ship that blew up and sank here in 1588.

"Twelve feet deep under the silt, say the diving experts, rest the twisted African oak timbers of the treasure galleon *Florencia*. Day by day, the search for them goes on, financed by the present Duke of Argyll, whose ancestors received the royal charter to this and similar wrecks in 1641.

"At the bottom of the bay, a few feet off, a British expert seems to be gliding with ballet grace in his light rubber diving suit and flippers. Suddenly he reaches up and grasps a long slender metal shaft lowered from the surface. He moves to a spot on the floor of the bay, sits down, places one end of the shaft between his knees, tugs his signal rope, and in a twinkling what seems like a minor atomic explosion has occurred.

"This is the new type hydraulic jet probe, which shoots a tremendous stream of water deep into the silt with the force of 250 pounds a square inch. Flanges stemming from the nozzle at 30-degree angles reciprocate the power and keep the shaft from bucking like a wild horse.

"By oscillating it gently as it bores into the silt, and listening at the same time, the diver has soon located a hard object deep in the ooze.

"Now another funnel is lowered to him: ten feet of canvas fire hose attached to a seventy-foot metal tube. This is the suction pump for silt removal. Placing the end of the hose over the silt the diver quickly sucks away an ever-widening and deepening hole. In a few minutes a round, encrusted object comes into view. Sent to the surface, washed and carefully chipped, it soon discloses an ancient Spanish stiletto, its steel heavily rusted and its linen fabric scabbard in tatters.

"The divers here have brought to the surface a few odds and ends of the Spanish wreck but thus far no definite trace of the treasure has been found. Given three consecutive windless days they say they will have made definite 'strikes' to the timber or metal, and will thus have finally located the wreck."

By the 8th of May, 1950, the Royal Navy Commander, Reay Parkinson, was confident that the vessel was indeed the *Florencia*. Two silver medallions, very thin, bright when polished and about the size of an American quarter, had been brought up. Each bore the figure of a reclining nude woman, a star at her feet, and each had a hook on the back for fastening.

Said Commander Parkinson, "How, if it's not our ship, could these medallions, obviously of ancient, and probably Spanish, origin, have got down eighty feet in the mud of a Scottish harbor?"

But the Duke of Argyll was paying the Royal Navy only to locate the wreck, not to recover the treasure. The cautious British Admiralty stated only that there was "a lively possibility that the wreckage of a foreign vessel had been located." They called off the Navy divers, explaining that the basic terms of the Duke's contract had been fulfilled, and that the military purpose of the exercise, which was to test new underwater diving and salvage equipment and techniques, had been accomplished. If the Duke wanted to bring up the treasure, he would have to do it himself.

A British Treasury spokesman rather hoped he would. Since any gold found would by law have to be exchanged for pounds sterling, said the Treasury man in a somewhat wistful statement, the Duke would be in a posi-

Franz Windprechtinger, an Austrian inventor, claimed to have a secret device for locating the treasure of the *Florencia*. He convinced the Duke of Argyll, but his gadget yielded nothing.

The Duke of Argyll's chamberlain (in tam) checks charts of Tobermory Bay with Lieutenant Commander Parkenson, head of the British Navy's treasure hunt.

tion to contribute "a very useful" 30 million gold ducats to Britain's gold reserves.

On the 19th of May the Royal Navy's bill fell due. The Duke of Argyll paid between £3,000 and £4,000 to cover the costs of what had been, in the Admiralty's guarded opinion, no more than a military field-test of new undersea equipment. The *Florencia* kept her secret.

But the Duke was nothing if not persistent. After all, in addition to his family records, his Cellini cannon, and the rest of his evidence, further study disclosed that the gold and silver plate brought up by the 1912 expedition bore a coat of arms with the initials "A.P." What else could it be but a part of the cabin plate of Andres Pereira, Captain of the fabled *Florencia?*

So in summer, 1954, the Duke hired divers and began again. The Royal Navy men had exposed large sections of the wreck's hull, which had been blown apart amidships, exactly as the old MacLean legend stated. The Duke's divers were engaged to break through the hull and bring up whatever was on the other side.

At least one officer of the Royal Navy, Rear Admiral Patrick McLaughlin, had been intrigued enough by the 1950 attempt to have thrown in with the Duke's long treasure hunt immediately upon his retirement from active service.

The Duke's effort centered on an eight-inch suction pipe similar to the one the Navy divers had used. The device, by now developed far beyond the steam-driven pipe of 1912, emptied 35 tons of silt an hour through sieves into a hopper-ship. The sifted contents of the mesh screens were

carefully examined throughout the summer of 1954. In September yet another tantalizing artifact came to light: a sword blade, encrusted with lime, was spat out of the pipe and saw the sun for the first time in 366 years.

The effort continued through the month. Divers descended in alternating two-hour shifts to handle the bucking pipe, which threw torrents of mud, silt, rocks, and shells into the hopper-ship. The team excavated a series of holes 30 feet across and five to six feet deep over the spot where the wreck was found. Eventually the plan was to merge the holes into a cavity 200 feet across, which would slope gently at a thirty-degree angle down to the exposed wreck.

But difficulties abounded. Rocks on the bay's floor frequently clogged the dredge pipe. Tides, mud and silt hampered the divers.

In the meanwhile, skeptical scholars produced evidence to contradict the Duke's belief in the identity of his wreck. Research done by Andrew Lang and R. P. Hardie in the last century was cited. The team had investigated Armada records, and had concluded that the real *Florencia* had escaped both Drake's fleet and the Scottish storms, to find her way home. The name of the Sicilian ship *San Juan Bautista*, a minor, treasureless transport vessel, was again brought up. Lloyd's of London, the famous maritime insurance company, was asked its opinion of the Duke's monomaniacal search. That august assembly opined that it was far more interested in salvaging the known wrecks of some 4,770 merchant ships lost during World War II (MARGIN NOTE: SEE *NAZI LOOT AND JAPANESE SPOILS*), whose cargoes, though not as glamorous as gold, were a surer bet.

Finally, in October, after spending a small fortune, Ian Douglas Campbell, eleventh Duke of Argyll, gave up. His last effort had yielded only a few bits of broken timber, some human bone fragments, and the remains of a five-foot spear. The only persons who benefited from the treasure hunt were local Scottish hotel keepers who catered to tourists attracted to the scene.

The facts in the mystery of the Spanish payroll are these: there is a vessel lying in 90 feet of water and silt off the Isle of Mull in Tobermory Bay. She is definitely a Spanish ship of the Armada period, and she has been blown in half amidships. Artifacts of great historical value which link her with Andres Pereira, known to have commanded one of the Duke of Medina-Sidonia's flagships, have been raised.

The questions remain. If Pereira did indeed sail the great Florentine galleon bearing the Armada's entire payroll into MacLean's harbor after escaping the debacle of 1588, why did he not pay for his provisions outright, instead of signing over his cannon, ship and crew to a wild Scottish Chieftain for a local blood-feud? Was he afraid MacLean would seize the whole hoard, once he suspected its value? Or is the whole story of Donald MacLean's defiant self-immolation simply another fireside tale to be related around Highland hearths to the greater glory of the Scots Clans?

Ian Douglas Campbell thought better. And if his wreck is the *Florencia*, and if she indeed bore the "bellyfull of gold" her Captain claimed she did in 1611, there are still 30 million *reales de oro* and a King's crown lying in ninety feet of silt at the bottom of Tobermory Bay.

Ships of "Operation Ducat," the Royal Navy's bid to find the payroll ship, arrive in Tobermory Bay in 1950.

3

Facing Page:
The Spanish enslaved the Indians they conquered, forcing them to work their own gold mines and executing them to keep the locations secret. Whole tribes of Indian slave laborers were buried with their gold when the hard-pressed Spanish gold-hunters north of the Rio Grande were forced to move on by more militant Indian bands, giving rise to persistent legends of Indian mines guarded by the bones of their original owners.

The Great Depression was a fertile ground for treasure legends. Especially in rural areas, where people had only recently made the transition from subsistence farming to cash-crop businesses, in most cases financed by banks and a commodity trading system at least as mysterious to the farmers at the far end of Wall Street's agricultural speculations as the derring-do of Spanish *conquistadores* and the pirates who preyed on them, the failure of the paper empire caused a wholesale revival of belief in buried gold. The same impulse which makes the more conservative members of today's somewhat shaky affluent society invest their surplus capital in South African Kreugerrands impelled the hardscrabble farmers in America's Southwest, who had watched as accidents of climate, bubble-headed New York speculation, and a worldwide hard currency panic combined to reduce their minimal farming profits to the dust left behind their local bankers as those worthies got out of town, to gather up their mining pans and their hunches and head for the hills in search of the fabulous "Lost Louisiana" mine. Hoover's "chicken in every pot" campaign promise had not worked out. But in the minds of a lot of busted farmers and hillmen in the Ozarks, the long-dead Spanish had left a gold-mine in every hill.

The legend of the Lost Louisiana gold mine, current throughout the south and the west, began back in the days of English privateering and Spanish greed in the New World. The story says that a fleet of nine Spanish galleons, homebound with treasures of gold and silver and jewels taken from Old Mexico, were set upon by privateers. Hard pressed by the English seadogs, they turned in at the Mississippi and anchored at a bend in the river which has since disappeared, according to Old Man River's notorious habit of changing his course every few years.

Anchored in their secluded riverbend, the Spanish heard rumors of more gold, worked by Indians who had dug mines among the hills far to the north in present-day Arkansas. The Spaniards loaded their Mexican treasure on rafts, sank their ships, and shoved off up-river in quest of new treasure. They found it, according to the story, somewhere beyond the confluence of the Arkansas and the Big Mulberry Rivers. The Indians were digging the gold from quartz ledges which overlooked the river fork, and the Spaniards, goldhunters by profession, captured the mines, enslaved the Indians, and forced them to continue the mining.

But ammunition and supplies ran low. Neighboring Indian tribes became increasingly hostile. Moreover, word arrived that the United States had purchased the Louisiana Territory, and that United States troops had been stationed at various ports down the Mississippi. The Spaniards decided to retire for a second time. They buried their Mexican spoils in a mineshaft, murdered the enslaved Indians, and threw their bodies down the same shaft. Then they set off downstream again, hoping to run the gamut of the new American forts, reach Mexico, and eventually return to claim their Lost Louisiana treasure. But the legend relates that they were beset by Indians and swamp fevers, and not a soul survived to carry the Lost Louisiana tale to Mexico.

If none of the Spaniards survived to pass on the story, presumably it was carried down to the prospectors of the 1930s by an Indian or two lucky enough to escape the Spanish holocaust. In any case, the tale persists to the present day, and if times turn out to be as hard as predicted, there will certainly be another hunt for the Lost Louisiana.

The quest for the "Lost Louisiana" has begun again. Following the recent chartering of the Cole Prospecting Company, the backhills of Franklyn County, Arkansas, are being methodically searched for a clue which may lead to that famous cache which has challenged venturesome spirits in the Southwest for more than a century.

And as this search for old treasure is renewed, new legends of buried wealth are in the process of being born. Traditionally skeptical, thousands of backwoods people have had their distrust bolstered by the recent failure of 147 Arkansas banks. Thousands of back-country depositors have been left penniless. As one obvious result a new regime of money-burying is beginning, and it will probably continue for years to come. So an entirely new crop of countryside treasure lore is due to come into being.

Spanish gold is a theme much in men's minds today, and the newly organized Cole attempt to recover the treasures of the Lost Louisiana mine illustrates the potency of this type of treasure legend.

The lure of hidden wealth is still strong, and today treasure hunters in patched blue overalls and faded work shirts swing pick and shovel. Toil-stooped prospectors plod forth with picks and pans and pack-burros. Weather-hardened men study tattered and mildewed maps. "Tracers" search far mountain ranges, following up rock gulleys, peering into bluff crevices, prowling into caves heavy with the clay of dead centuries, confident that some day they will blunder upon the protruding end of an iron chest too heavy for one man to lift.

The fact is that we are now entering upon a new era of treasure-hunting. The depression has whetted the common desire for an easy acquisition of wealth, and more than 700 stories of wealth-finding published in reputable newspapers during the past five years have whetted the hope. (MARGIN NOTE: SEE *FAKES, FOOLS AND FRAUDS*)

Treasure hunting is of three or four kinds, ranging from the most casual one-man search to well-organized ventures involving heavy investments both of labor and capital. The "Lost Louisiana" legend comes from a theme of Spanish gold long played upon. It dates back to the time when the French and Spanish rivalry in the Mississippi Valley was checkmated by Thomas Jefferson's unexpectedly imperial sally, the Louisiana Purchase. Though details of the Lost Louisiana story seem to belong to an earlier period of Spanish *conquistadores* and the rape of Mexico, nonetheless, otherwise sane and peaceful mountaineers of Franklyn County, Arkansas, are hard at work digging on the strength of the story.

The Lost Louisiana lore is far spread. Along a little river in the hills of southern Missouri an old man with enduring optimism is devoting his life to the search for Spanish gold. His name is Jim Woodruff. He was a tie-hack in his younger days, chopping down and trimming timber for the railroad line. One day he heard a story about a Spanish pirate who once came up the little river with a great treasure, only to be robbed and murdered by a band of French lead miners nearby. The Frenchmen, so the story says, carried away what treasure they could and buried the rest "in a cavern beside the waters." They sealed up the cavern, marked its site with crosses and signs cut upon adjacent trees and rocks. And they made a map of the location.

Jim Woodruff contends that he has found this map. On the first day of summer and again on the first day of autumn it is his custom to go forth to a bare hilltop, and there, just as the sun sinks out of sight, to measure off the paces to a certain spot. He assures everyone that he can dig up the treasure any time he chooses. But, so far as anyone knows, he hasn't yet chosen to.

Bear Holler, a remote hillcountry spot in McDonald County, Missouri, has also been associated with the Lost Louisiana. The Bear Holler version of the legend cuts the *conquistadores* down to a handful of Spanish "miners" who, in passing through the mountains, were attacked by Indians. Some of them were murdered, and the survivors, having buried their dead, hid their bags of golden treasure in a deep crevice into which they directed the channel of a mountain creek. Then they fled.

In 1880 a hillman named Van Wormer claimed to have a faded buckskin map which told the location of the cache. He found a line of graves containing a few fragments of firearms and some metal buckles apparently of Spanish origin. He set to digging according to the directions on his map, which specified a shaft bottomed by a vault "eighteen feet long and four feet wide, filled with silver but for one bushel of gold." He failed to find it. Four years later he turned the search over to his son, who pursued the quest halfheartedly for a number of years and finally handed his evidence over to one Charles Nidiffer, whose treasure-hunt fell out of sight in 1929.

It has been established that numerous Spanish expeditions penetrated far up the Mississippi Valley. The Plains Indians would not have become horsemen without the tough Spanish war- and packhorses which escaped or were captured in the course of the Spaniards' frequent clashes with the native inhabitants of the North American southwest. The Spanish imperial effort in the New World was based upon Spain's early supremacy at sea, and financed by her successful invasion of the gold-rich Indian nations of Central and South America. It is not wildly improbable that the same *conquistadores* whose horses formed the breeding stock of the North American mustang lost as well the secret of a Mississippi Valley goldmine they had been sent to find by Spanish Colonial authorities in Mexico. Gold drew the Spanish conquerors to the New World, and golden rumors pulled them up the Mississippi Valley, after they had pillaged the golden wealth of the southern regions. If those stern professional goldseekers came so far north on the strength of a rumor of golden treasure, is it any wonder the legend of lost mines continues to inspire the hillmen of Arkansas?

Francisco Pizarro, the grimly efficient conqueror of Peru, received triumphal honors from the King of Spain for the masses of treasure he sent home.

Various dates

THE BETRAYAL OF ATAHUELPA

Facing Page: Atahuelpa, last of the Inca Priest-kings, is about to be burned alive by Pizarro, in this fanciful 1882 engraving. Actually, "The Inca" died squalidly, strangled in his own palace on Pizarro's orders, when the *conquistador* had milked him dry of ransom and information.

The Spanish officially came to the New World, according to various Papal charters and royal commissions from the Holy Catholic Kings of Spain, to explore and to bring the natives into the bosom of Mother Church. In practice, of course, the Spanish conquest was a brutal land-grab, inspired from the first by a gold-fever unparalleled in the history of human cupidity. The *conquistadores'* royal patents were as loosely written as the letters of marque and reprisal borne by the early buccaneer captains. They were authorized to go anywhere and do anything, as long as they continued to send gold back to the Spanish King.

Foremost among these rapacious adventurers, with Cortes, the conqueror of Mexico, stands Francisco Pizarro, who singlehandedly destroyed the Inca Empire of Peru and Ecuador, putting an end to a highly developed culture which in many respects was superior to any European civilization at the time, except in the areas of weaponry and organized greed. Pizarro's gruesome relations with the gentle Inca priest-king Atahuelpa, his plundering of the gold and silver of Cuzco, and his final search for the temple treasure and mines of Pachacamac, make up a chapter as dark and bloody as any in the grim history of man's quest for Eldorado.

Pizarro and his small band of *conquistadores* were received graciously by the Incas when he first entered their empire, which at the time covered most of modern-day Peru and Ecuador. Although the Incas were too sophisticated to believe that the Europeans were gods, they did share with the other great nations of the Americas a culture-myth which spoke of the arrival of pale-skinned strangers in "winged" ships, and they honored their guests accordingly.

According to some accounts, Pizarro did not at first believe that the metal decorations, plates, huge vases and urns, some of which weighed well over a hundred pounds, were in fact of solid gold. Scattered almost casually all over the Temple and city of Cuzco, and treated negligently by the Incas, who admired the "yellow metal" for its beauty and malleability, but placed no great value on it, the gold of the Inca capital staggered the Spaniard. For him, as for most Europeans in the sixteenth century, gold was an infinitely rare and precious substance to be glimpsed from a distance glimmering from a church altarpiece or adorning the crown of a King. But to the Incas, in their mountainous, treeless empire, wood was of far more value, and at first they were amused by the Spaniards' startled reaction to their golden city. Their amusement did not last long.

Pizarro and his men went mad. The *conquistador* turned on the hospitality of the priest-king Atahuelpa and imprisoned him in a room of his own palace. Practical to a fault, Pizarro may not have understood anything about the Inca religion, but he recognized that Atahuelpa's position was higher, in the eyes of his people, than that of any European monarch. He was The Inca, the central symbol of the empire's culture and religion, and the living incarnation of a god. By seizing his person the small body of Spaniards had the heart of the nation in their hands, a fact which far outweighed the vastly superior numbers of the Indians.

Realizing too late the hold the yellow metal had on the heart of his treacherous guest, Atahuelpa promised Pizarro that in return for his life he would fill the room where he was confined as high as his arms could reach with gold. He also agreed to fill a smaller adjoining room twice over with silver. The offer was accepted, and The Inca's ransom began to pour into his cell from every part of the empire.

But for various reasons the gold came in slowly. Pizarro grew impatient, and began to plunder the city of Cuzco and the Temple of the Sun, adding its golden furnishings to the hoard accumulating in Atahuelpa's rooms. He accused the King of purposely delaying the payment of the ransom, and Atahuelpa, in a last effort to save his life and his empire, gave the Spaniard directions to the city of Pachacamac, which, he assured Pizarro, was even richer in the yellow metal than Cuzco.

Pizzaro, believing he had exhausted The Inca's usefulness, promptly strangled him. In 1533 he set off for Pachacamac, intending, once he had stripped the temple there of its finished gold, to extort from its priests the location of the Inca mines.

But the Incas, horrified by Pizarro's sacrilegious murder, and realizing belatedly that the Spaniard would not be satisfied until he had stripped the empire of its last nugget, hid the temple furnishings of Pachacamac in a mountain cave. Pizarro never found the hoard, nor did he ever discover the mines which were the sources of the vast Inca treasure. Despite having sent back to the King of Spain a flood of ingots melted down from the treasure of Cuzco and the ransom of Atahuelpa, a golden plunder which may have amounted to over a billion dollars at present valuation, and which at a stroke made Spain the richest and most powerful nation in Europe, Pizarro died a disappointed man in 1541.

Where are the mines from which the Incas drew their vast stores? Gold and silver are still produced in Peru, but the natives whom Pizarro found there had only the crudest forms of mining implements. They worked unscientifically and were ignorant of the use of mercury in saving gold by amalgamation. They picked up the precious metal from the beds of streams, or dug it out of seams in mountain sides. It is highly probable that these half-touched mines are yet to be rediscovered.

It is known that the Incas, seeing the store set by the Spaniards upon the metals which they had never coined, but used for ornament and manufactures, hid their gold and silver in the earth, in caves and burial-places. The tradition is that the treasure of Pachacamac was buried in one of the royal tombs, the mouth of which was sealed, and the whole covered with earth, rocks and trees, so that all trace of the entrance disappeared. The same was done with the gold mines nearby, and the people who where employed to secrete these stores of wealth were sacrificed by the priests, with whom remained the secret of these hiding-places. From generation to generation this valuable information had been kept in the priesthood of ancient Peru, the last of the line having died within this century (the nineteenth), aged precisely one hundred years, as we are informed and asked to believe.

It is this secret, wrested from the dying hold of the last head of an ancient priesthood, which is to guide the expedition of a certain wealthy American gentleman, more or less learned in geomancy and other occult sciences, into the Peruvian mountains in search of Inca gold.

September 22, 1875

THE GOLD MINES OF THE INCAS

The troops of the Spanish conquest found it hard to believe that the finely-molded urns they carried off were made of pure gold. But they learned.

November 21, 1929

SCENT INCAS' GOLD IN CAVE DISCOVERY

Prospectors in a mountain pass of Azuay near Chuchi (Ecuador) have reported the discovery of a cave containing an Inca idol and many skeletons. The discoverers are convinced they are on the trail of part of the fabulous treasure Pizarro missed after his murder of Atahuelpa, last king of the Incas.

The legend of lost Inca gold mines and hidden treasure has haunted these mountains ever since a Spaniard named Valverde, many years ago, claimed to have discovered a treasure cave in the vicinity, suddenly becoming ver, rich.

At the time of his death, Valverde allegedly gave the King of Spain directions to the cave. These directions have been followed as far as Margasitas Mountain, where the trail was lost.

Richard Spruce, an English botanist, followed the trail in 1857 as far as Margasitas, and reported that up to that point Valverde's instructions "corresponded perfectly with the actual locality."

Some scholars doubt the cave's connection with the legend of the lost Inca mines. They point out that the pass of Azuay was the location of a great battle in which the Incas conquered the rival empire of the Shiris some four and a half centuries ago, many years before Pizarro's conquest of Peru. The cave, according to skeptics, could be nothing more than an Inca memorial to that battle.

5

August 12, 1969

**'PIRATES'
LOOT SPANISH
TREASURE FROM
SHIPS WRECKED
OFF TEXAS**

Facing Page:
In shallow waters off
the dunes of Texas'
Padre Island, the
treasure of Luis de
Velasco's ancient
galleon fleet was
found in the late
1960s.

Padre Island, a long spit of dunes and beaches which parallels the southeast Texas coast between Corpus Christi and Brownsville on the Mexican border, is largely under the control of the National Parks Service today, which operates it as a national seashore. It is also the site of one of the richest treasure finds of recent times. Spanish ships carrying looted Aztec silver went down in the Gulf of Mexico at various spots along the island's eastern shore, and a major salvage effort, begun in 1967, has succeeded in bringing much of the silver, together with valuable historical artifacts, to the surface. But the Texas treasure story only started with the salvage. Modern-day pirates in scuba outfits made raids on the unsalvaged treasure in 1969, and in the meanwhile six different claimants initiated lawsuits over rights to the find. The wrangles, legal and otherwise, which went on over the Padre Island discovery somewhat deflate the romantic notion of lucky divers getting rich on Spanish loot. For the modern salvor, all too often the real treasure hunt goes on in the courts.

The captain of a Spanish treasure galleon, driven westward across the Gulf of Mexico by a hurricane in 1553, set both anchors when the western shore of the Gulf appeared. But the hawsers snapped and the ship was dashed aground. Lighter equipment on deck was strewn forward of the ship herself. Subsequently the ship and the gear were covered by ten feet of sand.

The ship was one of a fleet of galleons carrying booty seized in Mexico from the Aztecs by Spanish soldiers. Silver ingots and coins minted in Mexico from the melted-down Aztec ornaments, and bejewelled religious artifacts, made up the treasure. It was on its way back to Spain, sent by the Spanish viceroy of Mexico, Luis de Velasco, for use by the Emperor Charles V "in defense of the Catholic religion and of his kingdom." But of the twenty vessels which reached Cuba on the voyage, fourteen went down in the storm, which drove the fleet back westward to destruction on the sands off Padre Island.

A state official said today that "pirates and plunderers" had stolen tons of valuable historical treasure from the floor of the Gulf of Mexico off the coast of Texas.

He said he would ask the Federal Bureau of Investigation to conduct an inquiry.

The stolen treasure was believed to have been part of the first sizable booty taken from the Aztecs after the Spanish conquest of Mexico in the first half of the sixteenth century. The booty was said to be worth "millions of dollars."

Jerry Sadler, the state land commissioner, said that he discovered over the weekend that "pirates" had plundered at least three shipwrecks off the coast of Padre Island.

"Nothing remains but scooped-out craters," Mr. Sadler said. The holes were 450 feet long and 150 wide, he added.

The theft apparently took place before July 23 of this year. Mr. Sadler said

that a radar-equipped boat had been patrolling the area since that date to protect the shipwreck site.

The stolen treasure was believed to have been similar to that which was recovered in the last 18 months from another ship in de Velasco's fleet.

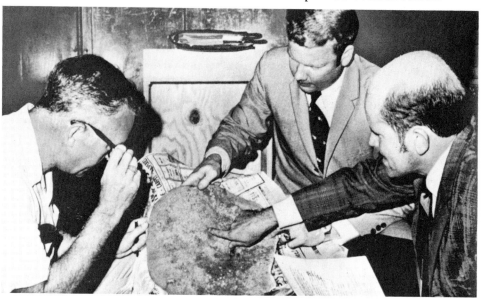

SALVAGED TREASURE ISSUE IN TEXAS COURT SUITS

The United States Customs Bureau has claimed jurisdiction over some ancient Spanish treasure that was salvaged from shipwrecks off the Texas coast.

The treasure was first claimed by the private company that salvaged it, Platoro Ltd., Inc., of Gary, Indiana. Since then it has been claimed by the State of Texas; by the City of Corpus Christi; by two Texas counties; and by a group of private citizens who want the treasure for museums. Three court suits to settle the ownership are pending, and a fourth is being prepared.

Cleburne Maier, the regional commissioner of the Customs Bureau in Houston, said that the Tariff Act of 1930 requires that all salvage from shipwrecks be cleared through customs.

Mr. Maier said that the historic artifacts, including bulk silver and silver coins, probably were not subject to taxes, but that the law requires that an inventory be filed with customs. If one is not filed, he said, the United States Government can claim the treasure.

Texas Secretary of State Martin Dies, Jr. said that he and the State Attorney General, Crawford Martin, would resist the Government's claim on the treasure.

"There wasn't even a United States when those ships were sunk," said Mr. Dies. "Besides, these shipwrecks are on Texas-owned land."

After conferring with Texas officials, including Governor Preston Smith, Mr. Maier said he would not put a time limit on the filing of the inventory because of the squabble over who owns the treasure.

Jerry Sadler, the Texas Land Commissioner, has possession of most of the smaller items, which were dug up from under 30 feet of water and 10 feet of sand off Padre Island. Larger items, including old cannonballs and cannons, are being preserved by the Memorial Museum at the University of Texas.

Mr. Sadler, who has been criticized by several state legislators for "carelessness" in his handling of the treasure and the salvage, said two weeks ago that "pirates and plunderers" had raided the salvage site off the Texas coast and had stolen the treasure from three other ships that the state had planned to salvage. He said he would "track down" the thieves, but so far has not done so.

Mr. Sadler himself proved not above some rather piratical strong-arm tactics in defense of part of the salvaged treasure, which he had locked in an Austin vault for safe-keeping in July, 1969. A state official, Representative Jake Johnson, tried to get a look into Sadler's vault. The burly Land Commissioner, barring the way with all the vigor of Sam Houston at the Alamo, grabbed Johnson by the throat and shoved him away.

The state legislators, who contend that much of the treasure disappeared after it was salvaged, have a pending resolution to censure Mr. Sadler, whose position as Land Commissioner gives him authority over state-owned land, as far as three leagues out into the Gulf of Mexico.

Mr. Sadler said he would testify tomorrow before the State House Rules Committee, which is considering the resolution.

The site of the shipwrecked fleet was first discovered about 30 years ago, but salvage operations did not begin until 1967. Divers say that they have found 14 of the ships.

In addition to silver, coins and religious artifacts, the recovered treasure includes some rare early navigational instruments.

Texas State Representative Jake Johnson shows the press how Jerry Sadler grabbed him by the throat when the legal scramble over the Padre Island treasure got physical.

Jerry Sadler, Texas Land Commissioner, led his state's forces in the legal fray.

SCIENTISTS TRACE A 1553 SHIPWRECK

A 15-member team of scientists has just completed a 30-day reconnaissance of shipwreck sites off Padre Island. They have performed extensive research on a sunken vessel they believe to be one of at least eight Spanish galleons which went down in a 1553 hurricane.

Dr. Eugene Herrin, a geophysicist at Southern Methodist University, used a magnetometer to spot chunks of metal under the Gulf sands, zeroing in on the wreck's position from a pattern of "magnetic anomalities" that was found at the site.

But Eugene McDermott, chairman of a non-profit group that helped state agencies in Texas to finance the Padre Island reconnaissance, said that only one of the eight shipwreck sites was proved.

Divers at that site recovered a falconer cannon, ballast stones and ancient wood fragments believed to have been part of the galleon's keel. Dr. Fred Wendorf, chairman of the Texas Antiquities Commission and of the department of anthropology at S.M.U., identified the cannon as one of a type carried by Spanish ships more than 400 years ago.

Spanish history has been thoroughly studied for references to the fleet of 20 galleons which left Vera Cruz, Mexico, with a load of silver for the king's treasury.

Dr. Wendorf said the scientists have located at least eight of the shipwrecks, seven of which have never been disturbed. He plans to ask the Texas Legislature for more money to finance excavations of the sites.

Members of the team include scientists and officials from S.M.U., Texas A & M. University, Texas Technological University, the Texas General Land Office, the State Historical Survey Committee, and the National Park Service.

The scientists searched for and charted sites for future underwater archaeological explorations aboard *El Pescador*, a diving ship. Jerry A. Sadler, the State Land Commissioner, used the same ship two years ago when he learned that Platoro, Inc., of Gary, Indiana, was recovering artifacts from another Spanish shipwreck off Padre Island.

The magnetometer that Dr. Herrin used is about the size of an attache case, with a sensor carried in a dory behind the diving ship. The $35,000 electronic sensor measures the magnetic field of the earth. When it passes over metallic objects buried in the ground, the sensor registers the increase in gammas of magnetism.

The magnetometer was demonstrated for newsmen this week, when *El Pescador* located the shipwreck site and sent down three divers. They brought up several ballast stones. They had hoped to find a cannon, but visibility on the bottom was zero.

The divers told of feeling what was obviously the keel of the ship, with ribs of wood every six feet.

Seventy-year-old Leo Barker was head diver for Platoro, Ltd.'s Padre Island treasure find.

The Tower of London, begun in the eleventh century on the left bank of the Thames, has endured throughout the stormiest period of English history, in the process accumulating a mantle of legend for the most part as dark as its weathered stones. Prison and execution place for noble traitors and losing aspirants to the throne of England during the bitter fifteenth and sixteenth centuries, the Tower has seen more than its share of unjust imprisonments, extortions and downright murders. Many a noble prisoner has been relieved of his personal wealth, as well as his head, within the Tower's frowning walls. But until the rediscovery of the diary of Samuel Pepys, the tireless Restoration-era man-about-town, few people since the seventeenth century suspected that some of the treasure which changed hands during England's years of turbulence may have remained buried within the Tower itself.

After Oliver Cromwell and his Roundheads vanquished the last of the Royalists in the seventeenth century English Civil War, a certain London jeweler, John Barkestead, was appointed Lieutenant of the Tower by the Protector.

Cromwell's stern Puritanism seems to have had little effect on Barkestead, who extorted vast amounts of gold from the imprisoned aristocratic Royalists in his charge. But by 1662 Cromwell was out, and Barkestead fled the wrath of the restored Royalists, escaping to Holland, a country which had long provided shelter for advocates of the Puritan cause. He was arrested there, at Delft, and brought back as a prisoner to his own Tower. Then, on April 19,1662, he was hanged, drawn and quartered at Tyburn.

Barkestead is thought to have buried his extorted wealth during his lieutenancy, and the belief that it still lies buried under the "King's House", in the southwestern corner of the Tower, adds still another legend to the many which encrust the most historic fortress in England.

Barkestead having been executed on April 19, 1662, Pepys made his first effort to find the gold on October 30 of that year. On that date he writes:

"To my Lord Sandwich, who was up in his chamber and all alone, did acquaint me with his business; which was that our old acquaintance, Mr. Wade (in Axe Yard) hath discovered to him £7,000 hid in the Tower, of which he was to have two for discovery; my Lord himself two; and the King the other three, when it was found, and that the King's warrant runs for me, on my Lord's part, and one Mr. Lee for Sir Harry Bennet, to demand leave of the Lieutenant of the Tower to make search . . .

"After dinner Sir H. Bennet did call aside the Lord Mayòr and me, and did not durst appear the least averse to it, but did promise all assistance forthwith to set upon it.

"So Mr. Lee and I to our office, and there walked till Mr. Wade and one Evett, his guide, did come, and W. Griffin, and a porter with his pickeaxes, &c.; and so they walked along with us to the Tower, and Sir H. Bennet and my Lord Mayor did give us full power to fall to work. So our guide demands a candle, and down into the cellars he goes, inquiring whether they were the

6

Reprinted, April 1, 1928
EXCERPTS FROM SAMUEL PEPYS' DIARY

Gadabout diarist Samuel Pepys hunted for treasure in the cellars of the Tower of London in the 1660s, at the request of his King, only to wind up imprisoned there himself for a time during the panic surrounding the "Papish Plot" of 1679.

Overleaf:
The Tower, forbidding symbol of the power struggles and civil strife of England's bloodiest centuries, is shown in a rare early photograph. This back view of England's premier fortress is impossible today: most visitors are familiar only with the riverward side.

same that Baxter (Barkestead) always had. We went into several little cellars, and then went out a-doors to view, and to the Cole Harbour (Cold Harbour, in Upper Thames Street), but none did answer so well to the marks which was given him to find it by as one arched vault. Where, after a great deal of council whether to set upon it now, or to delay for better or more full advice, we set to it; to digging we went to almost 8 o'clock at night, but could find nothing. But, however, our guides did not at all seem discouraged; for that they being confident the money is there they look for, but having never been in the cellars, they could not be positive to the place, and therefore will inform themselves more fully, now that they have been there, and the party that do advise them. So locking the door after us, we left work tonight, and up to the Deputy-Governor (my Lord Mayor and Sir H. Bennet, with the rest of the company, being gone an hour before); and he do undertake to keep the key of the cellars, that none shall go down without his privity."

The diary records that two days later Pepys made another unsuccessful attempt to discover the gold. On November 3, further information came to light, and on November 5 Pepys relates:

"Up and by appointment called upon Mr. Lee, he and I to the Tower to make our third attempt upon the cellar. And now privately the woman, Barkestead's great confidant, is brought, who do positively say that this is the place where he did say the money was hid in, and where he and she did put up £50,000 in butter firkins; and the very day he went out of England did say that neither he nor his would be better for the money, and therefore wishing that she and hers might. And so left us, and we full of hope; did resolve to dig all over the cellar, which by 7 o'clock at night we performed . . .

"But at last we saw we were mistaken; and after digging the cellar quite through, and removing the barrels from one side to the other, we were forced to pay our porters, and give over our expectations, though I do believe there must be money hid somewhere by him (Barkestead), or else he did delude this woman in order to oblige her to further serving him, which I am apt to believe."

Pepys made one last effort. On December 19, he says:

"Up and by appointment with Mr. Lee, Wade, Evett and workmen to the Tower, and with the Lieutenant's leave set them to work in the garden, in the corner against the mayne-guard, a most unlikely place. It being cold, Mr. Lee and I did sit all day till 3 o'clock by the fire in the Governor's house, I reading a play of Fletcher's being 'A Wife for a Month,' wherein no great wit or language. Having done, we went to them at work, and having wrought below the bottom of the foundation of the wall, I bid them give over, and so all our hopes ended."

T. F. May, who had charge of repairs in the Tower from 1892 to 1915, believes that if Pepys was well informed the gold still lies buried somewhere in the "cow shed", as the basement of the King's House is called. This is just inside the southwestern entrance of the Tower, a place familiar to all visitors.

Owing to the fact that Pepys' diary was lost in obscurity for so many years, Mr. May believes that there is little possibility that the search for Barkestead's gold was kept up after Pepys himself abandoned it. Pepys is not

Pepys and his party mounted three hunts by torchlight for the Barkestead hoard in the subterranean vaults of the Tower.

believed to have tried the old cellar which the present-day Beefeaters at the Tower call the "cow shed." After a careful study of the diary, Mr. May has come to the conclusion that Pepys dug in the wrong place. Pepys' statements that he and his guide "went to several little cellars" and that "we dug a great deal under the arches" are taken to mean that he dug under the recesses in that part of the old wall which, with its Norman transitional arches, runs north.from the Bloody Tower. Both the cellars and that point "in the garden in the corner against the mayne-guard," which even Pepys termed "a most unlikely place," have been identified by Mr. May. Neither, he believes, is identical with the cellars of the King's House which Barkestead occupied as Lieutenant of the Tower. Mr. May holds that if the tale of Barkestead's burying gold is true, the burying was done in the cellars immediately below Barkestead's official quarters.

Whether a serious effort to find it is to be made, remains to be seen.

May 22, 1957

GOLD HOARD IS HUNTED IN THE TOWER OF LONDON

Excavations began today in search for a seventeenth-century blackmailer's treasure reputedly worth $2 million.

The gold hoard belonged to John Barkestead, who was suspected of having hidden vast sums he extorted from his prisoners while serving as Lieutenant of the Tower of London.

The main purpose of the excavations is a search for a buried Roman wall, but the hunt organizers hope that the diggers may stumble onto the treasure.

Instigator of the search is Charles Quarrell, 60-year-old author and journalist, who badgered the Ministry of Works for five years to get permission for the work.

Since Don Manuel de Velasco, commander of a Spanish treasure fleet of seventeen galleons, scuttled his ships in 1702 to prevent a treasure amounting to some $70 million from falling into British hands, more than a dozen attempts have been made to recover the lost trove on the bottom of Vigo Bay in Spain. The salvage of the treasure was tried four times in the eighteenth century, five in the nineteenth, and at least four times more in the twentieth, the last in 1955.

In 1940, Spanish engineers recovered "some copper and lead objects" and located eight of the sunken galleons. The 1955 attempt brought up part of the treasure itself, as did a previous try in 1934. But most of the lost Vigo treasure remains where it sank, and Vigo Bay should rank high on any would-be treasure-hunter's list of documented treasure sites.

In September, 1702, a fleet of seventeen Spanish treasure galleons carrying a cargo of gold, silver, pearls and other precious objects were returning from the New World, heading for Cadiz, Spain's major Atlantic port. The Spaniards were about to reach their destination when Don Manuel de Velasco, commander of the fleet, heard that British Admiral Sir George Rooke, with "200 vessels and 13,000 men," was waiting for him off Cadiz.

Don Manuel changed course to shake off the pursuer and took shelter in Vigo Bay, farther north. He ordered the crews to cut down trees from the nearby hills and to link them with ropes. He placed the linked logs across the entrance to the bay, to bar access to it.

At the same time, he commandeered 1,500 carts pulled by 6,000 oxen to ship the treasure overland. But not even a tenth of the precious cargo had been unloaded when Sir George's fleet appeared outside Vigo.

The British attacked on the night of October 22nd. They easily broke through the log defense at the harbor mouth. A fleet of French frigates (France being at that time allied with Spain against the British) which had been stationed outside the bay to protect the treasure fleet, proved no match for Sir George's heavily-gunned men-of-war.

Red-hot shot from thousands of cannons swept the decks of the French vessels, felled masts, opened wounds fore and aft above the waterlines, and started fires.

Having sunk or disabled the majority of the French force, Sir George sailed on the helpless treasure galleons. Don Manuel saw that the treasure was about to fall into the hands of the enemy, and scuttled his galleons, torching them abovedecks and holing them below. The galleons, "after burning to the water's edge sank in hissing foam and through billows of smoke," according to an account on record with the Spanish Ministry of the Navy.

Frustrated in his attempt to seize the Spanish treasure, but gratified by the decisive victory he had scored over the combined French-Spanish force, Sir George sailed home. A formidable figure in Britain's naval annals, two years later Rooke was the commander who seized Gibralter from Spain, a feat for which the Spanish to this day have never forgiven him.

Facing Page:
A rare engraving of 1871, showing salvors of the time at work in Vigo Bay.

May 29, 1875
EXPEDITION FOR SUNKEN TREASURE

Date unknown, probably 1870s
THE CARBONIC GAS EXPERIMENTS OF A GERMAN SCIENTIST— NEW HOPE FOR TREASURE SEEKERS

February 18, 1934
$1,635,000 TAKEN FROM GALLEONS

The steamship *Dido*, belonging to the London and Edinburgh Shipping Company, left Leith for Vigo on May 11, with a number of divers on board. The vessel has been chartered by a London salvage company for the purpose of carrying on operations to recover treasure sunk in the harbor at Vigo in the form of specie and plate valued at several millions.

More than one attempt already has been made to recover the treasure, but these have failed, it has been stated, for lack of the proper equipment. In the event of the treasure being recovered, a royalty of forty-three and a half percent will be paid to the Spanish Government.

If there is any truth in a reported discovery which a German scientist claims to have made, marine treasure hunters may expect to recover wealth beyond the dreams of avarice from the deep. The most ingenious engineering devices presently used by treasure-seekers, it is believed, will be eclipsed by a product of the chemist's laboratory: carbonic acid gas (CO_2). Under pressure, the gas can be reduced to a liquid, which can then be stored and released in its gaseous form again at will.

The German scientist, a man named Reithmann, has already applied his discovery to the raising of sunken objects from underwater. He tested its efficiency in deep waters, on a large block of concrete. A diver was sent down to the sunken block carrying an iron box containing liquified carbonic acid gas. The box, equipped with five iron pipes fitted with faucets, was enclosed in a canvas bag folded like a collapsed balloon. Once having attached the box to the concrete block, the diver opened the faucets. The liquidied CO_2, immediately resuming its normal gaseous state as it was released, inflated the canvas balloon and carried the block to the surface.

It is hoped that this new way of raising sunken vessels will be applied to the question of the Spanish plate ships which the English sank in Vigo Bay. There has long existed a controversy concerning whether or not the silver and gold carried by the fleet is still there. There can be no doubt as to the ships, but the chances that the treasure is elsewhere are very high. No one knows what has become of it, or who recovered it. It is, perhaps, not absolutely certain that there was any to recover in the first place. By 1702, the Spanish had learned enough over the years of seeing their treasure fleets preyed upon by the English sea-dogs, to have formed the habit of masking their major shipments of treasure from the New World by dispatching one or more decoy fleets at the same time. It is possible the fleet that sank in Vigo harbor was one of these.

But although these facts may have come to light in the course of previous attempts to recover the Vigo treasure, the disappointed treasure-hunters have kept the truth to themselves. This is natural enough. No one is sorry to see others fall into the trap which caught him.

Treasure from sunken Spanish galleons amounting to $1,635,000 has been raised in Vigo Bay, and further rich hauls are expected. According to some authorities, from $70 million to $135 million in gold doubloons, ingots and silver plate lies on the harbor floor.

Spanish gold lying in the Bay of Vigo since 1702 will be the object of a diving expedition organized by the Spanish military engineer, Manuel Moxo, it was announced today. The gold will be sought with the aid of pneumatic caissons, hollow metal forms which are allowed to fill with water and sink near the site of a suspected sunken ship. Attached to the ship on the bottom by divers, the caissons are then pumped out, and rise to the surface carrying the ship with them.

The operation will be financed by a company from the United States.

March 2, 1935
FURTHER GOLD SOUGHT BY SPANISH ENGINEER

Buried treasure, believed brought to the Old World from America in 1702, has been unearthed by a farmer digging post holes near the village of Caldas de Reyes, it was disclosed today.

The village lies in the vicinity of Vigo Bay, site of a famous battle which sent a fleet of treasure galleons to the bottom in 1702. It is known that part of the treasure was taken ashore and loaded on oxcarts for overland transport before the battle. It is possible that this find is part of that hoard.

The Civil Guard set a watch on the gems and gold, which were said to weigh 14,945 grams, and include rings, combs and other ornaments. Under the law, finders of such treasures are required to report to the authorities.

June 14, 1941
SPANISH FARMER STRIKES OLD GOLD

After 250 years, Britain may finally get her hands on part of a treasure she tried to wrest from Spanish hands in the days when Admirals were both watchdogs of empires and glorified pirates.

The Spanish Government has just granted a concession to Ventures, Ltd., a British company, to recover from the bottom of Vigo Bay the $70,000,000 treasure lost there when a Spanish commander scuttled his fleet to keep it out of the hands of the English enemy in 1702.

Under the terms of the contract, which is to run for three years, Ventures, Ltd. will receive fifty percent of the value of the findings up to $25,000. Above that figure, the British percentage will drop to forty. The Spanish Government will be the exclusive owner of any actual objects salvaged. The value of such objects will be estimated by experts chosen jointly by the Spanish Government and the British company. Salvage operations are to start by November.

September 18, 1955
BRITONS TO HUNT SPANISH TREASURE

This team of divers was marshalled by John S. Potter, an American treasure buff who went after the Vigo Bay wrecks in 1958.

Various dates, 1964-1972

THE HURRICANE OF 1715

One of the richest treasure salvages of modern history began in 1955, when a retired construction engineer named *Kip Wagner* found a Spanish silver "piece of eight" on a beach south of Cape Canaveral. Wagner's modest beginning grew into a heavily capitalized company in the mid-1960s, and by 1972 three New York auction houses, including Sotheby-Parke-Bernet, had become involved in the sale of artifacts and coins rescued from the deep by Wagner and his associates.

Wagner's treasure strikes, of which the richest were made in 1964 and 1965, confirmed the old legend that an entire fleet of Spanish treasure galleons had gone down in a 1715 hurricane off the east coast of Florida. Gold fever seized the citrus-growing and cattle-ranching town of Fort Pierce, midway between Cape Canaveral and Palm Beach. And the strip where most of the sunken galleons were found, between Sebastian Inlet and Hutchinson Island, off the town of Stuart, earned the nickname "Florida's Treasure Coast."

The Wagner discoveries brought treasure-hunters flocking to the region, demanding permits to dive on the ancient wrecks. The State of Florida, torn between a desire to claim the lion's share of treasure for itself, and its tourist-wise sense that the Treasure Coast's real wealth would lie in the revenue the treasure-hunters would bring into the area, drew up some hard regulations regarding treasure-diving in its territorial waters. As recent events surrounding another hefty haul of Spanish gold bear out (MARGIN NOTE: SEE *THE CONTROVERSY OF THE KEYS*), the legal scramble between the State and private salvage firms has not net been resolved.

But at least Wagner, unlike the majority of men bitten by the gold bug, realized a solid profit on his find. By exercising care in his salvage procedures he was able to bring up a number of pieces of jewelry intact, and they fetched record prices at auction for their intrinsic beauty and historical importance. In effect, Wagner and his Real Eight Company legitimized treasure-hunting, which in the past had been a matter of battering through sunken ships in search of the obvious, the crude methods often destroying artifacts of unique artistic and historical value. And if, in the shadow of modern salvage's expensive and complex procedures, the glint of romance seems to have gone out of treasure-hunting, it is nice to remember that Kip Wagner made his first discovery wandering along a Florida beach with a *$15 Army surplus mine detector.*

The Spanish *Conquistadores* laid the foundation for 300 years of exploitation in the New World. The rich gold and emeralds of Colombia and the fine, rich silver of Mexico were shipped to the royal treasuries of Cadiz and Seville to support the political and religious adventures of the Spanish crown.

By the beginning of the eighteenth century the Spanish had adopted the "flota" system to discourage pirate attacks on ships returning to Spain along the well-known route known to pirate captains as the Spanish Main. Two fleets, each consisting of merchant vessels escorted by heavily-armed warships, were dispatched each year from different ports in the Caribbean

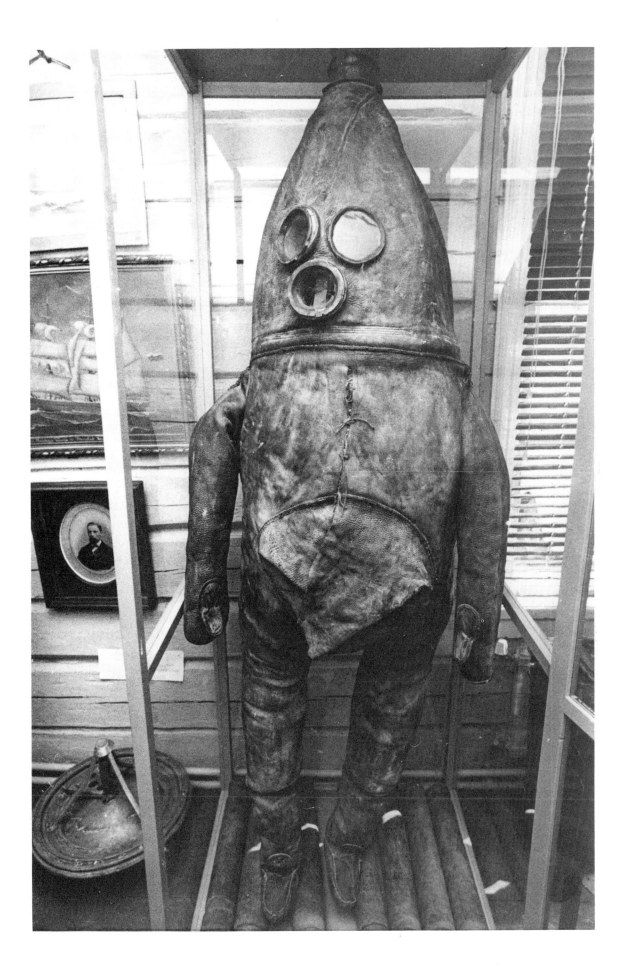

bean area. Making a rendezvous at a predesignated spot, the fleets would then combine for the perilous voyage across the open Atlantic.

In 1715, one such fleet loaded goods at Vera Cruz in Mexico. These wares included silks and china brought by sea from the Far East to Acapulco and then carried overland by mule to the Gulf coast.

A second fleet picked up a cargo of gold, silver, crosses, spoons, jewelry and other artifacts from the vast Spanish empire of Latin America. It sailed first from Cartagena in Colombia, westward to a point near the Isthmus of Panama, where it obtained goods from Peru that had been brought overland from that country.

In the spring of 1715 the two fleets met, as arranged, at Havana. Under the overall command of Captain-General Don Juan Esteban de Ubilla, the combined fleets, numbering eleven treasure galleons in all, proceeded northward along the eastern Florida coast. According to the established course, they intended to pass St. Augustine before turning east for the voyage to Cadiz or Seville.

But Ubilla's command never saw St. Augustine. The fleet was halfway up the Florida coast when, at 2:00 A. M. on July 31st, 1715, a violent hurricane struck. All but one of the eleven ships went to the bottom. The surviving vessel brought word of the disaster to St. Augustine, and the news was later confirmed by a handful of crewmen who had escaped the fate of their ships and had made their way up to the coast to the Spanish city.

The Spanish Government immediately dispatched salvagers to the site of the wrecks, to bring up a treasure valued at the time at four million pesos ($14 million today), according to elaborate records now on file in the Spanish National Archives at Seville.

The records also show that pirates and salvagers from all over the Caribbean hampered the Spanish activities, attacking the salvage ships and diving on the wrecks themselves. In 1718 Manuel Miralles, a diving contractor for the Spanish, arrived on the scene with a small squadron and surprised and captured eight sloops and riggers "fishing" on the wrecks.

After four years of salvage the Spanish Government abandoned the sunken hulks, leaving about half the treasure. It was to remain largely undisturbed for 235 years.

September 2, 1964-November 15, 1966

HUNT AT CAPE KENNEDY YIELDS TREASURE IN SEA

A treasure in jewelry and gold coins has been found on the sea floor near Cape Kennedy, Florida.

The National Georgrapic Society disclosed in Washington today that Kip Wagner, a construction engineer of Sebastian, Florida, and nine associates spent the least four years in salvage work.

The treasure was reportedly lost in a hurricane in 1715, when ships carrying New World plunder for King Philip V of Spain were wrecked off the cape.

It came to light again in 1955, when Mr. Wagner found on a beach south of Cape Kennedy, an irregularly-shaped silver piece of eight with a cross and the arms of Spain. Nearby finds, made with the aid of a $15 Army surplus mine detector, convinced him that he had discovered the site of a fortified

Kip Wagner, president of the Real 8 Company and one of Florida's pioneer treasure salvors, examines Spanish tableware and Chinese porcelain salvaged from the 1715 wrecks off Fort Pierce in 1968.

warehouse in which eighteenth-century Spanish salvors, dispatched to the site by the Spanish Government as soon as news of the disaster reached home, had stored what treasure they could recover. The site gave clues to the location of the wrecked ships.

Encouraged by his finds, Mr. Wagner and his associates formed the Real Eight Corporation in 1961 ("pieces-of-eight" was a common name for the old Spanish dollar, which was divided into eight *reales*). The corporation obtained permission from Florida authorities to undertake exclusive offshore salvage operations. Its take from the wrecks is shared with the State of Florida.

Mr. Wagner, in his search, has found bright gold rings, necklaces, flatware, vessels, lockets, religious objects, and blue-and-white porcelain from China, still intact in its packing.

More than $400,000 in Spanish gold and silver, all hidden in Florida waters for nearly 250 years, will be exhibited soon throughout the state. The items represent only one-fourth of the amount recovered recently off Fort Pierce and the nearby Sebastian Inlet by the Real Eight Corporation, a private salvage company. Under a licensing agreement, the state is entitled to 25 per cent of everything recovered from wrecked ships. The value of the entire find is about $1.6 million.

Included among the recovered artifacts are cannons, cannon balls, sounding leads, muskets, pewter plates, map dividers, fragments of olive jars and

November 1, 1964
NO DEEP MYSTERY

These articles from the New York Times help give Florida's Treasure Coast its nickname.

Hunt at Cape Kennedy Yields Treasure in Sea

WASHINGTON, Sept. 1 (UPI)—A treasure in jewelry and gold coins has been found on the sea floor near Cape Kennedy, Fla.

The National Geographic Society disclosed here that Kip Wagner, a construction engineer of Sebastian, Fla., and nine associates spent four years in salvage work.

The treasure was reportedly lost in a hurrican~ 1715, when 10 ~

N~

EARLY DIVER FO

Skeleton With Prim~ Is Near Sunken

MIAMI, Fla., Marc~ expedition seeking $~ sunken gold bullion h~ the skull and primiti~ an early American d~ whose skeleton was f~ wreck of an old Span~

Joseph Summers of~ Williamson expeditio~ divers had found doz~ craft between Key W~ and that the latest di~ back to about 1700.

A search of the~ ever, failed to disclo~ the gold which re~ cached aboard the~ ship Santa Rosa.

Commenting on th~ dead diver, Mr. Summ~

"There are two c~ about it. First, the h~ airlines or any provis~ cept what was in the~ ond, the skelet~ most 1~

Spanish Treasure, Lost at Sea in 17

By GRACE GLUECK

Gold ingots, pieces of eight and other samples of buried Spanish treasure have turned up at a site that would aston- ish Captain Kidd—the Madison Avenue auction galleries of Parke-Bernet.

The loot, lush enough to satis- fy even such grabby pirates as Pew and Long John Silver, is part of a cache recovered in rec~nt years from a 10-ship Spanish fleet wrecked off the coast of Florida in 1715. Its worth is estimated at more than $500,000. The gallery will auc-

tion it on Feb. 4, but local treasure buffs will have a chance to view it from Dec. 20 through Jan. 15.

"This is the pièce de résist- ance," said Howard Ricketts, antiquities expert for Sotheby —Parke-Bernet, pointing to a gold "captain's chain." The chain, 11 feet 4½ inches long and made up of 2,176 solid gold links, bears a gold pendant in the form of a dragon. The dra- gon's belly conceals a gold toothpick, its tail serves as an carpick, and the dragon itself is a whistle.

The chain, probably made in China, is of a type once worn by captains-general of Spanish fleets as their emblem of office. It is believed to be the only one of its kind still in exis- tence, and its value has been put by museum experts at over ~000.

hurricane struck the~ ships near Cape Cana~ Cape Kennedy). All b~ driven on to the ree~ valued officially at~ went down with th~

After four year~ efforts, the Span~ ment abandoned~ hulks, leaving ~ the treasure.

Encouraged ~ Mr. Wagner a~ ciates formed ~ Corporation in~ eight" was a ~ the old Span~ was divided~ The corpora~ mission fro~ ities to u~ off-shore s~ take from~ with the~

Divers ~ tarnished~ cluding ~ together~ ~ matter~

Treasure Hunt Approved If Florida Receives Half

WEST PALM BEACH, Fla., Jan. 15 (UPI)—The Central and Southern Florida Flood Control District gave a treasure hunter permission to search for a pirate's chest in a St. Lucie County Canal today—provided he gives the state half of what he finds.

The district board condition of the agree an employe be pres the hunt.

Paul A. McDowell the board in the na Indian River Coin C Fort Pierce to sea pirate treasure ches he believes was loca canal.

2D SPANISH GALLEON FOUND OFF FLORIDA

MELBOURNE, Fla., July 2 (AP)—The discovery of a Spanish galleon that is expected to yield great sunken treasures was announced today by the Real 8 Corporation.

Harry Cannon, a mem the corporation, at a onference the tol r exceed", up too th

Spanish Treasure In Holiday Display

y HERBERT C. BARDES

THE fabulous treasure recovered off the southeastern coast of Florida from the wrecks of anish fleet has been in ut of the headlines for tter part of three years. tive handful of collecve seen bits of it at a or coin shows.

ng Tuesday, and conuntil Jan. 15, hunthese salvaged items display at Parkealleries, Inc., 980 Avenue (at 76th urs are 11 A.M. to lays through Sat- 7 P.M. Sundays. n charge of $2.50 ludes a "Treasustrated in cole for children 1, and group ble on request. serve as the e to what be an even nt, a public the items. by Parkerospective lers may

effort that ended in 1719. Several American salvage companies, starting in 1961, have managed to bring up only an estimated million dollars worth of treasure from four of the 10 wrecks that have been located so far.

Many of the gold coins in the Parke-Bernet display are of date-mint combinations hitherto unrecorded. The same, to a lesser extent, is true of the silver coins. All were minted in 1715 or earlier. A sampling of the crudely struck gold coins is illustrated at right.

Items of the Day

In addition to the numismatic items, the display includes a variety of non-numismatic material—cannon balls, naval gear, pewter plates, silver forks and pottery, and porcelain utensils—much of it perfectly preserved. The gold coins, too, are in "mint state," but many of the silver coins are in large chunks, fused by the action of sea water.

Will Be Sold

"Because of its purity, the gold was brought up in bright mint condition," noted Mr. Ricketts, hefting in his hand a pie-shaped gold bullion block that weighs 120 troy ounces. "The silver and base metals became encrusted with sea matter that has to be removed by electrolysis."

Perhaps the most bizarre of the finds is a small silver cross, which cannot be separated from the spiky shell fragments that have adhered to it through the centuries.

The haul also included costume buckles of pewter and bronze, a huge silver ingot weighing 516 ounces, mess plates of pewter and silver, forks and spoons and teacups of Chinese export porcelain that have survived the centuries without a scratch.

The treasure recovered to date comes from just four of the wrecks. Mr. Ricketts explained that the salvage group was auctioning it in order to finance further explorations.

To display its haul, the first such cache ever shown at the Parke-Bernet will exhibition rooms

An in red of ver, the

A. hat ken ba, ted

ow- of was ish

the ngs no

finds, asso- Eight eces of me for which reals). ed per- author- exclusive tions. Its is shared lorida.

inging up coins, in- lumps stuck nt-like "sea ching a total ey also found a gilded ink- along

A pewter plate with the calcified remnants of a Spanish officer's last meal still on it, silver forks, and Kang' Hsi Chinese cups transported across Mexico from Spain's Pacific trading ports, made up part of the Real 8 Company's mid-1960s salvage.

other ceramic objects, pieces of timber, ballast stones and rigging.

Among the items made of precious metals are a number of gold chains—some are as long as six feet—as well as gold rings and round, pie-shaped gold and silver ingots weighing up to twelve pounds. Also found were silver forks, knife handles, candlesticks, and Spanish "cobs," which are irregularly-shaped, die-stamped coins of gold and silver. Some date from 1607.

The state's share of the treasure also includes 857 gold coins and 2,193 silver coins, plus a large number of coins imbedded in coral. Dates on these coins range from 1693 to 1714.

Many attempts have been made to recover valuables from wrecked ships, but most of these efforts have been unorganized, unscientific and sporadic, and the rewards usually have been minor. However, the successful salvage operation that recently enriched Florida, as well as the project's organizers, was carefully planned, and will continue for at least ten years.

The salvage company uses several kinds of diving gear, electronic detecting devices, dredging apparatus and water-pumping systems.

The salvagers have found that the wrecks, which are in a 50-mile area along the shore, bear little resemblance to the commonly held conception of a large hulk lying on the bottom. In fact, the divers have found little to indicate that this ocean floor was once strewn with wrecks.

According to the trustees of the state's Internal Improvement Fund, the salvagers "do not conform to the treasure-hunter image; to them, this is a business, and it is approached as such."

And it is a business that is expected to become even more profitable for the state of Florida. There are hopes for larger finds. Most of the treasure brought up so far came from just one wreck site, which is believed to have been a Dutch ship leased by the Spanish.

Many of the coins found are not in the catalogues of numismatists. Research has shown that the recovered coins were struck at several mints in the New World during the latter part of the reign of Charles II (1665-1700) and the early part of the first reign of Philip V (1700-1724). During that time there were at least four mints operating on the mainland of Spanish America: at Mexico City, Lima, Santa Fe de Bogota, and Potosi.

January 31, 1965
THE GOLD BUG

Port Pierce, Florida, a cattle, citrus and farming center midway between Palm Beach and Cape Kennedy, is now reaching out for the tourist trade with a glamorous glitter of doubloons and pieces-of-eight from Spanish galleons wrecked offshore nearly 250 years ago.

Stirred by nationally publicized treasure finds that have been made within the last year at a point only a few yards off Fort Pierce beaches, the town has adopted various means of cashing in on the salvage operations without actually joining the quest. To attract tourists to a degree never experienced here, the title of "Treasure Coast" has been officially adopted for this Indian River region.

Amateur treasure-hunters abound. Indications point toward a grand influx of scuba-minded youngsters to Fort Pierce during the coming college

vacation period, drawn from their traditional haunt, For Lauderdale, "where the girls are," to this community, "where the gold is."

The solitary Fort Pierce coin dealer, doing a sort of hobby business before the gold rush, now finds his trade increased by 400 per cent. He has just petitioned the state for permission to dredge a nearby canal for a pirate's chest.

"Do you really find treasure on the shore?" is the gist of hundreds of inquiries sent from other states, and even from foreign parts, to the Chamber of Commerce.

The answer is, "Yes." But without scientific equipment, a long study of charted wrecks, a large sum of luck, and leases from the State of Florida, which now takes a fourth of the salvage finds and may possibly take all, amateurs have to be satisfied with an occasional tarnished silver piece, a bright gold escudo or a coral-encrusted what-not defying identification.

There is talk of professional treasure- hunters flipping ancient coins for drinks in Fort Pierce bars. Businessmen and telephone conversations with jocular queries, such as, "How's the gold today?" Lawsuits even have been started here that reflect disputes among the treasure finders. Treasure maps and charts of reefs that have caused wrecks have ready sale, and counterfeit doubloons have started to appear.

However, it should be stressed that Fort Pierce, with a population of 45,000 and an economy soberly based upon thriving cattle, citrus and sportfishing industries, has not really gone treasure-mad. The treasure finds would be litle more than a diversion to the town, were it not for their impact on the local culture and the fact that many in Fort Pierce feel the place has never had its rightful share of the tourist dollar. A citizens' group has been formed to organize a Fort Pierce museum, to display treasure loaned by the State of Florida. Imporvements to bridges along State Route A1A are planned, to handle the expected influx of tourists, many of whom from the Cape Kennedy space center 70 miles up the coast. Treasure-mad or not, local officials are delighted.

As an aftermath to the recent recovery by the Real Eight Corporation of a fortune in Spanish treasure off Florida's east coast, the state has been considering a plan that would give it complete possession of all such discoveries made in the future. In the meantime, state officials have decided to stop issuing permits for treasure hunting in Florida waters.

It has been suggested by A Special Advisory committee appointed by the state and headed by anthropologist Dr. Charles Fairbanks, that Florida also revoke permits currently in force, take over all salvage operations, and keep everything that is found.

Trustees of the Florida Internal Improvements Fund, the state agency which monitors treasure salvage, acted immediately, voting unanimously to stop issuing treasure-hunting permits, pending a review of the present situation.

Among the subjects to be reviewed is the criticism that has been leveled at

January 31, 1965
**FLORIDA
RECONSIDERS
THE SHARING
OF TREASURE**

the manner in which the recent findings have been divided between the state and the Real Eight Corporation. At the recent division, in which the state's share was set at $400,000 in gold, jewels and artifacts, the state was represented by a highway trooper and a certified public accountant, individuals whose qualifications as experts on the value of Spanish treasure are dubious, to say the least.

The state's Marine Salvage Advisory committee is now working on tightening supervision and control of treasure-hunting operations.

June 13, 1965

FLORIDA CURBS TREASURE HUNTS

Florida has passed a new law, the Florida Antiquities Act of 1965, to restrain treasure hunters and to "protect, and preserve treasure trove, including sunken, abandoned ships or any part therof." The act requires that "all salvage operations must be carried out under the immediate supervision and control of official representatives of the State Board of Antiquities." The board will be made up of the Governor and his aides.

The act also establishes controls over historic sites, buildings and objects of antiquity that have scientific or historical value.

The recovery of $1.6 million worth of treasure from a sunken Spanish galleon off Fort Pierce focused attention on the state's loosely-worded and little-enforced laws covering such discoveries.

Now, a treasure hunter must enter into a binding contract with the state before undertaking a search. Any treasure found must be appraised by three professional appraisers. The Board of Antiquities then determines the salvor's "fair share" with the remainder going to the state. The salvor's share cannot exceed 75 per cent and can be less.

The state is already in the process of hiring archaeologists and persons expert in determining the value of antiquities, to serve as its agents under the new law.

Various dates, June, 1965-June, 1969

GOLD FEVER CONTINUES

Facing page:
Silver pieces-of-eight, fused together by oxidation and the encrustations of marine organisms, were found in profusion by Wagner's divers. Many others, more perfectly preserved, made up the richest numismatic find of the 1960s.

The stiff new regulations in Florida did not stop new waves of treasure-hunters from flooding into the Fort Pierce area. Wagner's Real Eight Corporation was but one of many salvage companies that resumed the search in the summer of 1965, after seasonal spring storms had calmed down.

Edwin A. Link, inventor of the Link Trainer system of simulated aircraft for pilot schooling, came to the area to film some episodes of a movie on diving, "Descent to Greatness." An oceanographer by vocation, Link was accompanied by Dr. Jacques Piccard, holder of the world record for depth diving, and John Perry, a pioneer in the development of small, deep-diving research submarines. Link was also in Florida for treasure. As chief of operations for the Salvage Research Corporation of Vero Beach, he planned to use his research vessel, *Sea Diver II*, supplemented by an 18-foot mini-submarine from the Woods Hole Oceanographic Institute, to investigate the wrecks of the "Treasure Coast."

Other salvage companies proliferated. Expeditions Unlimited, operating in conjunction with the Martin County Historical Society, began explorations off Hutchinson's Island, where additional wrecks from the 1715 fleet

were believed to have gone down. Competing with the company in Hutchinson Island waters was another, the Perdido Corporation. Real Eight's policy of operating in strict secrecy obviously could no longer be sustained, in the golden glare of publicity focused ont he Fort Pierce area.

The publicity was stepped up by the exhibition, in a museum in Gainesville, Florida, of part of the state's share of the Real Eight Corporation's 1964 find. That exhibition later traveled to the Florida pavillion at the New York World's Fair, and the treasure fever grew apace. The Florida Antiquities Act of 1965, drawn up hastily to deal with the swarms of amateur and professional treasure-hunters who flocked to Fort Pierce in the wake of the exhibition, limited the issuing of state permits for treasure- diving. But enforcement could not keep pace with the gold fever, and at least one lucky amateur, John Charles Sykes, proceeding without a permit, managed to keep title to at least part of the value of a pair of solid god Aztec statuettes he found on Florida's Gulf Coast. Not associated with the 1715 wrecks, these statuettes, plus a large number of silver coins Sykes also found, were probably part of a Spanish shipment from Mexico in the late 1600s.

Meanwhile, in July, 1965, the Real Eight Corporation struck gold a second time. This time the treasure galleon, another vessel from the 1715 fleet, was found just south of Sebastian Inlet, 35 miles south of Cape Canaveral (Cape Kennedy at the time). More than 3,000 pounds of gold and silver, including ten disks weighing between 60 and 100 pounds each, wedge-shaped and cylindrical ingots, and coral-incrusted clusters of pieces-of-eight, were put on display at Real Eight's private treasure museum in Melbourne, Florida.

The second discovery, which eventually topped $1.8 million in value, bringing the company's total treasure strike to over three and a half million dollars, sent the State Board of Antiquities into a flurry over enforcement of the Antiquities Act. Dr. Fairbanks, advisor to the Board on treasure matters, stated in November, 1965, that some salvors were refusing to make treasure items available for inspection by appraisers. The state decided to toughen regulations, and refused absolutely to grant new permits. By the end of the year only the Real Eight Corporation and the Martin County Historical Society still held treasure licenses.

In February, 1966, Florida got one quarter of the second Real Eight find, its share amounting to $460,000. This time the appraisal was far more searching, conducted by experts on both sides. The following June Real Eight went back to work, operating this time through a subcontractor called *Treasure Salvors, Inc.* The new effort, again off Sebastian Inlet, netted 68 silver "cobs" 15 unidentified iron objects, four cannon balls, a dagger, a human bone, a petrified tooth, a silver wedge of about seven pounds, and a smashed lead box. But buried in this grandmother's trunkload of odd jetsam was a priceless emerald ring, proving that Wagner's professionalism, and painstaking methods had again paid off.

The Florida State Museum was designated sole custodian of the state's share of the treasure, and it began to work on the problem of providing adequate security for the displaying of its valuable collection.

Amid the disputes over divisions and shares of the spoils, some citizens of

Vero Beach remembered that Spain, after all, was the original owner of the treasure. But as far as the state and the hard-headed professional salvors were concerned, Spain's claim was as out of date as its New World empire; a rather apologetic token of a few coins was eventually delivered to the Spanish Embassy in Washington by members of the Indian River Coin Club, which had benefited extravagantly from the treasure fever and its attendant publicity.

Disputes over shares continued into the fall of 1966. The Florida Association of Marine Explorers, a group whose membership included weekend scuba-diving amateurs as well as professional salvage firms, threatened to go to court to force the Board of Antiquities to liberalize its regulations. The association objected to the Board's ruling that a state agent must be aboard every treasure-seeking craft to log its activities. It further protested that the state's 25 per cent share was exorbitant, considering that the state contributed nothing to the financing of treasure expeditions.

But Wagner and the Real Eight-Treasure Salvors amalgamation continued, largely exempt from the broils which affected other salvage firms. To begin with, their first major find was made before the 1965 law was passed. The company had kept some of the best-preserved and most beautiful artifacts from their years of salvage, and in 1966 the choicest items were released for sale at auction, to the prestigious Parke-Bernet Galleries in New York (see below).

Nor did the company rest on its laurels. As late as June, 1969, a marine biologist, Carl Clausen, announced that a diver for Treasure Salvors, Inc. had discovered what was believed to be the *Capitaña*, the flagship of the 1715 fleet. With most of its wrecks charted completely, and a substantial amount of treasure the early Spanish salvors had missed, brought up from the bottom to gleam in display cases at auction galleries and in museums, the fleet of Don Juan Esteban de Ubilla had completed the perilous voyage from local legend to world-renoned reality, a journey in many ways far longer than the distance from the New World to Spain.

Robert Johnson, Real 8's chief diver, displays one of the ten large silver disks recovered from the Florida treasure coast site in 1965.

Various dates, November, 1966- December, 1972

TREASURE AT AUCTION

The auction of treasure from the Ubilla fleet was not the first major public sale of Spanish gold and silver, but it proved to be one of the richest. The first auction took place at the Parke-Bernet Galleries (now Sotheby Parke Bernet, Inc.) on Madison Avenue in New York, after the auction gallery had put the treasure on display over the 1966 Christmas holidays. The exhibition which preceded the auction was lavishly mounted, the display rooms being accurately redecorated in the style of the eighteenth century. Gold and silver coins provided the majority of items on display, the sale being directed toward the numismatic market. But cannon balls, naval gear, pewter plates, silver flatware and porcelain utensils, much of it perfectly preserved, were also displayed, helping to provide a dramatic and historically accurate setting for the suptuous coin show.

The most unusual artifact displayed was a *gold chain 11 feet 4 1/2 inches long*, made of 2,176 hand-crafted links. Suspended on the chain was a gold

Hans M. S. Schulman, a New York coin dealer, indulges in some justifiable gloating over prizes from Kip Wagner's treasure. The dealer was one of many who profited handsomely in the auctions of Real 8 salvage, which made numismatic history in 1969 and 1972.

Real 8 Company's historian, Bob Page, exhibits a display complete with grinning skulls, of the cream of the Wagner treasure in 1969. Spanish officers of the eighteenth century carried the thin rapiers and ornate flintlock pistols. The cutlass in the foreground was a more rough-and-ready weapon, the combat tool of choice of both the Spanish ordinary seaman and his buccaneering counterpart.

Gold chains of office, Chinese porcelain, jewelry and pieces-of-eight are displayed prior to the historic Parke Bernet auction of February, 1967. Kip Wagner was one of the first professional treasure salvors to respect the artistic and archaeological value of his sunken galleons' cargoes, and his care paid off very nicely.

pendant in the form of a dragon, about the size of a man's thumb. The dragon itself was a whistle; hinged into its stomach was a golden toothpick; and the tail was designed to be used as an earpick. The whole device, as handy as a Boy Scout knife and much more beautiful, was recognized by experts as the emblem of office of the Captain-General himself, Don Juan Esteban de Ubilla, overall commander of the plate fleet in the fateful year of 1715. The dragon-whistle, made in China, ended its strange journey over years and seas by vanishing into the possession of an unnamed collector, who purchased it through the agency of Elinor Gordon, an antique dealer of Villanova, Pennsylvania. It sold for $50,000.

The anchor of the treasure fleet's flagship, the *Capitaña*, more than eleven feet long, was purchased by L. P. Lee, a London firm, for $1,000. The British purchase was appropriate, since the *Capitaña* had formerly been the *Hampton Court*, a London-built vessel of 1678, captured by the French and presented to their Spanish ally. Other participants in the great auction, which took place on the 4th of February, 1967, included the Smithsonian Institution, which won a 33-ounce quartered ingot of gold for $1,700; the Newark Museum, which bought gold and silver coins; the University of Illinois, which carried off a breech-block, cannon balls, and some of the rare, intact Chinese porcelain cups, still nested in their original packing; and the American Numismatic Society, which bought several gold pieces, one a full doubloon of 1713. The sale grossed $227,450.

Although serious antiquaries, collectors and museum experts accounted for the majority of the important purchases, Parke-Bernet's auction was charmed by the presence of quite a few children, who participated vicariously in the romance of treasure and treasure-hunting by bidding against adults for affordable items like ships' nails and single pieces-of-eight. Twelve-year-old

Brad Staub of Ridgewood, N.J., won out over a Spokane, Washington doctor, carrying home 10 nails from a Spanish galleon for $5 more than the physician was willing to pay. "I've been saving a long time, and I still have a little money left," said Brad as he left with his trophy. Another twelve-year-old lugged home 20 lead grapeshot and $90 worth of antique lead plating which had once protected the bottom of a treasure galleon from salt-water corrosion. The experts may have collected the cream of the treasure, but the kids made the auction at the normally staid Parke-Bernet Galleries into a media event, by capturing the lion's share of attention from the television news cameras which covered the affair.

In September, 1969, more of the Real Eight Cororation's treasure salvage went on sale at Stack's, a well-known numismatic auction house, also of New York. Schulman Coin and Mint, another highly-regarded auction house catering to the coin specialist, sold more of the treasure in October of 1972. But Kip Wagner did not live to enjoy the proceeds of the latter sale. He died in February, 1972, having made history as the first major salvor to apply advanced technology and a concern for the artistic and historical value of treasure trove to the age-old golden quest. His example has guided modern treasure-hunters ever since, simply because he proved that there was more money to be made by proceeding carefully and systematically than had ever been realized by the old doubloon-grabbing salvage attempts of the past. Perhaps it is not too sentimental to suggest that Wagner, who had begun his golden career as a treasure-hunter by beachcombing in his spare time, was most pleased by the children who attended the Parke-Bernet auction and, ignoring the meticulously coded signals and conventions of their elders, simply shouted out their bids for romantic fragments of the vessels sunk so many years ago off Florida's Treasure Coast.

THE SECRET OF THE BLACK CITY

Introduction

9

Alexander of Macedon conquered the Persian Empire and pushed his armies as far east as India in the fourth century B.C., leaving a string of newly-built cities named after himself in his wake.

Facing page:
The high plains of Outer Mongolia are dotted with the leavings of nomadic cultures which have ranged here since prehistory.

The subject of Russian treasure immediately conjures up visions of the last days of the Romanovs, when fleeing aristocrats attempted to smuggle bejeweled Fabergé "eggs" and other glories of the Tsars into exile, while Bolshevik armies ransacked abandoned palaces looking for the remainder to finance their fledgling Soviet state. Treasure hidden during the Russian Revolution does exist, and the Soviet Government successfully unearthed a good deal of it during the 1920s, the richest single haul being several million dollars' worth of jewelry discovered in 1925 in the Leningrad palace of Prince Yussopov, head of the cabal that killed the last Tsar's evil genius, Rasputin.

But there are other treasures of far more romantic provenance associated with Russia. Three great conquerors once swept through areas of the country, from present-day Kazakhstan (Kazakh Soviet Socialist Republic) to the Chinese border of Mongolia. In their wake they may have left ancient hoards far exceeding the lost loot of the Romanovs.

Alexander the Great, on the march of conquest which took him across the old Persian Empire into northern India (330-328 BC), is rumored to have cached some of the immense plunder of Susa and Persepolis in earth mounds near the city of Turkestan, K. S. S. R.

Tamerlane, or Timur Lenk, "Timur the Lame" (1336?-1405) sallied forth from his capital at Samarkand near the Afghan border with an army of Tartars and Mongols, to overrun desert, plain and steppe from Poland to the Persian Gulf and from Constantinople to the China Sea. The treasures of Baghdad, Aleppo, Damascus, Moscow and a host of other cities fell into his hands, and was borne on caravan trains of camels and elephants back to his capital. A Spanish envoy from the court of Henry III of Castile visited Tamerlane's court in 1403 and described the conqueror's gaudy furnishings:

"There were gold tables, each standing on four legs, and the tables and legs were all one. And seven golden vials stood upon them, two of which were set with large pearls, emeralds, and turquoises, and each one had a ruby near the mouth. There were also six round golden cups, one set with large pearls inside, and in the center of it was a ruby two fingers broad, and of a brilliant hue."

Tamerlane, too, was reputed to have left a large portion of his treasure in the tumuli of Turkestan, after his death in the field during his attempted conquest of China.

But the empires of Alexander and Tamerlane died with their founders. There are scholarly objections to the rumors of buried treasure associated with each. Alexander, it has been established, was in the habit of sending the greater part of his spoils home to Macedonia the moment he had conquered a city, to prevent dissension among his forces. And Tamerlane's loot was probably dispersed and scattered during the period of turmoil which shattered his empire after his death.

It is the booty of Genghis Khan (1162-1227) which still promises rich rewards for the persistent treasure-hunter. Slashing out of Mongolia with his warriors, Genghis conquered China and established an empire which for a time stretched from Peking to Kiev. It lasted long enough for permanent outposts to be built and for an orderly system of provincial governments,

regulations and taxation to be established. His successor Kublai established the Mongol (Chin) dynasty in China, and was the "Great Khan" referred to by Marco Polo in the Italian entrepreneur's account of his trading travels to the East.

Treasure connected with the empire of the Khans has been unearthed in the area of Samarkand and present-day Alma Ata, but rumors of a legendary hoard associated with a mysterious "lost city" in Mongolia's Gobi Desert provide the most tantalizing clues for the hunter in search of the loot of the Mongol Empire.

May 2, 1926
VAST STORES OF LOOT SEIZED BY CONQUERORS SOUGHT IN TURKESTAN

Genghis Khan led his Mongol hordes out of Central Asia to conquer China and establish an empire stretching from European Russia to the China Sea.

The paths that once were made by the chariot wheels of conquerors are to be followed again by treasure-seekers. This time it is the tumuli of Turkestan that are to be explored by an expedition dispatched by the Russian Soviet Government in search of the riches which Alexander the Great, Genghis Khan and Tamerlane are believed to have concealed during their campaigns.

Whatever may be the outcome of the quest, the announcement of its initiation has served to point attention to the looting methods of the early conquerors. The wholesale demand for a city's wealth that was once the ruling doctrine of the victor is typically expressed in the words of the great Genghis Khan, leader of the hordes of Mongolia, when he stood outside the walls of Bokhara:

"Oh men of Bokhara, you have been guilty of enormous crimes; hence the wrath of God, of whose vengeance I am the instrument, hath employed me against you. Of all property in this city which is visible, it would be needless to require an account. What I demand is the immediate surrender of all that is concealed."

Two enclosures of stones screened by curtains mark the burial place of Genghis Khan today at Rache Tchurin in the country of the Ortous Mongols. In 1206 he became Emperor of the Mongols; in 1226 he died in his traveling palace after scourging all Asia, yet tribute is still paid to his memory. Only a few years ago a wandering priest, one of the guardians of the tomb, described ceremonies of reverence staged in memory of the nomad conqueror:

"The twenty-first day of the third moon in every year is the date for sacrificing at the tomb. In the open space on the northeast side a large tent is erected, and the white stone coffin is respectfully carried out by a white horse and a white camel, and carefully placed in the middle of the tent. In front of it are arranged the bows, arrows and carts belonging to the deceased; also the sacrificial animals. They then worship and pour out libations according to the rites. Those who live far away to the north or west send their official representatives to present sacrificial offerings.

April 24, 1927
THE BLACK CITY

By Avrahm Yarmolinsky

A recent dispatch from Moscow says that General Peter K. Kozlov, the celebrated Asiatic traveler and geographer, intends this year to excavate a mysterious well situated among the ruins of the ancient Mongolian city of Kharo-Khoto, and said to hold many carloads of treasure.

It was during Kozlov's expedition to Central Asia in 1907-1909 that he discovered and partly excavated the deserted ruins of the city in the Gobi Desert, on the lower reaches of the Etsingol River in Inner Mongolia. Earlier travelers had heard reports of the mysterious city, known to local nomads as Kharo-Khoto, or the Black City, but Kozlov asserts that he was the first European to behold its half-buried towers and tombs.

In his account of the trip, published in 1923, Kozlov related the following legend in which the above-mentioned well figures. The last ruler of the fortified city, Hara-Tzyan-Tzyun, made an attempt to capture the throne of the Emperor of China. A series of battles took place east of the city, and the hard-driven Kharo-Khotans finally had to take refuge within its walls. Unable to capture the city, the Chinese imperial army built a dam to divert the River Etsingol, from which the Kharo-Khotans drew their water. The besieged proceeded to dig a well in the stronghold, hoping to strike water. No matter how deep the shaft went, not a drop was forthcoming. It was then that Hara-Tzyan-Tzyun decided to go forth a last time to give battle. Anticipating defeat, he first slew his two wives and his children, lest they suffer a worse fate at the hands of the enemy. He also buried his most precious possessions—there were eighty carloads of silver alone, according to the legend, plus priceless hoards of gold and jewels—in the waterless well.

Having completed his preparations, he had a breach made in the northern wall and sallied forth. The ruler perished with his whole army in battle. The Chinese entered the city and devastated it, but failed to find the hidden treasure. Later attempts to discover it have been equally unsuccessful, for the reason, concludes the legend, that its owner had laid a spell upon it.

The dead city is located on a low sandstone terrace. Part of the massive clay ramparts remains, but in places a camel can walk across the city walls over the sands piled up by the desert winds. Here and there the dreary skyline is broken up by brick mausoleums.

One of these, known as "The Famous," yielded a treasure of immense value to Kozlov and his assistants, during the explorer's second expedition. Artistic finds included a fine collection of Buddhist sacred images painted on silk and canvas, in the Chinese and Tibetan manners. "The Famous" also yielded an assemblage of books and scrolls, chiefly manuscripts, more than 2,000 items in all.

Among the Mongolian texts Kozlov found a fourteen-line fragment apparently part of a collection of the sayings of Genghis Khan. There are also documents in the original Tangut script, the written language, not yet deciphered completely, of the Tangut tribes. The fragments and other evidence support the theory that Kharo-Khoto was the chief city of the Tangut State, an important administrative department of Genghis Khan's empire. The warlike Tangut tribe was of Buddhist faith and spoke a language akin to Tibetan. Racially distinct from Genghis's Mongols, the Tanguts were never fully assimilated by the conqueror, and it is possible that the assault of the last ruler of the Black City upon the then-Mongol emperor of China reflected a residue of the hostility that continued to smoulder among the Tangut tribes long after their land had become part of the empire of the Khans.

KOZLOV AND THE TREASURE OF THE MONGOLS

It is not recorded whether or not General Kozlov found the legendary well of the Black City, with its eighty carloads of silver. His most successful dig in Central Asia occurred in 1923, when he discovered a vast Mongol necropolis at a point some 100 kilometers northeast of Urga, the holy city of the Mongols. The ancient burial ground consisted of over 200 tumuli situated in three parallel valleys of the Noin-Ula Mountains, not far from the River Hara.

At a certain depth beneath the surface of the earth mounds Kozlov and his assistants discovered burial chambers built of wooden logs. Within each of these were found internal chambers which held coffins. The walls of the chambers were hung with woolen and silken draperies, and under the coffin, which was richly decorated, there was invariably a large rug made of felt surmounted by woolen fabric and edged with silk.

The treasure found by the archaeologists included gold, amber and jade ornaments, brass objects, silk robes trimmed with fur, and braids of human hair in silken cases with funerary talismans attached. Some broad-handled wooden cups, painted black and lined with red lacquer, and bearing on their outer surfaces a thin design in red, dated from the Chinese Han Dynasty, which would make them more than 2,000 years old. Details of design among the numerous rugs discovered were found to be similar to ancient Scythian design modes, and certain purple fabrics embroidered in white and brown thread are undoubtedly of ancient Greek workmanship.

The arrangement of the drapery-hung coffin-chambers, with their felt rugs, however, resembles closely the decor of the funeral tent in which the sarcophagus of Genghis Khan continued to be honored yearly well into the twentieth century (see above). It is possible, therefore, that some of the ancient artifacts from other cultures were buried at the Noin-Ula site by Mongols of the period of the Khans, who had collected their precious spoils in the course of their conquests all over Asia.

Present tension between the U.S.S.R. and China has turned the Gobi Desert area into a no-man's-land and the Black City of Kharo-Khoto, as well as other locations of Mongol fortresses and tombs, remains shrouded in mystery. It is possible that Soviet workers—or their Chinese counter-parts, depending on the outcome of the territorial struggle—may yet come across the Black City's legendary well, containing the treasure of a last outpost of the Mongol Empire.

Of the many ships on both sides sunk during the Revolutionary War, only a few have been associated with treasure, and these are all British. This is not surprising, since the Continentals waged war on a flimsy paper framework of Congressional notes redeemable in the event of victory. Hard currency had always been in short supply in the American Colonies, and it got a good deal scarcer once the war broke out.

On the British side, although shipments of gold and silver specie were sent at intervals to pay King George's troops, because the British retained control of the sea until late in the war, for the most part these shipments made port safely and were duly dispersed to regimental paymasters. However, some American actions against British vessels did succeed, even in the first years of the war, and among the British ships sent down, a small number have taken their places in legend as treasure ships.

On October 23rd, 1777, the British frigate *Merlin*, a transport carrying 18 cannon, entered the Delaware Channel bound for Philadelphia. Under the orders of Admiral Lord Howe, the *Merlin*, accompanied by the 64-gun ship-of-the-line *Augusta*, was reputedly carrying $1 million to $2 million in gold, pay for British troops who were occupying Philadelphia after the battle of Germantown. Attempting to run past American-held Forts Mercer and Nassau on the Jersey shore, the two ships were caught in a fierce cannonade of red-hot shot. Their powder magazines were touched off, and they went to the bottom.

The man-of-war, *Augusta*, was the object of two successful salvage ventures off Hog Island in the Delaware, one in 1876 and another in 1948. The salvage yielded timber, pottery, and a British coin, but nothing of more than historical value. Of the *Merlin* and her precious cargo not a trace has been found.

Another British payroll ship, carrying money to British soldiers up the Hudson River during the Battle of Saratoga, went down between Bemis Heights and Fort Miller. Sporadic searches for the wreck have yielded little more than rumors over the years.

Of all the British treasure ships, the best-documented and most sought-after is H.M.S. *Hussar*, which went down in New York City's East River. She has been the goal of treasure-hunters since 1830. The quest for her rumored gold in the 1930s caught the attention of Simon Lake (MARGIN NOTE: SEE *RAISE THE LUSITANIA!* AND *THE MYSTERY OF THE SPANISH PAYROLL*), a submarine pioneer whose promotional abilities were at least as formidable as his ingenuity as an inventor.

H.M.S. *Hussar*, a 26-gun frigate carrying gold belonging to wealthy British citizens, American Tories and the British Army, was taking part in the British evacuation of New York City in 1780. Attempting to navigate the treacherous rip tides and currents of Hell Gate, *Hussar* struck Pot Rock and sank. According to the best calculations of various would-be salvors, she lies on the bottom of the East River between Port Morris and North Brother Island, about 50 yards off the Bronx's East 138th Street. The estimates of her cargo of gold bullion have ranged between $1.8 million and $5 million, the sum varying with the enthusiasm of the salvors.

Various dates, 1935-1940
THE TREASURE SHIP OF THE EAST RIVER

September 26, 1936

LAKE THINKS HULK IS TREA-SURE SHIP

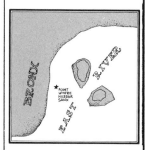

The East River off the Bronx, New York, has a secret. In 1780 a British frigate, H. M. S. *Hussar* sank here, carrying a treasure reputedly worth $4 million in gold.

August 6, 1935

"HUSSAR" GOLD QUEST RESUMED BY INVENTOR

Facing page:
Simon Lake, indefatigable submarine pioneer, shows a diagram of his bold method of reaching the *Hussar* treasure, one of many such schemes for which he was responsible in the 1930s.

Simon Lake's quest for the half-legendary gold of the British ship *Hussar* was resumed again yesterday in the swift rips and currents of the Hell Gate vicinity.

Mr. Lake, the submarine inventor, has been working intermittently for months, adapting and perfecting his diving apparatus of a "baby" submarine and hinged steel tube to the difficult conditions encountered in the East River. He stopped work some time ago, after finding three hulks at different spots in the vicinity of the *Hussar*'s supposed resting-place, all of them covered with about fifteen feet of silt. In the interval Mr. Lake installed a glass window in the bottom of the bow of the submarine. The craft is serviced by a long tube from a surface vessel. Lake also made a probing device which can be operated outside the submarine, controlled by those within it.

The work will now consist of an investigation of the three hulks, in an effort to learn if one of them is the *Hussar*.

The *Hussar*, according to a report that has never been fully substantiated, carried treasure, variously estimated at $4 million to $5 million, when she sank. Other reports placed the value of the treasure at a much lower figure, and still others deny that she had any gold aboard.

Simon Lake has notified the Treasury Department in Washington that he has discovered a hulk in the East River which he believes to be the almost fabulous H.M.S. *Hussar*, carrying $1.8 million (sic) in gold.

Summoning reporters to his room at 108 West 43rd Street yesterday afternoon, the inventor declared: "If I were a betting man, I would lay 100 to 1 the *Hussar* has been found at last. For fifty years I have been speculating on the likelihood of locating this ship, and within six weeks I expect to step within her hold. Now, nobody can tell what gold there is. It's not the gold so much as the satisfaction of solving a riddle, though some gold would do no harm."

On September 4th, his seventieth birthday, Mr. Lake struck the *Hussar*, he contends. Sounding operations were being conducted by him about fifty yards offshore between East 130th and East 140th Streets, the Bronx, on the East River.

Here, within the shadow of the busy College Point ferry terminus, his 80-foot beam was plunging into the murky water and through two fathoms of soft silt.

"All on board recognized the telltale sound of wood when the beam landed," Mr. Lake said, "and we more or less expected to find a spongy, water-logged raft, but instead the screw revealed hardwood, probably teak, and we felt we had the *Hussar*.

"Previous salvage operations established her position as just over a ledge, with her bow in fifty feet of water and her stern twenty feet lower," he continued. "I find such a ledge extends nearly a mile along the shore and drops down in some places to the depth mentioned. The hulk located lies in a posi-

tion corresponding to that of the *Hussar*.

"It is covered with twelve feet of silt which must be pumped off before I send a submarine down to settle on the frigate's decks. From that point divers can step into the hold with jets and suction pumps to see whether the treasure is fact or fable.

"My probing leads me to believe the *Hussar* could very well be raised for exhibition at the World's Fair. I hope to begin work under the supervision of the Coast Guard within a month."

February 12, 1940

BRONX PRESIDENT LYONS OFFERS GOLD

James J. Lyons, president and press agent extraordinary of what he invariably refers to as the Beautiful Borough of the Bronx, thought up another way yesterday of getting those inseparable names into the newspapers again.

He has a proposition to make. He's offering 20 per cent. All anyone needs to do to earn that sum (the principal is $4,000,000) is possess engineering

skill, provide a boat, and a diving bell, and have faith in Mr. Lyons. A kind and honest heart is another prerequisite, for the other 80 per cent, Mr. Lyons says, must go to the "deserving needy and poor of our city," including the Bronx.

The $4,000,000 lies on the bottom of the East River off Mr. Lyons' beloved borough. It got there, according to the borough president and the book he consulted (Charles B. Driscoll's *Doubloons*), when His Majesty's frigate *Hussar* sank on the spot in 1780, carrying a cargo of gold bullion, including, perhaps, some from another treasure ship, H.M.S. *Mercury*.

Since then there have been many efforts to salvage the fortune that President Lyons so generously donated to charity yesterday.

In 1830 an English expedition tried to raise it with a diving bell and failed. In 1880 Captain George Thomas got permission from the government to try it, but all he seems to have raised was the price of some beautifully engraved stock certificates he sold.

In 1900 divers, trying to salvage a sunken yacht, found an anchor with "H.M.S. *Hussar*" inscribed on it. The anchor was made of iron and brought $20 in a junk shop.

In 1930–1936 Simon Lake went looking for the gold. He didn't find it either.

Mr. Lyons thinks someone ought to find it.

"I have no desire to start a 'gold rush' to the Bronx," Mr. Lyons said yesterday, "but I hope this appeal for the revival of the search for the sunken *Hussar* will attract some attention."

"To the Bronx?" Mr. Lyons was asked.

"Exactly," he replied, going back to his book.

The tragic case of His Majesty's frigate *Hussar* has just been recalled by the offer of Bronx Borough President Lyons to give 20 per cent of the ship's treasure (estimated to be $4 million) to anyone who will salvage it. This tale of fabulous wealth lying just out of reach recalls other stories of buried and sunken treasure, gold and pieces of eight, believed or known to be hidden near New York City. Great riches await the finders, if rumor is to be credited.

Generally speaking, the swirling tides which gnaw at Manhattan and nearby shores cover authenticated treasure the value of which exceeds by far all the loot buried beneath the earth of the city. Off Cape May, New Jersey, to mention one example, lies the hulk of the *City of Athens*, with $3 million in her strong room. In addition to the *Hussar* at least one other sailing ship with gold and silver on board is reportedly sunk in the East River.

But the vicious tidal rips, cross-currents, and the soft ooze of which the bottom of New York's waters is composed present formidable obstacles to the treasure seeker. If the *Hussar* was indeed carrying gold when she sank in 1780, tides, currents and the shifting bottom have no doubt scattered the treasure from Hell Gate to the Battery by now.

SUNKEN PIECES OF EIGHT

THE BALLAD OF CAPTAIN KIDD

Introduction

11

(NOTE: Sources for this Introduction include The Pirates, by Douglas Botting, © 1978 Time-Life Books Inc., a wholly owned subsidiary of TIME INC.)

"My name was William Kidd, as I sail'd, as I sail'd;
And so wickedly I did, God's laws I did forbid,
As I sail'd.

I roam'd from sound to sound, as I sail'd, as I sail'd,
And many a ship I found, and them I sunk or burn'd,
As I sail'd.

I'd ninety bars of gold, as I sail'd, as I sail'd;
I'd a crew both brave and bold, and dollars manifold,
As I sail'd.

I murder'd William Moore, as I sail'd, as I sail'd,
And laid him in his gore, not many leagues from shore,
As I sail'd.

Farewell to young and old, for I must die, I must die;
And jolly seamen bold, you're welcome to my gold,
For I must die."

Or so one version of the broadside ballad, "Captain Kidd's Farewell to the Sea," would have us believe. The ballad, sold to the holiday-making crowd that thronged to watch Kidd and six members of his crew hang at London's Execution Dock in 1701, began the legend of the bloodthirsty pirate Captain who left millions in treasure all along the coast of the northeastern United States and Canada. But the ballad had nothing to do with the man himself, who never took an unlawful prize before his last voyage, was forced into piracy by his own crew, proved both inept and monumentally unlucky at the game, and died as a scapegoat in a political and financial cover-up which involved the innermost circles of the Court of King William III of England.

William Kidd was born in Scotland circa 1645. Details of his early life are unknown, but by 1689 he had seen active service as a privateer captain, fighting for Britain against the French and Spanish in the West Indies. In the 1690s he was well established as a merchant seacaptain in New York, and owned a large house at Pearl and Hanover Streets in today's financial district. He also owned property at 119-121 Pearl Street, 52-56 Water Street and 25-29 Pine Street, as well as a country retreat north of the seaport, near present-day East 79th Street. His house boasted New York's first "Turkey," or Oriental, carpet, and was sumptuously furnished with silver plate and silk hangings, all profits from the trading voyages of the merchant vessel he owned. He was married to a beautiful and wealthy Englishwoman, Sarah Oort, was a pillar of the Anglo-Dutch society of the town, and in general seems to have been a citizen of impeccable reputation both in business and private life.

But New York at the end of the seventeenth century was something of a wide-open town. The American colonists, hamstrung economically by Britain's Navigation Acts of 1651, which created a trade monopoly in the colonies for English merchants and shippers, had for some time been openly trading with pirates, then engaging in plundering the richly-laden vessels of the Red Sea

Facing page:
A conventionally villainous image of Captain William Kidd by illustrator Howard Pyle. The real Captain was distinguished more by bad luck than blood-lust.

and the Indian Ocean. Arab coffee sheikhs, Indian Moguls, and the British, Dutch and French East India Companies engaged in a golden trade in those waters, and the pirates, most of whom, like Kidd, had learned their trade as privateers during the recently-concluded wars, took prizes of enormous value. Needing a steady market for their stolen goods, and recognizing the American eagerness for a more open commerce than that provided by the strictures of the British Crown, the pirates, with the open connivance of almost all colonial governors of the period, openly walked the streets of New York, Newport, Salem and Boston, a vital element in the economy of British America. The Governor of New York, Colonel Benjamin Fletcher, was so deeply involved in the pirate trade that eventually he became an embarrassment to H. M.'s Government, and had to be replaced.

His replacement, a wealthy Anglo-Irish lord, the Earl of Bellomont, was to become the harbinger of Captain Kidd's ignoble end. Kidd had taken his trading sloop to London on a routine merchant voyage in 1695, and there he was introduced to Bellomont by one Robert Livingstone, a New York entrepreneur. Bellomont was involved in an elaborate scheme, prompted both by duty and avarice, to rid the seas of pirates and at the same time grow rich on the proceeds of their glittering stolen loot. He had the backing of four of the most powerful men in England: Sir John Somers, Lord Keeper of the Great Seal and afterwards Lord Chancellor; the Duke of Shrewsbury, Secretary of State; Sir Edward Russel, First Lord of the Admiralty; and the Earl of Romney, Master General of Ordnance. All they needed was the right captain, and Kidd, a sober, reliable shipmaster with combat experience as a privateer, was their man.

But the venture was a disaster. Kidd sailed from London in March, 1696, in the *Adventure Galley*, a newly-commissioned three-masted frigate built for speed and battle. She carried 34 guns, and her sail-power was supplemented with 46 oars to keep her moving even in calm air. She also carried a hand-picked crew, chosen for honesty and experience.

Kidd lost this crew almost immediately, in a *contretemps* with a Royal Navy ship, whose commander impressed every man for service, according to the highhanded practice of the time, before Kidd ever left the Thames. They were replaced by a pack of scurvy dogs who had failed to meet the Navy's by no means exacting standards for service. Kidd filled out this bunch with a group of semi-pirates recruited in New York. But in order to sign them for what was an official pirate-catching voyage, he had to increase the crew's share of the spoils to the usual privateering 60 per cent. This was in complete violation of the terms of his commission with Bellomont, which stipulated a share of only 25 per cent for the *Adventure Galley's* spoils of war. The articles of agreement he had signed with Bellomont and his noble backers further stipulated that there was to be no sharing-out of the takings during the cruise, the whole to be reserved for an official division by the British Admiralty upon Kidd's return. Kidd, knowing the tenor of the men he sailed with, had misgivings about the voyage before he ever left New York.

He had a further argument with the Royal Navy over the replacement of a set of sails he had lost in a storm near the Cape of Good Hope. Kidd's com-

mission, signed by the King and giving him the right not only to police the seas for pirates, but to attack ships bearing French papers (England being nominally at war with France at the time), may have given him delusions of grandeur. In any case, he comported himself rather arrogantly with the Navy, and later, when he anchored at Johanna Harbor near the pirate island of Madagascar, he appeared so suspicious to a British East Indiaman lying there, that she trained her guns on him and forced him to leave.

His crew, racked with fever and grumbling openly about short rations and the lack of prizes taken in more than a year at sea, was becoming a problem. Kidd proceeded to Perim, an island that had long provided pirates with an ambush point for attacks on Arab shipping coming down the Red Sea. For three weeks he lay in wait, but no pirates appeared. Finally, to satisfy his crew, he was persuaded to attack and fire upon a mixed convoy of English, Dutch and Arab merchantmen. Obviously of double mind about turning pirate in this manner, he quickly withdrew when an armed East Indiaman protecting the convoy moved in to engage him. His first half-hearted attempt at piracy had ended foolishly.

Kidd proceeded to the Malabar coast of India, where the ruling Moguls and the various East India Companies maintained a coastal shipping rich in gold, spices, jewels and precious fabrics. Commited, however reluctantly, to piracy, he captured a Moorish vessel and took her English captain and Portuguese interpreter on board his own ship. Shortly thereafter, he encountered an English ship, and his conscience reasserted itself. He refused to attack her, and his crew, led by chief gunner William Moore, became furious. Even if their master was having qualms, they had opted for piracy. They were on the verge of mutiny by October 30th, 1697.

It should be remembered that the life-and-death authority possessed by the Royal Navy captains of the period by no means obtained with privateersmen, who stood on a footing of uneasy democracy with their crews, and only assumed true command when going into battle. Kidd's hold on his men was precarious at best, and when gunner Moore, resting on deck after an illness, flared up at Kidd for failing to take the British ship, he lost his temper and killed the man with an unlucky blow to the temple with an iron-bound wooden shot-bucket.

A murderer in the eyes of landlubber law, if not by the rules of the sea (indeed, his crew settled down after the incident and seemed to respect him better for it), Kidd reconciled himself to at least part-time piracy. His next prize was another Moor, but he was happy to find that she bore French passes, making her at least minimally legal acccording to the terms of his commission. And on January 30th, 1698, he took the *Quedah Merchant*, skippered by an Englishman and owned by Armenian partners, but also bearing French passes.

Kidd knew perfectly well that the French passes were at best a thin excuse, since all sensible captains in disputed waters carried the papers and the flags of every nation whose ships they expected to encounter. Kidd himself carried French flags, which he displayed as a ruse on occasion. But he carefully locked away the two French passes from the first Moorish vessel, which he

Frustrated by weeks at sea without a prize, Kidd's gunner, William Moore, confronted his captain angrily. Accusing him of inciting the crew to mutiny, Kidd lost his temper and broke Moore's head with an iron-bound shot bucket.

Overleaf:
The Earl of Bellomont (at right), then Governor of New York, looks on as Kidd bids farewell to his wife before setting off on the ill-starred voyage of the *Adventure Galley*.

had renamed the *November* in honor of the month of her capture, and the *Quedah Merchant*. For he knew that rumors of his piratical turnabout had by now reached his backers and the Admiralty. He would have a lot of explaining to do when he returned, and he trusted the French papers to provide him with a tissue of legality.

The reluctant pirate put into the notorious pirate haven of St. Mary's Island, off Madagascar. The first thing he saw was a genuine pirate ship, the *Mocha Frigate*, and in an effort to clear his name by obeying the letter of his orders, he tried to persuade his men to take her. Instead, they deserted en masse to the pirate captain, a cutthroat named Culliford. After burning and looting the *November* and the *Adventure Galley*, and leaving Kidd only thirteen loyal crewmen, the mutineers, by an act of whimsical generosity which was as much a hallmark of pirate behavior as mindless brutality, awarded the Captain his full privateer-master's 40 per cent of the treasure of the *Quedah Merchant*, a big 500-tonner with a rich cargo of gold, jewels, silver, iron and sugar. They even left him the ship, too big and clumsy for piracy, before departing with Culliford.

Kidd sailed for home in the *Quedah Merchant*, still hoping that his 40 per cent share of the treasure would square his accounts with his backers and the Admiralty. But the rumors of his activities had become blacker and blacker in the telling. Bellomont's four titled backers, members of the Whig party, had been found out, and their Tory opponents were busily trying to smear them politically by associating them in the public press with a known pirate expedition sent out under the guise of a privateering venture. Bellomont, in turn, was scrambling to save his political reputation. Before Kidd ever made landfall in the British Leeward Islands, he was as good as hanged, served up to the Admiralty and the Tories as a scapegoat.

He knew his only hope lay in soliciting the aid of Bellomont, and he sold the conspicuous *Quedah Merchant*, leaving her in Hispaniola with some loyal crewmen. He bought a sloop, the *Antonio*, and sailed for New York with his treasure. At Oyster Bay, Long Island he anchored, and began to offload the treasure, sending parts of it in the care of various friends to hiding places all over the New York area, and caching more of it in a warehouse in Stamford, Connecticut. Most of it was buried on Gardiner's Island, and he got a receipt for it from John Gardiner, the island's owner. By the terms of his commission, he should have retained his entire share intact for examination by the Admiralty appraisers, but Kidd knew he was in trouble, and the scattered caches could be picked up again if he got out of his difficulties with the Admiralty. The locations of the treasure would also provide him with leverage with which to plead his cause with Bellomont, who had summoned him to Boston to appear before his Council.

As a preliminary gesture, he sent his precious French passes to Bellomont. Landing in Boston, he sent to Lady Bellomont a further proof of his good faith: £1,000 in gold, part of his share from the profits of the *Quedah Merchant* prize. Bellomont, pressured by the noble backers, took Kidd's offer to his wife as an attempt to bribe him, and reported it to the Council, who ordered the Captain's immediate arrest. Bellomont had Kidd's Boston lodgings

ransacked, finding some treasure, and clues which led his searchers to Gardiner's Island, Stamford, and every other location where Kidd had hidden booty.

The inventory is on record, and it matches Kidd's own testimony, given under oath to Bellomont after the arrest. It consists of 1,111 ounces of gold, 2,353 of silver, one pound of precious stones, 57 bags of sugar and 41 bags of merchandise, chiefly muslins and silks.

Kidd was captured and held without trial in Boston and London for two years before the Tories called him to a hearing before the House of Commons. They hoped he would implicate his Whig backers in his testimony. But the closest he came to implicating the lords was to state that he had had bad advice. The House of Commons concluded that he had turned pirate on his own, and delivered him over to the Admiralty Courts.

He was quickly disposed of. Eyewitnesses of the Moore murder appeared against him, mutineers who had deserted him to sail with Culliford in open piracy, now turning King's Evidence to save their own necks. Bellomont conveniently managed to mislay the vital French passes, and Kidd had no hard evidence to prove he had not committed plain piracy in taking the *November* and the *Quedah Merchant*.

He maintained his innocence to the last, stating after his sentencing that he was "the innocentest person of all" involved in the case.

Some benevolent soul managed to smuggle spirits to Kidd on the morning of his execution, and when he was brought out to stand in the tumbril he was shambling drunk. The hangman muffled the first attempt, to the delight of the crowd. The rope broke, and the dazed old seaman was fetched up from the low tide muck of the Thames and hanged again.

After his death his treasure was sold at auction by the Crown. It brought £6,472, and the sum was used to build a hospital at Greenwich, a building which now houses the Royal Maritime Museum. Kidd's body was tarred and clapped in iron hoops and chains and hung from a gibbet at Tilbury, where every ship which entered or left the port of London had to pass it. The hoops kept the skeleton from falling apart with the flesh, and Kidd's bones may have swung in the breeze for years. Although they may have frightened a few seacaptains away from the freebooter's trade, most pirates knew exactly what had happened to Kidd. His end only reinforced their determination to blow themselves to hell together, rather than facing an Admiralty Trial. The new century brought with it fresh outbreaks of piracy, culminating in the career of Bartholomew Roberts. Compared to Roberts, whose crews regularly returned with up to £700 apiece in booty, after a cruise which may have involved over a thousand men, Kidd can hardly be said to have been a successful pirate. His brief venture into piracy was distinguished primarily by relentlessly bad luck.

Naturally the public could not accept that a pirate so luridly painted by the Admiralty prosecution and the broadsheets and papers of the time, could have been so inept as to have landed with only £6,472 as his captain's share, after a three-and-a-half year cruise into the treasure-rich eastern seas. Kidd's hapless attempts to hide his wealth on Gardiner's Island and among his friends became a series of romantic voyages to remote beaches along the en-

tire northeastern seaboard, and treasure-hunters have never given up on the legend.

William Kidd died because of an eight-penny shot-bucket, but the ballad-monger's bloody Captain is credited with having buried more gold than the entire wealth extant in British America, at the time when the real man's bones swung bleaching in the sun at Tilbury Point.

Various dates, 1872-present

A VOYAGE IN THE WAKE OF CAPTAIN KIDD

As mentioned, Kidd secreted caches of the treasure of the *Quedah Merchant* with friends and at various locations along the North Atlantic seaboard, during the interval between his return from the east and his arrest. Although that treasure has been accounted for, and no one has proven that Kidd had anything else to bury, the legends remain. Crewmen left aboard the *Quedah Merchant* in Hispaniola are rumored to have hidden loot here and there in North America. The exploits of a pirate named Bradish, whose vessel, like Kidd's first ship, was called the *Adventure*, and who was hanged in Execution Dock in as many irons as bedecked Kidd, have been confused with those of Kidd himself over the years. Bradish may or may not have left treasure in Turtle Bay, New York; at various locations on Long Island; in the Hell Gate area of the East River; and near Croton, on the New York bank of the Hudson.

Whatever the truth of the legend, it is a persistent one. For the devoté of muffled oars, dark-lanterns, heavy chests, deserted beaches, and secret spadework by night, who is also fortunate enough to own a yacht, we here offer *The New York Times* Captain Kidd Treasure Hunt, which retraces, to the best of our knowledge, the ports of call associated with Kidd's booty. Things have changed in the 270-odd years since Kidd died in Execution Dock. The yachtsman sailing in the wake of the Captain will find himself competing with oil tankers and tugs for searoom in some areas. But on the other hand, the northern leg of the voyage will take him into the largely unspoiled coastal waters of Maine, Nova Scotia and Prince Edward Island, areas which, if he can afford to make the trip in the first place, he has probably already visited. There is no guarantee whatsoever that he will find so much as a single piece-of-eight, but the voyage should be its own reward. And he could just get lucky.

Set sail from your home port and chart your best course to Cape May, New Jersey, the southernmost point of the voyage. Anchor in the old resort's harbor, and make for Cold Spring, a site which was very popular with Kidd buffs in the last century.

May 21-25, 1872

CAPTAIN KIDD'S TREASURE IN NEW JERSEY

From Cold Spring, Cape May County, New Jersey, comes a story of the discovery of a chest containing $30,000 on the Dick Thompson farm, near Fishing Creek. Two men, one named Garretson, were digging ditches on the farm when they hauled up the money chest. The larger part of the treasure is gold, the coins being about the size of twenty dollar gold pieces. It is said that

tain Kidd's name was found imprinted on the chest . . .

The coins are old and very much worn. The few that bore distinct dates were coined in the year 1604, "cob" dollars probably made in Peru.

Later evidence suggests that the find may have been a hoax, or just wishful thinking. But citizens of the area have rushed to the area, hoping to find evidence of the truth of the local rumor that the old pirate left some of his booty buried nearby.

Now sail north along the Jersey Coast, round Sandy Hook, and put in at Port Monmouth, proceeding overland to Red Bank, where Kidd enthusiasts still talk of buried treasure despite a discouraging report in 1955.

March 27, 1955
NO PIRATE GOLD BARED

No trace of any of Captain Kidd's buried treasure was unearthed during extensive excavation work for the 165-mile Garden State Parkway, officials of the New Jersey Highway Department reported today.

The announcement was disappointing for many inquirers who thought some of the legendary pirate gold might turn up. The highway parallels the Jersey shore where Kidd was said to have made lengthy visits.

One Monmouth County property owner insisted on reserving his claim to any buried treasure turned up on a parcel of his land that had been used in parkway construction, according to commissioners.

From Port Monmouth your course is NE by E to Great South Bay, Long Island. If treasure-hunting on the mainland yields nothing, there is always Fire Island.

July 19, 1925
CAPTAIN KIDD'S TREASURE: A NEW YORK MYSTERY

The Mariners' Chronicle of the year 1834 published a circumstantial account of a fisherman of Great South Bay, who dreamed on three successive nights that at a certain spot on a nearby beach Kidd's doubloons lay buried. He arose before daybreak, untied his boat and rowed to the place. Next morning he was found lying unconscious across his own doorstep. His boat was never seen again. His spade, wet sand still adhering to it, was discovered in a graveyard miles away. When aroused, he declared he had no recollection of what had happened after he commenced to dig, nor of how he got back home.

Putting out from Great South Bay, thread the needle between the tip of Fire Island and Pikes Beach, and proceed coastwise to Montauk Point. Keep your heading NE until you strike Block Island.

July 24, 1955
KIDD'S TREASURE

Pirate Captain Kidd's buried treasure is supposed to be worth $700,000. Probably more than that sum has been spent in efforts to find it. It is not certain where the supposed treasure is buried. A scientific effort to find it is about to be made with electronic devices, on Block Island, which lies off the coast of Rhode Island.

From Block Island you must double back, steering due west. Look for a following wind to carry you through the Race, between Plum and Fisher's Islands, and into Long Island Sound. Sail along the Connecticut coast for the Thimble Islands, west of Sachem Head.

A curious gold ring, said to have once been owned by a British King, as it tallies in detail with one which disappeared from the English Court in 1610, and has since been listed in the records as of unknown whereabouts, was found by Charles Burns, hoseman of the New Haven Fire Department, in the sand of the Thimble Islands, noted as a rendezvous of Captain Kidd. It is believed that the ring was a part of the treasure loot of the pirate, who, according to legend, buried his spoils in this vicinity.

Burns was on a clamming trip when he uncovered the ring. It is composed of four bands, joined by clasped hands. The nearest resemblance to the ring was one worn by Lady Catherine Grey, which is said to have signified her marriage to the Earl of Hereford. Queen Elizabeth I, displeased with the union, sent Hereford to the Tower of London in confinement and subjected Lady Grey to many hardships until the validity of the marriage was proved. The marriage was later dissolved by a commission, and was so pronounced in the palace of the Bishop of London in 1562.

Burns has deposited the ring in a vault and has refused an offer of $2,000 for it. He said he intends to make a further search of the beach in the hope of uncovering other trinkets.

From the Thimbles, continue along the coast westerly, until you strike Great Captain Island, and put in to the mainland, striking inland to Rye, New York.

One of the traditions of the town relates that a mysterious stranger, evidently a seafaring man, begged a farmer's wife for shelter one stormy October night. Next morning before he left, he filled her apron with gold pieces. The stranger was said to have been Captain Kidd. Hence the tale that he concealed gold and jewels somewhere along Rye Beach.

Setting off again, sail to the western end of Long Island Sound and weave your way through Jamaica Bay, heading for the East River. Sail south downriver and find safe harbor at Manhattan's South Street Seaport, where the reconstructed glories of the last of the windjammers will give you noble company. Come ashore for awhile, and visit Captain Kidd's old neighborhood in Lower Manhattan. His ancient holdings along Pearl, Hanover, Wall, Pine and Water Streets (see above) have long ago been swallowed up by the financial marketplace which occupies the area, but the paper fortunes traded aboveground once reflected more substantial subterranean treasure troves.

Gold and silver coins turned up the other day in the excavation at the corner of Wall and Broad Streets. Laborers flung themselves, pale with avarice, on the rusty pieces in the Wall Street cellar, fighting and cursing over possession of the "rascal counters."

Re-embarking, round the Battery and sail up the Hudson to the town of Croton-On-Hudson on the New York shore. Croton was once the site of Westchester County's "Money Hill", a mysterious mound associated with the Captain's treasure, which was levelled during highway construction in the 1920s.

Westchester County may very soon receive great riches. The county Parks Commission solemnly decided yesterday that when it awards contracts for the removal of Money Hill it will insert a clause that if the name of the earth mound turns out to be accurate, the money found therein shall be the property of the county not the contractor. The suggestion was made by James Owen, one of the park engineers. When the commission met at Bronxville to open bids for the removal of the hill at Croton, a 55,000-cubic-yard obstacle to the widening and raising of the Albany Post Road.

The commission is inserting its treasure-claiming clause because of Captain Kidd. There has long been a legend up around Croton that that predatory person buried his wealth in the mound, giving it its name. No one saw Captain Kidd bury anything there, and no one knows that he did. But pieces-of-eight and other coins of ancient mintage have been found in the area, and it may be that under a thin covering of earth the whole hill is solid treasure. If it is, the commission wins; if it isn't, that's that.

When Captain Kidd was homeward bound after his last privateering voyage, he made a stop at the island of Hispaniola, today the large landmass divided between Haiti and the Dominican Republic. In the seventeenth century Hispaniola was a favorite rendezvous of pirates and buccaneers, and Kidd is rumored to have left a ship there, crammed with treasure. The ship, a prize captured on the cruise, the *Quedah Merchant*, figures in the Westchester legend of Money Hill. It is said that "Whisking" Clarke and James Gilam, two officers of Kidd's crew, set out for New York with the treasure, in the wake of Kidd's own sloop. Reaching New York Harbor, they were pursued up the Hudson by a British man-of-war. They scuttled the ship after dividing the swag between them, and went ashore near Croton. Mysterious "pamphlets" which turned up in the nineteenth century allegedly prove that at least part of

December 5, 1924

WESTCHESTER RESERVES RIGHTS TO MONEY HILL TREASURE

December 21, 1924

AGAIN THEY DIG FOR CAPTAIN KIDD'S GOLD

In March, 1951, a young turtle-fisher named Stanley Cramer was working the banks of Ship Bottom, N. J. His turtle-pole struck this corroded bronze plate bearing the words "William Kidd, Master, Quedagh." The *Quedagh Merchant*, Kidd's richest prize ship, was sold in Hispaniola, but the 3½-by-5-inch plate, could well have been brought north by Kidd with his share of the *Quedagh's* cargo. The plate, whose authenticity is still in dispute, is one of the very few surviving artifacts associated with the luckless "pirate."

the treasure was buried in Money Hill. But later reports from the Westchester County Parks Commission state that if that was the case, the highway crew missed the treasure. All that turned up during the levelling of the earth mound was earth.

Aboard again, your course is south, downriver to the 79th Street Yacht Basin, Manhattan's West Side marina. A crosstown bus will take you to East 79th Street, where a prodigious act of imagination might be able to make you transform the glittering Silk Stocking neighborhood into the wooded slopes and fields of the seventeenth century, when Kidd maintained a country retreat there. Take a last jaunt downtown to Turtle Bay, another site long associated with Kidd's loot. Return to your ship and provision her for the long haul to Maine and Canada. Circumnavigate Manhattan and retrace your course across Jamaica Bay to Long Island Sound. Cruise the length of the Sound until you fetch Orient Point. Take a southeasterly heading and sail through Plum Gut, between Orient Point and Plum Island. Continue your heading until you strike Gardiner's Island.

December 21, 1924 (continued)
THE ONLY RECORDED TREASURE OF CAPTAIN KIDD

Kidd himself sailed his sloop back from Hispaniola to Gardiner's Island, off Hog Creek Point, Long Island. Anchoring, he got the island's owner, John Gardiner, to bury on his property a chest and box of gold, a bundle of quilts, and four bales of goods, either booty from the prizes of Kidd's last voyage or purchases he had made in Hispaniola for his mercantile enterprise in New York. The gold was intended for Bellomont, Kidd told Gardiner, part of his share of the spoils of the cruise.

Three sloops from New York had sailed out to the island to meet Kidd, and they busied themselves for three days unloading the cargo from Kidd's own craft.

An inventory was taken on Gardiner's Island during the unloading and burial of the cargo, and another was taken at Stamford, Connecticut, where the three New York sloops offloaded the unburied portion of the loot to a warehouse. A third inventory was taken when Kidd was arrested in Boston, and the house he was in was searched.

According to the records, the totality of Kidd's treasure in the three locations amounted to the following: 17 precious stones, 1,111 Troy ounces of gold, 2,353 of silver, 57 bags of sugar, and a few additional pouches of gold and diamonds. Perishable goods aboard the sloop brought the total worth of the cargo to a meager £10,000, with perhaps another £60,000, mostly in foodstuffs and cloth goods left aboard Kidd's first ship in Hispaniola. The total of some £70,000, added to the £6,472 which made up Kidd's personal fortune, forfeited to the crown upon his conviction, is a far cry from the millions ascribed to him by legend. But the Gardiner's Island cache and the contents of the other two inventories, make up the only documented list of Captain Kidd's booty, and the chest and box buried on the island by prearrangement and dug up under the official scrutiny of the Governor's men, are all that has ever been dug up in the whole Kidd tradition, at least as far as the records show.

After looking around Gardiner's Island for a few doubloons the inventory-takers might have missed, you must stand boldly out to sea, for Captain Kidd had no Cape Cod Canal to provide him with a short cut to the Maine coast. Clear Martha's Vineyard and take the Muskegat Channel between that island and Nantucket. Leaving Monomoy Point to port, round the elbow of Cape Cod and proceed north to Maine. Clear Cape Elizabeth and enter Casco Bay, which may have been the site of an authentic Kidd find in the last century.

April 1, 1928
A PIRATE TREASURE

On Bailey Island, one of the 365 islands in Casco Bay near Portland, Maine, was found a treasure supposedly buried by Captain Kidd. A man named John Wilson, who lived on the island in 1853, seeking the legendary treasure, dug up a copper kettle which had been buried deep in the ground. It contained $12,000 in Spanish gold. Although the search for other pirate treasure has been pursued along the Maine coast for many years, only the Bailey Island find has rewarded the eager seekers of easy money.

The resort industry and the bustle of a modern port have replaced treasure-hunting in the Portland area by now, but the most tantalizing clue to the Kidd mystery is yet to come. Set a course ENE from Casco Bay until you fetch Cape Sable Island and Baccaro Point on Nova Scotia's southern coast. Sail NE up the coast to Mahone Bay, some 80 nautical miles, where among the bay's generous sprinkle of islands, near its head and the town of Chester, lies Oak Island.

June 6, 1926
(The New York Times Magazine)
THE TREASURE OF OAK ISLAND

By Catherine Mackenzie

One of the most mysterious buried treasures known to history or legend is believed to be hidden on Oak Island, in Mahone Bay, Nova Scotia. The bay's name comes from the old French term *mahonne*, the low and rakish craft used by coast pirates, who were by no means strangers to its anchorages.

Whether the treasure was left on the island by these pirates, or by the legendary Captain Kidd, is not known. The elaborate precautions supposed to have been taken to conceal it, which include enlisting the tides of the bay in its defense, is deemed proof of its value, and likewise proof that it was not left there by any picayune coast pirates.

Whoever the mysterious visitors were, they had men enough to dig a hole a hundred feet deep and a dozen feet across in the flint-like clay of the island. They carried stores of protective materials in quantities sufficient to surround seven oak chests and no one knows how many other containers.

Still more amazing, they had the skill to plan and build an elaborate system of drains connecting the pit with tide water, which floods the shaft deeply twice a day. Their efforts to conceal the chests and other material have defeated six organized treasure-hunts since 1795. Although excavators have brought up wood and packing material over the years, the chests have never been raised intact.

In 1795, three young men named Vaughan, MacGinnis and Smith ran their canoe ashore on the island, and in the course of exploring it, happened upon a great oka with a limb sawed off close enough to the trunk to provide a

natural derrick, unobstructed by foliage. The branch showed the ancient marks of a block and tackle. The three youths explored further, and found, on the rocky beach not far away from the tree, a stout iron ring-bolt fastened to a boulder below the high-tide water level, clearly an old mooring ring detectable only at extreme low water.

The trio was intrigued enough to begin digging in a circular depression they found beneath the oak-limb derrick, and immediately struck a clearly-defined shaft bearing pick-axe marks in its hard clay sides, which had been loosely filled in with earth. Ten feet down they struck a heavy oak planking with more loose earth beneath it. A second layer of planking lay at twenty feet, and a third at thirty.

The three young men could go no further without assistance. For six years they tried to interest heavy money in a formal expedition, and finally, in 1801, a company backed by prominent Nova Scotia businessmen returned to Oak Island. This time the shaft was sunk to 95 feet. A stone with an illegible inscription was brought up, with some fibre resembling cocoanut-matting, probably part of a packing material intended to protect whatever was buried. But the expedition was defeated by the old excavators' system of drains, which brought the tide in overnight to drown the shaft in water to within 25 feet of its mouth.

The next treasure-hunt on Oak Island was not mounted until 1849. This time the hunters provided themselves with a crude pump and an augur bit, which was designed to bore below the bottom-most layer of planking and pierce the chests themselves. The bit cut through clay and old oak planking until it struck what was thought to be the side of a chest. Oak splinters, fragments of metal resembling part of an ancient watch-chain, and more cocoanut-fibre packing material were carried up on the flanges of the drill. But once again, the flooding system defeated the treasure-hunters, and they backed off.

Four more tries were made over the years, and in each case the treasure-hunters found evidence than some large wooden containers, chests or casks, were lying in a compartment below the last layer of planking. The contents of the containers, which the original owners took such elaborate means to conceal, remain a secret.

Ex-diver Harry L. Bowdoin, who once found some Confederate gold worth $2,000 in South Carolina, outfitted an expedition for the treasure of Oak Island this year. He and his partner, M. V. Andrews of New York, intended to approach the problem as an engineering question.

"We will not attempt to bail out the ocean, as some other searchers have done," Mr. Bowdoin stated. "We have with us several new inventions in the way of diving apparatus that will make the task easy for us. We have a diving suit in which a man can go down 500 feet, a thing which has not been tried by any other person except myself. I expect to have the treasure inside of two weeks, and if we cannot get it in a month, it will be because there is no treasure there."

But by November the expedition, organized as the Old Gold Salvage and

*March 18-
November 7, 1909*
**THE BOWDOIN
EXPEDITION**

Wrecking Association of New York, gave up. They had failed even to find the ancient shaft and planking, and proclaimed it a myth.

AGAIN HUNT KIDD'S GOLD

Sprague & Henwood, a drilling corporation of Scranton, Pennsylvania, began operations three weeks ago. They are cleaning out a shaft last operated by the Campbell interests of Sydney, Nova Scotia in 1931.

A New York financier has been reported willing to pay $50,000 for the search this summer.

Working with the Scranton firm is Sylvester Carroll, veteran Porcupine, Ontario gold miner, who has charge of cribbing. Large, electrically driven pumps have been installed.

A follow-up indicates that this expedition, like all the others, ended in failure. Well over $200,000 has been spent in hunting for Kidd's elusive treasure on Oak Island.

If the hapless Kidd did manage to engineer the elaborate shaft and sluice-works to protect a portion of his treasure, one wonders how he himself would have retrieved it.

Leaving Oak Island, continue NE along the southern coast of Nova Scotia, clearing Andrew Island and tacking northwesterly across Cedabucto Bay to the channel that separates Cape Breton Island from the mainland. Emerging into St. Georges Bay, shape a course NW for Prince Edward Island and put in at Abel's Cape.

December 28, 1924
To the Editor of *The New York Times*:

Referring to your article on Captain Kidd in the Magazine Section of December 21st, I should like to say that the wild and rocky shores of Prince Edward Island are supposed to hold a considerable portion of this noted searover's loot.

Treasure holes are to be seen on many of the wooded promontories of this beautiful spot ... Fearsome stories of the search for this treasure were told to me by the farmer-fishers of Abel's Cape. While digging there one night, they heard the roar of an anchor chain being let out in the bay. Through the trees they dimly descried the misty outlines of an old-fashioned, high-pooped ship, her sails slatting like thunder as the anchor held and brought her to the wind. Over her side swarmed a horde of figures cursing and jabbering in strange tongues. The excavators fled, returning the following day to find a newly-dug hole, but no treasure.

—Henry Warwick, New York

It is fitting that your last port of call in the wake of Captain Kidd should involve a ghost story, in which the myth of the man reigns supreme, untainted by fact. Whistle up a wind, crowd on sail, and return to New York City before the autumn storms. A codicil to the legend of Kidd's treasure calls up the ghost of John Jacob Astor, who may have stolen a march on all other treasure-hunters as long ago as 1802.

In 1970 a Canadian group called Triton searched Oak Island, drilling holes at the bottoms of the enigmatic shafts. When the drill-bits came up carrying fragments of ancient steel (shown here), the group was convinced it had found clues to the hidden pirate loot. But further search yielded nothing.

December 21-March 24, 1924
THE ASTOR CONNECTION

Professor Herbert Bolton, historian of the University of California, said recently that Kidd's buried treasure gave John Jacob Astor his start in life. He based his statement on evidence gathered in the last century by Frederick Law Olmstead, the landscaper who created New York's Central Park. Olmstead's family owned an island off Maine in the eighteeth century and early nineteenth centuries, where a trapper, Jacques Cartier, in Astor's employ, may have found old gold and jewelry worth $1.4 million, in 1802. Coincidentally, that was the year in which Astor's bank balance rose from zero to exactly $1.4 million.

But Lady Astor denied the story, which she said was romantic, but untrue. "The foundation of the Astor fortune," she said, "was not laid quite so easily. John Jacob Astor left England, learned something of the furrier's business, and traded in furs in America for years, expanding his enterprises until his ships sailed all over the world."

Regardless of the truth or falsehood of the Astor story, Kidd himself almost certainly died broke. The reluctant pirate was finally granted a formal pardon by Mayor Hylan of New York City in November, 1924. Kidd's bones, wherever they are, are at rest. But the legend continues to flourish in the romantic hearts of treasure buffs, unfettered by historical verities. The gulf between the real man and his myth is an indication of the lengths to which people will go to sustain a legend, if that legend has to do with Eldorado.

KING
JOHN'S LAST
CAMPAIGN
Introduction

12

Facing page:
King John of En-
gland, forced to sign
the Magna Carta in
1215, set off in a fit
of understandable
bad temper to pun-
ish some of his
weaker barons, and
lost his personal gold
and plate en route.

January 28, 1934
A NEW SEARCH FOR KING JOHN'S TREASURE
By John Kenmuir

King John may have been as bad as he is painted in popular tradition, but he had immense difficulties to overcome when he assumed the English throne following the death of his brother Richard I in 1199. The Lion-hearted had captured the popular fancy by his chivalric participation in the Crusades, but his adventure had beggared the kingdom. More important, his long absence from England had left the realm rulerless, and a prey to numerous baronial factions aided and abetted by the intrigues of the French king. The great barons, by the time of John's accession, had carved the country into numerous fiefdoms which they ruled autonomously. John's derisive nickname, "Lackland," was just: in theory ruler of all England, he was in fact but an impecunious baron among many whose holdings far exceeded his own.

His reign was characterized by his ruthless attempts to build up his Treasury and reassert, by intrigue and force of arms, the royal authority over the barons which his vigorous father, Henry II, had established. To do so, he was not above employing one of the first European pirates on record, a renegade monk named Eustace. John set the piratical ex-cleric loose on French shipping in the Channel, but Eustace interpreted his instructions loosely, and was soon attacking John's own convoys as well. Exiled by the outraged monarch, Eustace sold his services to the French, and attempted to lead a French invasion fleet against England. Defeated in naval battle by his ex-employer's forces, he was executed summarily.

King John's other money-making ventures, which included merciless taxation and wholesale seizure of his vassals' lands, proved more successful. But his highhanded methods infuriated the barons, and led to the confrontation at Runnymede in 1215, in which the powerful baronial faction forced him to sign away most of the authority and holdings he had striven to wrest from them.

Much diminished, but still King, John set forth on a punitive expedition against some of his weaker opponents. As was the custom in those days of traveling monarchs, who seldom spent more than six months in any one spot within their fractious kingdoms, John carried his still-considerable treasure with him. Somewhere between King's Lynn and Long Sutton, in the treacherous tidal bogs of the Wash, the baggage train and the King's treasure were lost.

About 717 years ago the baggage train of King John of England attempted to take a short cut across the treacherous sands bordering the Wash. An incoming tide and the descending current of the river Nene trapped the cavalcade. The King's horses and the King's men, carrying all the royal luggage and treasure, were swallowed up. King John witnessed the disaster. Its effect on him is assumed to have contributed to his death a few days later.

Since then no trace of the lost baggage train has ever been found. Historians and archaeologists recently have pieced together a considerable amount of data about the movements of John's army in October, 1216, and particularly those on the fatal twelfth when the baggage train perished.

As a result, a company has been formed to recover the treasure. Apparently the Fenland Research, Ltd., as the company is called, expects no easy

John's reign was chiefly distinguished by his relentless efforts to refurbish the royal treasury, which had been exhausted by his brother Richard the Lion-hearted's crusade expenses. When the absentee-king Richard was captured during his return from the Holy Land, England was further beggared by the exorbitant ransom demanded for his release. John's nickname, Lackland, is indicative of the low state of the kingdom's holdings and finances at the time when the luckless monarch assumed the throne.

SEARCH FOR KING JOHN'S TREASURE BREAKS DOWN IN LITIGATION

time of it. Not only is the trail extremely cold, but the geography of the region has changed to such an extent that, where once vast areas of sand lay bare at low tide and were covered at high tide, tall rushes now wave on firm meadows that only here and there slough off into miry places. The fens between Norfolk and Lincolnshire have steadily pushed back the shoreline of the Wash. Additional ground was gained through manmade drainage canals. When the approximate spot where the baggage train was engulfed is determined, the company expects to have to dig to a depth of at least thirty feet.

Examination of documents disclosed that in certain aspects the generally-accepted version of the disaster is not correct. The original story asserts that King John, in high dudgeon because the barons forced him to sign Magna Carta at Runnymede, was moving northward to punish the weaker barons of the fens by plundering and burning their farmhouses and abbeys. Recent studies of the writings of Matthew Paris, Abbot Ralph of Coggeshall and other contemporary chroniclers reveal that King John and his advance guard did not cross the sands, but followed a longer route via Wisbech and higher ground. Two separate routes from Kings Lynn to Long Sutton have been worked out; one followed by the impatient King and the other by the baggage train.

Although even the barons of the regions would hire a "fen slodger" before attempting the passage across the tidal sands of the Wash, there is evidence that John's baggage train crossed without a guide. There was no chance of retreat once the tide had turned, because the water hid patches of quicksand that could be avoided only at high tide.

Modern scholars deduce that King John witnessed the loss of his convoy and all his accumulated wealth from higher ground. In mournful silence he rode on to the Cistercian Abbey of Swineshead, where he spent the night.

An apocryphal story relates that a monk at Swineshead prepared two goblets of poisoned wine, offering one to the King. John, suspecting a trick, seized the other and made the monk drink the one he had refused. When the monk obeyed, John drank his, fell violently ill, and died a few days later at Newark. The monk survived the King for only a short time.

But diligent search among the writings of the period discloses no mention of the poisoning episode, although there are references to the gluttonous meal John ate at the abbey, and to his chagrin at the loss of most of his wealth.

Fenland Research, Ltd.'s search for King John's lost treasure turned up nothing but bad feelings between its principal backer, a wealthy American named James A. Herbert Boone, and its British contractor, Edward Gaspard Ponsonby, son of Sir Frederick Ponsonby, then Keeper of the Privy Purse. The two fell out over Ponsonby's refusal to appoint a mysterious "gold diviner" named Charles Gladwitz as exclusive independent contractor. Gladwitz seems to have had considerable influence with the romantic American, and when the latter dismissed Ponsonby for refusing to give Gladwitz all powers to excavate land that he claimed lay along the track of King John's

legendary baggage train, Ponsonby took him to court.

The case was soon dropped by Ponsonby, whose counsel stated, "Mr. Ponsonby now realizes that, although he acted in the interests of Mr. Boone, he was not justified in failing to carry out Mr. Boone's instructions, whether he thought they were, or were not, in the interest of Mr. Boone."

Boone, who had already spent about £20,000 in the search, was soured by the experience. "Very little has been done, except spending money," he said. But although the search was abandoned, the American clung to his belief in the existence of the treasure, which had fascinated him since childhood. If nothing else, King John's legend has provided some gentlemen of aristocratic names with employment, in the depths of the Depression. For the first time, Bad King John had managed to do some good for someone other than himself.

13

Jean Lafitte was born a hundred years too late to participate in the glory days of piracy, which lasted only 30 years, from the end of the seventeenth century through the first quarter of the eighteenth. The wars between Britain and Spain, which had created the buccaneers (NOTE: SEE *THE NOBLE BUCCANEER*) of the earlier seventeenth century, who were technically privateers, taking their prizes under legal letters of marque, ended in 1689, and a host of skilled and ruthless captains who had learned naval warfare under the various flags of the belligerents were turned loose on commercial shipping. Untold amounts of booty were accumulated by the pirate captains of the period, who ruled the seas virtually undisputed, and set up lawless pirate capitals at such widely-separated spots as New Providence Island in the Bahamas, and Madagascar in the Indian Ocean. But by the 1720s, conditions had changed along the sea-lanes. The American colonies, which had once provided the pirates with safe ports, a flourishing market for their loot, and a steady source of recruits for their crews, were better administrated, and colonial governors began to mount punitive expeditions against the seawolves to protect their own fledgling maritime commerce. The nations of Europe began to co-operate in efforts to rid the seas of pirates, and the warships of the great seafaring nations became ever more formidable. One by one, the pirate capitals were closed down, re-colonized, and drawn into the imperial folds of the Western nations. From a multimillion-dollar illicit industry, piracy degenerated to a petty irritation carried on by occasional desperadoes, who were usually slapped down before they had had a chance to accumulate more than a pittance of booty. The terrible captains—Blackbeard (NOTE: SEE *BLACKBEARD'S BOOTY*), Roberts, Tew, Taylor, Low, Every—passed into myth.

But the outbreak of wars which ended the eighteenth century and continued into the nineteenth trained a whole new generation in the privateering art. Since the distinction between privateer and plain pirate was always hazy, it is not surprising that many of the new privateersmen exceeded the terms of their commissions whenever they ran out of legal targets. Even so, most of these latter-day pirates were small fry compared with the great captains of the earlier period. Their exploits were distinguished more by their desperate brutality than by the values of the prizes they took, and determined efforts by well-organized British and American navies wiped them out by the 1830's.

But a few of the renegade privateers were successful, and in this small group Jean Lafitte stood head and shoulders above the rest. As skilled a politician as he was a fighting seacaptain, he traded flags to suit his convenience, played Governor off against Emperor, and built up a legend of buried treasure which can take its place among the immense hoards of the captains of the Golden Age.

Jean Lafitte, with a reputation long confined to the South, has been coming up. Recent honors in a light opera and a movie have helped popularize him. As such gentry go, he was a much more successful pirate than Captain Kidd. At least he never bungled his business to the extent of getting himself hanged for it. Instead, he earned Presidential amnesty.

Lafitte's battle-hardened pirate gunners, though ill-accustomed to fighting on land, turned the tide against the invading British in 1815. The most famous battle of the War of 1812 was actually fought after peace had been declared.

August 12, 1940
JEAN LAFITTE

Lafitte, personally handsome and possessed of a charm which matched his fighting abilities, successfully played his various opponents off against each other throughout his career.

Lafitte's story begins with an almost Horatio Alger touch. He was the son of poor but honest parents in Bordeaux, France. An adventurous youth, he ran away from home to make his fortune at sea. Alas, he next turns up as a full-fledged pirate in the Indian Ocean. He is said to have completed his education in an English prison, which may have accounted for the ferocity with which he preyed on British shipping.

A patriot (when it suited him), Lafitte operated out of New Granada during the Napoleonic Wars, carrying French letters of marque against his government's British enemy. He became a familiar figure off the coast of Charleston, South Carolina. But a slight case of murder ended his welcome in that city.

But in 1807 the American embargo on foreign trade, levelled principally against the British, gave him his chance in a big way. Calling his brother Pierre into partnership, he soon had most of the honest merchants of New Orleans corrupted with illicit transactions in slaves, forbidden imports, and stolen treasure. Like the pirates of a century earlier, Lafitte recognized that free enterprise was no respecter of politically- motivated embargoes, and by providing New Orleans, a town whose French and Creole population was by no means reconciled to its new status as American territory, with vital (if illegal) grist for its economic mill, he rose to a high place in society.

Indeed, his success became so scandalous that in 1812 the hardpressed American Governor Claiborne put a price of $500 on Lafitte's head. Lafitte, knowing where the loyalties of his fellow townsmen lay, promptly countered with an offer of $15,000 for the Governor's head. He added insult to injury by stating that he knew he could raise the bounty, but he doubted if the American could.

Thus goaded, Claiborne dispatched a company of militia after the free-booter. Unfortunately, the expedition was commanded by one of Lafitte's former lieutenants. It was neatly surrounded in the bayous below New Orleans, loaded with presents, and sent home without a shot being fired.

This was an excellent comic opera touch. But the dignity of the United States was offended. President Madison ordered Commodore Patterson with a fleet of gunboats and a company of regulars to reduce the pirate stronghold at Barataria. These orders were carried out with thoroughness. Lafitte's fleet of pirate ships were sunk or captured, but he and most of his followers managed to escape.

His situation was now precarious. New Orleans, now occupied by General Andrew Jackson's troops in anticipation of a British attack, the War of 1812 being by now in full career, was closed to him. Without his fleet he was helpless, and it looked as if Claiborne would make good on his original bounty offer for the pirate's head.

But the British unwittingly played into Lafitte's hands. The fugitive captain was offered command of a British frigate for the attack on New Orleans. Playing for time, the Frenchman pretended to accept, and learned much about the British attack plan. He promptly contacted his old enemy Governor Claiborne, revealing the British scheme and at the same time bargaining for a pardon by offering his services to the American cause. Claiborne

had no choice but to accept, under the circumstances.

Lafitte and his pirate crew joined forces with General Jackson's army. Manning their guns on land as recklessly and courageously as they had as freebooters on the high seas, they helped to repulse the British attack at the Battle of New Orleans. Jackson, a practical commander, was impressed, and sent his recommendation to President Madison, who replied with a full pardon for Lafitte and his men.

But Lafitte's piratically independent nature was not long in reasserting itself. Leaving New Orleans, he took his crew up the coast of Texas and commandeered Galveston Island, which he set up as an autonomous republic, some say with the connivance of Aaron Burr, who was then embroiled in his scheme for the conquest of Mexico. He was finally ousted from his little duchy in 1821 by American naval forces.

There are half a dozen accounts of Lafitte's death, but the pleasantest one carries him back to France and permits him to end his days in his boyhood home.

September 12, 1921

DISCOVERY OF LAFITTE TREASURE RUMORED

A report that part of the supposed treasure of Jean Lafitte, the pirate, has been found in the vicinity of Jefferson Island, the onetime home of actor Joseph Jefferson, has sent excitement in that neighborhood to a fever pitch, according to reports from the South Louisiana coast.

The fact that several gold coins of ancient date have recently found their way into circulation on the island, two of them bearing the date 1754, has given strength to the reports, according to which two pots of buried gold were found.

According to legends, large sums were buried in the neighborhood by Lafitte, who preyed on gulf and river shipping in the late eighteenth and early nineteenth centuries.

August 12, 1940 (continued)

LAFITTE TREASURE IN TEXAS

There is considerable excitement in the town of Anhuac, Texas, over reports that some of the pirate-patriot's hoard has been discovered. A resident there has asked the State authorities for permission to salvage a strange ship which on clear days can be seen glimmering deep in the sand of an inlet in Galveston Harbor.

It was first located around 1850 by a man who kept the secret in his family for three generations. Some thirty years ago several Spanish doubloons dated 1803 were found on the beach nearby. The theory is that this vessel bore most of Lafitte's strong boxes when he fled from Galveston in 1821. Tradition has it that the ship was sunk in local waters by the United States Navy gunboats which drove Lafitte from his private republic.

Lafitte was a shrewd businessman. Estimates of his fortune run from several hundred thousand dollars to several millions. So in Anhuac, hopes are high.

(A modern footnote)

Nothing of major interest came to light in the Galveston Bay hunt, and citizens of Anahuac (modern spelling) had to be content with the "several Spanish doubloons" already found.

But if there is a Lafitte treasure to be found, Galveston Island is still the most likely place to search. Lafitte, canny entrepreneur that he was, certainly did not set up his Galveston colony on good faith alone.

BLACKBEARD'S BOOTY

Introduction

14

Edward Teach, or Blackbeard, matched his personal style to the violence of his profession. Some of his victims were reputed to have abandoned their guns at the mere mention of his name, surrendering in the vain hope that their terrible attacker would let them off with their lives.

Edward Teach, or Blackbeard, was the "Compleat Pyrate." Like so many others of the golden age of piracy, he began as a privateersman, sailing for England in the West Indies during the War of the Spanish Succession (1701-1713). As had been the case with previous wars, the outbreak of peace meant the end of profitable and congenial employment for privateer captains and their crews. By nature violently opposed to the sort of tyrannical authority which was then the rule aboard His Majesty's Royal Navy ships, and too used to easy money for the cautious, patient life of a merchant skipper (the peace-loving Kidd's choice, until his final cruise), Teach (or Thatch: his real name is as obscure as his early history), with hundreds of others, turned pirate. By 1716, aboard his 40-gun flagship, the *Queen Anne's Revenge*, Blackbeard was busily carving for himself the most terrifying legend in the annals of piracy.

He prepared for his piratical image like an actor, cultivating a ferocious appearance which matched his blood-and-thunder personal style. He let his hair and beard grow long, plaiting it in long forks and tying it up with red ribbons. He also affected bandoliers carrying six primed matchlock pistols, which he fired with the long, smoking matches he carried under his hat. Upon one occasion he replaced the ribbons in his beard with lighted candles, which set the whole affair afire. But the singeing he sustained was amply repaid by the terror he inspired in his victims, who threw down their weapons and babbled for mercy. Arrayed for battle, he awed even his own hellacious crew, one of whom, startled by his master's berserker behavior, once exclaimed, "Why, Captain, you look as if you were coming straight from the gallows!" He flew a ferocious variation of the Jolly Roger, showing a horned skeleton carrying an hourglass (signifying that time was running out for his victims) and shaking a spear at a bleeding heart.

Under the precarious democracy which obtained between pirate captains and their crews, authority could only be sustained by terror-tactics. Blackbeard ruled his men simply by being more outrageous, more bloody-minded, and more unpredictably savage than they were. He shot his mate once on a whim, and forced his men to compete with him in games of violence which reflect the gallows humor of the fraternity of freebooters, who knew the odds were in favor of their dancing a jig one day at the end of an Admiralty rope. On one occasion, according to Daniel Defoe, who published a copious account of famous pirates in 1725, Blackbeard dared his men to dangle with him by the neck from the end of a rope, to see who could endure hanging the longest.

Blackbeard operated from the notorious pirate island of New Providence, which by the second decade of the eighteenth century had replaced Madagascar as the freebooters' capital. The Indian Ocean had become too hot for open piracy, but the pickings were excellent in the Caribbean and along the coast of North America; and the Royal Navy, corrupt and low on manpower due to disease, was largely ineffective in protecting shipping.

Ranging from his home port, Nassau, Blackbeard had his most profitable year in 1718. Commanding a fleet of four heavily-armed ships and upwards of 400 men, he rampaged from Virginia to Honduras. At one point he even managed to blockade the harbor at Charleston, South Carolina, pillaging

Lieutenant Maynard's crew celebrates as Blackbeard's head is hoisted to his flagship's bowsprit. So ferocious was the pirate's reputation that Maynard's Virginia commissioners required the head as proof that Blackbeard was truly dead.

ships and holding ranking members of the colonial government for ransom.

His free-and-easy ways along the Carolina coast were not entirely of his own making. Like many colonial governors, North Carolina's Charles Eden was starved for trade, and he allowed Blackbeard safe havens for careening and provisioning his vessels in North Carolina's rivers and inlets. At one point the Governor even granted Blackbeard a pardon, in return for a share in his booty.

But not all governors were as friendly. Virginia's Governor Alexander Spotswood was infuriated by Blackbeard's audacity. He posted a reward of £100 for the corsair's head, and sent two Royal Navy warships, H. M. S. *Pearl* and H. M. S. *Lyme*, on Blackbeard's trail.

The men-of-war caught up with Blackbeard in Ocracoke Inlet, North Carolina, where the pirate and his crew were holed up with two ships, the *Adventure*, which had replaced the *Queen Anne's Revenge* as his flagship, and a captured merchantman. Lieutenant Robert Maynard, commander of the punitive expedition, maneuvered his ships with difficulty among the shallows and sand bars of the inlet, sustaining many casualties from the pirate's defiant broadsides. At last he closed with the *Adventure*, and Blackbeard, impetuous

as always, led a boarding party onto the deck of H. M. S. *Pearl*. He himself engaged Maynard in a hand-to-hand battle with cutlass and pistol, which has served as a model for dozens of pirate movies ever since. Out-numbered by the Navy crew, Blackbeard refused to surrender. Larger-than-life to the end, he sustained dozens of wounds from sword and ball before he succumbed. His crew, undone by the death of the "unkillable" pirate captain, gave up. Maynard sailed back to Virginia to claim his reward in triumph, with the gory head of Blackbeard swinging from his bowsprit.

Various dates, 1926-present
BLACKBEARD'S BURIED GOLD

"Only the devil and me know where my gold is hid," the flamboyant pirate used to proclaim in his cups (which he was most of the time: Maynard and his men might have had an even harder time defeating Teach if he and his entire crew had not been badly hung-over during the fight at Ocracoke Inlet). The likelihood is that Blackbeard, who played as recklessly as he fought, followed the pattern of most of the hard-core pirates of New Providence Island, who cruised until they struck it rich, returned to their pirate havens and spent the proceeds of their voyages riotously, and set sail again when they had run out. Be that as it may, as might be expected with such a formidably rapacious figure to deal with, legend has bestowed upon Blackbeard millions in hidden doubloons. Hunts for Blackbeard's booty have taken place in all his haunts, from New Providence in the Bahamas to the Isle of Shoals, off the New Hampshire coast.

October 8-9, 1926
DIGS FOR PIRATE'S HOARD

A century-old legend telling how the pirate Blackbeard buried his plunder beneath an old black walnut tree as a marker, has gained so much credence in New Jersey that Miss Florence E. Steward of Trenton directed a group of laborers in digging for the treasure around such a tree, located on property she owned in nearby Burlington.

Miss Steward said her family had known of the legend for two generations, and that as she expected to sell the house, she did not wish the property to leave the family without every effort being made to determine whether the walnut tree in the yard was the one associated with Blackbeard. She will continue to dig, she says, until certain of the result.

According to the tradition, Blackbeard buried a Spaniard upright over the treasure chest and then sailed away, never to return. In the course of time the walnut tree on Miss Seward's property has become known as "The Pirate Tree."

In further developments, a human skull unearthed by school children gave renewed zest to the hunt. Believing the skull might be that of the legendary slain Spaniard, Miss Steward asked police to guard her property against further digging by volunteers until she can supervise personally the work of her own excavators.

The children found the skull, along with fragments of other bones, in a corner of an excavation made recently by Miss Steward's workmen. The report persists that the workmen pried a large, heavy object from the excavation and took it with them when they quit work two days before the

Overleaf: Blackbeard died as furiously as he had lived, sustaining numerous sword and bullet wounds before he finally went down before Maynard and Ocracoke Inlet.

children's find.

Barred from the Steward property, the same children set to work on the other side of the fence on property owned by Miss Anna Pugh, actually nearer than Miss Steward's lot to the site of the historic "Pirate Tree." A few feet below the surface they found a large cache of bones, and excitement again reigned until a veterinarian examined them and found they were cow bones, relics of the time when the tract was a tannery.

Local experts from the Burlington Historical Society deny the story of the Spaniard's skull, stating that the area of Miss Steward's lot was a well-known Indian burial ground.

Now a reservation under the protection of the United States Government, Blackbeard Island lies, surf-beaten and inhospitable, fifty miles south of Savannah and ten miles off the Georgia coast. So it is far away from Ocracoke Inlet, where the pirate met his end at the hands of Lieutenant Maynard.

After Blackbeard's death there was not an island from North Carolina to Florida that the credulous failed to visit in search of his treasure.

Captain W. H. Parker of the Confederate Navy, in his *Recollections*, says of an island in Pamlico Sound, off the North Carolina coast, where Blackbeard often lay in a hut watching Hatteras and Ocracoke Inlets:

> I visited this island, and every square foot of earth on it had had a spade in it, in searches for Teach's money. Also, everybody believed that Teach had buried a large amount of money somewhere on the shore of the (Pamlico) Sound.

Ten miles off New Hampshire the surf-rimmed Isle of Shoals may be seen on a clear summer day. Rocky as Appledore is, treasure seekers have dug and blasted all over it to upturn a box secreted by Teach. The whole Atlantic coast has been prospected, to no avail.

March 13, 1932

BLACKBEARD ISLAND

The rocky New England coast is sprinkled with bleak headlands and lonely coves associated with the loot of Blackbeard.

coast has been prospected, to no avail.

To Blackbeard Island men came by scores with tattered maps and divining rods of witch hazel or metal.

Yet the only treasure there, according to Ben Ames Williams, in an article, "Treasure Trove," written for *American Forests* magazine, is natural beauty, the bird life of the surf line and tangled forest and the animal life of an interior little changed since the coming of the Spaniards. Sixty varieties of birds may be seen by the naturalist in the spring. White-tailed deer abound, and in the swamps alligators still swim sluggishly. No trace of Blackbeard can be found, although, according to Williams, "no man can set foot on the shore without being conscious of the ancient mystery of the place; without feeling in himself an atavistic stirring and a whispering fear."

November 15, 1934
QUEST OF TREASURE GRAVE

Pirate treasure bobs up on Blackbeard's Island off the Georgia coast. There an exploring citizen has discovered a subterranean wooden chamber in which he believes the famous pirate's life savings are deposited. The government has granted the necessary permission to excavate.

The spot is not far from the site of Edgar Allan Poe's "The Gold Bug," and it is a question which would do the world most good, a couple of million dollars' worth of doubloons or another short-story gem like Poe's masterpiece.

The story is of a piece with similar products of the treasure fever and the hunger for easy money called up by hard times. The success of the Artiglio in the Bay of Biscay (NOTE: SEE *THE SALVAGE OF THE EGYPT*) has inflamed many adventurous imaginations. But the Artiglio's experiences have shown that treasure-hunting is not an easy life, nor one for amateurs.

February 27, 1938
TEACH'S TREASURE IN FLORIDA?

Hovering over the streamlined civilization characterizing the scene around Delray Beach and Boca Raton, Florida, is the ghost of Edward Teach, the legendary Blackbeard, as alive today in the imaginations of many as he was on that day in 1718, just before Maynard's men gunned him down in Ocracoke Inlet.

A few miles south of Delray Beach along the coast is the inlet old maps listed as Boca de Ratones, "the mouth of the hidden rocks," and today the rocks are still there and still hidden. Now, as then, the rocks would protect those vessels able to thread the passage from the open sea, and trap those attempting a straight pursuit.

That Teach, Morgan and other pirates knew of this hideway along their sweep from the Carolinas to the Spanish Main seems reasonable, and it is firmly believed by many persons here. Some people readily admit their past ventures in excavation and dredging; others refuse to comment as they continue with their plans for new, secret treasure hunts.

Among those who have dug and will talk, a local grocery-store owner tells

of taking a "treasure witch," made of wires and magnets, to an oceanside cave just north of Boca Raton, at a time in the past when the mouth of the cave, now visible from the boulevard running to Palm Beach, was hidden by scrub and vines. Digging to water level at a spot indicated by the machine, the grocer got only the thigh bone of a deer. But he is not daunted, believing the bone to be an old Indian sign of "treasure beyond."

Another Florida man located an ancient wreck just north of Boca Raton inlet. He hired a dredge, posted guards, and proceeded to dig in the sands, to the tune of thousands of dollars. He didn't even get a deer bone for his troubles.

Numbers of old maps owned by collectors of the section spur the hunt for pirate gold. All of them show the inlet close to where it is known to be now, and as far as the long-ago pirates were concerned, it was an ideal location, situated equidistant from their usual range's northern and southern limits, for careening their ships in safety and, perhaps, hiding a chest or two of gold to be picked up again later.

THE NOBLE
BUCCANEER
Introduction

15

March 20th, 1927:
Sunday Magazine
**THE BUCCA-
NEERS OF THE
SPANISH MAIN**

Sir Henry Morgan (1635-1688) is the model upon which all romantic notions of pirates and buccaneers are based, and the facts of his life are even more stirring than their Hollywood versions. His career encompassed the golden age of buccaneering on the Spanish Main, the time when sea-robbery was a legitimate occupation for Englishmen, leading often, as in Morgan's case, to a knighthood and vast riches. John Steinbeck's portrait of Morgan, in his novel *The Cup of Gold*, is probably less romantic than the truth about this cavalier of the high seas, who plundered scores of galleons, took Panama in an audacious overland raid, and left legends of vast treasure hoards all over the Caribbean and the Pacific coasts of Spanish America.

In all the pages of romance there never was another company of men like the buccaneers—Morgan, Drake, and a dozen others, famous around the world. There is a common confusion between buccaneers and pirates. Although both roamed the Spanish Main and sunk many a ship in the day's work, officially the buccaneers ranked as "privateers." Their captains bore royal seals on their commissions to go forth and plunder the Spaniards. More than one King of France or England shared the spoils, while protesting to the King of Spain that they could not control their rapacious subjects in remote seas.

The story of the buccaneers is a phase of empire building. They were the unacknowledged vanguard of French and British colonization in the New World tropics. By the middle of the sixteenth century, Spain had occupied the best islands of the West Indies, conquered Mexico and looted Peru. The French and British looked on while Spain sought by every means to assert her sovereignty. The French had yet to venture into Canada, and the British were only precariously established at Plymouth and Jamestown, at the time when British buccaneers were already well established on the Spanish Main.

While neither nation dared to confront Spanish power openly, many private captains, with the covert approval of their Kings, were willing to risk hanging at the yardarm for a prize of Spanish gold. At the beginning of the buccaneers' age of glory—the seventeenth century—they were often titled gentlemen like Morgan, with plumes in their hats and heraldic arms on their cabin plate. By the end of the century they were merely savage cutthroats. Romantic encounters on the high seas had become plain piracy.

Sir John Hawkins was one of the first and boldest of the buccaneers. Named "Admiral of the Ocean Sea" by Queen Elizabeth I, Sir John robbed Portuguese slavers on the African coast and took their human cargoes to the Spanish Indies for sale, returning later as a freebooter. In 1567 Hawkins entered the harbor at Vera Cruz, pretending to be a trader, but intending to sack the town. The Spanish fleet caught him before he had a chance to mount his assault, and only two ships of his fleet escaped. One was commanded by Hawkins himself. The other was under the control of the young Francis Drake, who five years later was a commander himself, burning towns along the Spanish Main. Crossing the Isthmus of Panama years ahead of Morgan, he swore one day he would sail an English ship in the Pacific. By

Facing page:
Henry Morgan's attack on the Spanish at San Lorenzo was a fully-mounted military operation, a far cry from the usual pirate raid.

124

Overleaf
Morgan's men sack
Panama City, in
this illustration by
Howard Pyle, whose
romantic drawings
and paintings (with
some basis in fact)
created our modern
image of pirates.

Various dates
SIR HENRY MORGAN

1578 he succeeded, mounting devastating raids against the Spanish settlements on the west coast of Central America.

The rules which governed Drake and his fellow buccaneers' unofficial warfare against Spain were to capture or sink prizes at will, so as to demoralize and endanger the Spanish presence in the New World. When not fighting the Spanish, the buccaneers turned upon the numerous pirates of the area, most of whom were Spanish renegades, competitors, after all, and fair game.

The buccaneers' first period of glory continued from the 1630s to 1671, when Morgan took Panama City. After his unprecedented feat the distinction between privateers and pirates began to blur. The political situation in England changed, and European affairs increasingly preoccupied the British Crown. But Morgan's and Drake's feats were discussed wherever freebooters gathered, and pirates, nominally flying the French or British flags, set out to emulate their buccaneer forerunners.

New figures appeared: the Frenchman L'Ollonois ravaged the Gulf of Venezuela, and the Englishman John Coxon crossed the Isthmus of Panama, following the Morgan pattern. With only 300 men he took Spanish ships in the Pacific and raided coastwise in the Drake and Morgan styles. John Cook and his successor Edward Davis similarly plundered the rich Pacific coast of Spanish South and Central America, Davis at one point having ten ships under his flag.

For eighteen years, their second period of prosperity, the buccaneers plundered at will along the west coast. But 1689 brought a radical shift in alliances at home. Britain joined with old enemies against France over the question of the Spanish succession, and French and British buccaneers found themselves at war with each other. The institution of the "privateer" fell apart, and by the second decade of the eighteenth century the buccaneers had abandoned all pretence of lawfulness, plundering all nationalities (and each other) at will. Their fierceness and rapacity accomplished what Spain had been unable to do: their own destruction as a coherent force. The buccaneers' calling was replaced by the trade of sea robbery on a small scale. In later years no one came close to the exploits of Drake and Morgan.

But the early efforts of the buccaneers were hardly in vain. British and French colonies in the meantime grew up around the old buccaneer settlements in the West Indies, checkmating Spanish power in the New World. Sir Henry Morgan may not have been everyone's idea of a patriot, but his swashbuckling paved the way for the extension of the British Empire into the Caribbean Islands.

Sir Henry Morgan was born in Llanrhymay, Wales, in 1635. According to legend, as a boy in Bristol he was kidnapped and sold as a slave in Barbados. From there he escaped to Jamaica and took up buccaneering. By the time he was 28 he had a ship of his own, and three years later commanded a ship under the English privateer Edward Mansfield. Under Mansfield, Morgan aided in the capture of Santa Cataline and Old Providence Islands, and the latter later became one of his home ports. He is rumored to have buried much of his treasure there.

When Mansfield died Morgan succeeded him as Captain of his fleet of buccaneers. In 1668 Sir Thomas Modyford, British Lieutenant-Governor of Jamaica, dispatched him under Royal commission to Cuba. With 10 ships and 500 men he captured and sacked Puerto Principe, and sailed on to Porto Bello in Panama. When he returned to Jamaica after taking the Panamanian town and levying heavy tribute, he was mildly reproved for exceeding his orders. But the loot of his victory outweighed his insubordination, and he was made Commander-In-Chief of all the ships of war at Jamaica.

With this commission he again ravaged the Cuban coast in 1670, and the following year he made his famous march across the Isthmus of Panama, capturing and plundering Panama City, then one of the richest towns in Spanish America.

Unfortunately England and Spain were temporarily at peace at the time of Morgan's Panama City conquest, and he was arrested and sent home in 1672 to face charges of treason and piracy. But the gold he brought with him to England stood him in good stead and enabled him to make a court fight which cleared him. He was restored to Royal favor to such an extent that he was knighted and sent back to Jamaica as Lieutenant-Governor. He lived out his days in peace and died in 1688.

Delayed by fierce fighting under the city's walls, and furious at finding less loot than he had expected, Morgan tortured his Spanish prisoners to get the locations of their hidden treasure.

(R): "Broadside and broadside, and at it they went," in this version of a Morgan sea-fight. Ashore, well-drilled ranks of Morgan's sailor-soldiers mount an assault on a Spanish New World settlement.

CHAMPION DIVER TO SEEK MORGAN'S GOLD IN WEST INDIES

At Maracaibo, Morgan set derelict ships on fire and floated them against the Spanish fleet, breaking the blockade.

The buried treasure of Sir Henry Morgan will be sought for within the next few days by Bernard Joachim Keegan, deep sea diver and Second Mate of the U.S. working tug *Favorite*, of the Panama Canal. Tradition says that the treasure is hidden in a cave at Old Providence Island in the West Indies. The cave mouth, above water in Morgan's day, is now 75 feet below the water.

Keegan, a veteran of submarine warfare in the World War, made a record descent of 309 feet in a diving suit, and is not worried about the treasure dive, which will involve a 150-foot swim up to the cave's main chambers after the initial 75-foot descent. These chambers, above the surface but inaccessible from the land, are thought to contain Morgan's doubloons.

The waters off New Providence abound in man-eating sharks, but Keegan's chief threat will be barracuda, which are attracted by the white of flesh. For this reason Keegan will wear dark-colored gloves when he dives.

Once safely into the cave, Keegan will face two more menaces: a huge colony of bats (including the dreaded vampire bat) and a native tradition that the Devil protects the loot of his servant Morgan. But, says Keegan, "My Irish luck will be with me. Besides, who minds a little danger when there's a chance at a fortune?"

Treasure trove has been found in Panama City, and the torch of romance again illuminates the page of history. But instead of a faded map written on parchment and a grisly skeleton pointing the way, we have a modern scientific instrument as the revealing force. This new version of the divining rod is variously described as a violet ray or a radio device that indicates the presence of treasure.

It is only a year or two since sunken treasure hulks began to be penetrated with any success. With the triumph of the new radio device ashore, we may soon expect to see an organized search for lost treasure on a large scale.

Though the search has just begun, dispatches from Panama City indicate that treasure may be expected in at least five other places about the city. The present enterprise is under Government supervision, and the Anglo-American team may yet discover the hoards of doubloons which await the scientific treasure hunter. It is reasonable to suppose that at least a part of the vast loot legend ascribed to this area exists.

We know, however, that Morgan and his men got little for their pains in the 1671 sack of the city except renown. Fighting outside the city and beneath its walls delayed him, and the besieged Spanish had plenty of time to bury their gems and gold. When Morgan finally scaled the walls his men shattered the city, finding booty, but much less than expected. San José Church was destroyed in the looting, and it is among its old foundations that the Anglo-American team has made its find.

Any further success in applying the new radio treasure finder will undoubtedly bring about intensive search of the West Indies, the Florida Keys, and the Mexican coast. Certainly we shall see the world's two greatest treasure islands explored anew—Cocos, off the Chilean Coast (MARGIN NOTE: SEE "TREASURE ISLAND") and Trinidad in the South Atlantic, not the West Indian island, but a volcanic patch long associated with pirate gold.

Gold ornaments and chains, precious emeralds, rubies, diamonds and sapphires, comprising a treasure as yet unvalued, were discovered today in a tunnel beneath the ruins of San José Church, which was destroyed when the old city was burned down by the pirate Henry Morgan in 1671.

Two Englishmen, George Williams and Fred Kelly, and an American, Wallace Bain, found the loot under a special concession for treasure hunting granted by President Chiari of Panama. Kelly and Williams financed the treasure hunt at Cocos Island (MARGIN NOTE: SEE "TREASURE ISLAND") last year, but they never reached the island and were charged with fraud in British newspapers. Their concession gives them the exclusive right to hunt for treasure in Panama for four years.

President Chiari visited the site of the excavations today and congratulated the explorers, who are using a ground radio apparatus to locate the treasure. According to the explorers, the instrument indicates other treasures buried in the old city, and already they are excavating on five sites. The tun-

nels are filled with water, and it is necessary to pump them out for further excavations.

The amount of treasure so far recovered is not considerable, but a large amount is supposed to have been buried at the time of Morgan's sack of the city.

The search for Eldorado goes on forever. Hundreds of years after the pirates and buccaneers roamed the Spanish Main, expeditions are still going out with high hopes of discovering the plunder they are traditionally supposed to have buried.

The latest expedition is headed by Louis Morgan, a Texas descendant of the celebrated buccaneer Sir Henry Morgan. The Morgan expedition will go

October 16th, 1927: Sunday Magazine

TEXAS MORGAN SEEKS BUCCANEER ANCESTOR'S GOLD

Morgan's assaults on the Spanish were well-supplied, highly organized combinations of land and sea maneuvers. To reach Panama City, he and his men made a grueling overland march through the steamy jungles of the Isthmus.

Overleaf
Naval combat in the days of the buccaneers was a chaotic affair. Ships grappled together in a welter of shot-down masts and spars, burning sails and tangled rigging, maneuvering to fire broadsides and release boarding parties under blinding clouds of smoke from cannon and flaming timbers.

to Central America in search of some of the loot Sir Henry's followers carried off after the sack of Panama City. Tradition has it that the buccaneers buried their booty somewhere near a bayou in the region of Darien Bay, on the west coast of Panama.

The modern Morgan will be guided by a map which he claims was left by Sir Henry to his descendants after his death in Jamaica in 1688. The drawing, on old parchment, came to the present owner from his father, Frank Pierce Morgan, once District Attorney of Victoria, Texas. The story is that eight of Sir Henry's men buried the treasure and were promptly murdered by their leader, leaving him in sole possession of the secret.

The Morgan expedition will set sail from San Francisco aboard the 40-foot auxiliary launch *Saxon*, hoping to obtain permission from Panamanian authorities to make excavations at the Darien Bay site indicated on the map. Since, according to Louis Morgan, a distant relative of his is already searching for Sir Henry's treasure in the ruins of the old city of Panama, the search assumes the aspect of a family contest over family heirlooms.

The American yacht *Queen of Scots*, owned by Anthony J. Drexel of Philadelphia (MARGIN NOTE: SEE *THE QUEST FOR THE MERIDA*) arrived today at Teneriffe, Canary Islands, carrying a scientific expedition reported searching for buried treasure. They were said to be en route to a local island where the pirate Morgan was believed to have hidden sea loot in gems and gold.

U. S. YACHT SEEKS GOLD

Facing page:
Howard Pyle's ver-
sion of a Tory family
fleeing their village
before a mob of
enraged patriots dur-
ing the American
Revolution. What
valuables such refu-
gees could not carry,
they often buried,
giving rise to the
legend of Tory trea-
sure.

*March 15, 1873-
June 6, 1877*

**TORY
TREASURE
IN SUSSEX
COUNTY**

In addition to the payroll money lost when Continental guns sank British treasure ships during the Revolution (NOTE: SEE *THE GOLD OF NEW YORK HARBOR*), the British and their Loyalist sympathizers provided America with another source, if not of gold, at least of golden lore. At the outbreak of hostilities in 1775 the smart money was by no means on the American side. The wealthy families of the northern colonies were almost universally Tory in the beginning, the Revolution having been preached chiefly by a New England faction of small merchants, shippers, editors and lawyers who adroitly manipulated the plight of the desperate urban poor of Boston and the hardscrabble farmers of outlying areas to drum up support for the cause of separation. It was only gradually that the followers of Samuel Adams began to reconcile their version of Revolutionary aims with the quite different grievances of the great independent planters of Virginia. The Union thus created can be said to have contained the seeds of the Civil War, even as the American nation was being born.

Meanwhile, the first families of New England, who had grown rich on a British colonial policy which attempted (unsuccessfully, as it turned out) to apply the same exploitive plantation concept which had worked in the south, to northern colonies where commerce and industry were already far more profitable than agriculture, naturally regarded the efforts of the Sons of Liberty to upset the applecart with fear and contempt. Even when the southern planters joined the cause, and the Continental Congress was formed to declare independence formally, raise an army, and draw up a constitution for the new nation, the wealthy Tories of New York were sure that Washington's rabble-in-arms would be crushed in a matter of weeks by the awakened wrath of the mother country.

But when the war heated up and the revolutionaries began tarring and feathering Tories and seizing their goods and land, the beleaguered Loyalists changed their complacent attitude concerning the probable course of the revolution. Most fled to Canada after the Continental Army's successes in upper New York State and New Jersey, taking their treasure with them. But a few of the fugitives failed to escape in time, and some Tories deliberately stayed on, serving as spies and otherwise aiding the British cause to the best of their abilities. These latter provide the source of the persistent rumors of hidden Tory treasure, which survived well into the twentieth century in New Jersey and New York.

One of the oldest traditions in this corner of New Jersey concerns a chest of gold and silver coins worth an estimated $100,000 (1873 valuation), buried on Crabtree's Island, near the town of Vernon. The year was 1776, and the Tories of the Delaware Valley were engaged in a sort of minor guerilla warfare against the patriots, which occasionally involved robbery. Six of them managed to plunder the treasury at Philadelphia (although another version of the tale claims they simply robbed a rich Whig on the outskirts of town). They intended to turn the money over to the British Army, but being

Newspaper accounts of caches of eighteenth century coins keep the legend of Tory treasure alive in New Jersey and New York State.

Coins of 1770 Start Gold Rush in Jersey

By The Associated Press.

HIGHLANDS, N. J., April 9—The finding of several eighteenth century coins started a "gold" rush here today.

Several hundred persons armed with rakes, picks and shovels scratched and dug at the banks of the Navesink River near the place of the first discovery. Darkness and a chill wind discouraged the "prospectors" temporarily, but most said would be back tomorrow to continue the search.

It all started with the by William R. Cottr French gold coin dat the top of the river Wednesday. Mr. Co and his son, Will the next day an more gold piec the 1700's. H friend estim the coins at

DREDGE GIVES HINT OF 1775 TREASURE

Hunt for Tory's Gold Is Spurred at Whitehall After Box Is Brought Up, Only to Drop.

Special to The New York Times.

WHITEHALL, N. Y., Sept. 29.—The tale of a treasure chest dropped in the harbor here by Robert Gordon at the breaking out of the American Revolution and never recovered has been revived by dredging work now being done in the Haven by the big State dredge.

Gordon, a Scot, was born in London in 1738. After various adventures over the world he finally fell in with Philip Skene, original proprietor of Whitehall, and about 1770 became his stock of goods to known as and Indians. west

A HIGHLAND EL DORADO

SEEKING RICHES IN ULSTER COUNTY.

LEGENDS OF UNTOLD WEALTH HIDDEN AWAY BY PIRATES AND TORIES—A PROPOSED EXPLORATION OF THE GREAT CRO' NEST CAVERN—COOPER'S STORY OF "THE SPY" AND ITS FOUNDATION —A VEIN OF GOLD FOUND NEAR NEWBURG.

From an Occasional Correspondent.

NEWBURG N. Y., Tuesday, June 5. 1877.

The mania for treasure-seeking seems to have attacked all parts of this section of the State, from the dwellers among the Shawangunk in this and Ulster County to the credulous portion of the community that centres in the Highlands of the Hudson. Family records and the memories of the "oldest inhabitant" are being overhauled and taxed for legends of the times when the rocky confines of our mountain chains were the resorts of pirates and Tory robber bands, and when this region was overrun by enthusiastic seekers after traditional El Dorados; the first people that visited the Highlands and old Shawangunk hills were adventurers in the mines of gold and silver of which the navigators carried back to foreign lands the most extravagant stories. In 1609, the Half Moon, the pioneer sail of the Hudson, Cornwall Mountains, Master Juett this journal that: "the mountains look or minerals was in them." Then

---

HIDDEN TREASURE.

From Our Own Correspondent.

VERNON, N. J., Wednesday, March 12, 1873.

Every locality in this country has its pet legends of immense treasures buried somewhere within its limits. The oldest inhabitant hereabout remembers, when a boy, hearing his whitehaired grandsire relate how his father used to tell of the depredations of Brandt, the Indian chief, and Claudius Smith, the cowboy, and their respective 'ollowers throughout this section, and of the large amounts of gold and silver they compelled the settlers to disgorge, all of which they were in the habit of hiding in caverns and caves, and burying in different localities. A time came when those desperadoes were driven off, leaving untold riches behind them. This has ever since been tarnishing and corroding in its secure hiding places. Now and then some farmer's plow turns up a pot of glittering coin, a wood-chopper's ax reveals a fortune in some ancient hollow tree, or some ambitious student of geology, digging and picking among the rocks and ravines of Sussex County, is rewarded by finding a portion of the hidden wealth.

One of these traditions is to the effect that there is buried near this place gold and silver

---

PLOW REVEALS BURIED GOLD.

Champlain Farmer Finds Fortune Supposedly Stolen from Burgoyne's Army.

PLATTSBURG, N. Y., Oct. 2.—A farmer named Vostburg, living near Champlain, while plowing yesterday turned up a quantity of ancient gold coins. Digging further he found more coins that he could carry home at one time. Their value is several thousand dollars.

It is believed the treasure was buried by persons who stole it from the British Army which camped near Champlain during the Burgoyne campaign against New York State. The robbers probably lost their lives subsequently, so that no

---

at said he returned several ll dated in a collector the worth of $200 each.

Mention has containing $100 hidden by a par a swamp in the J., in 1776; to sage way to the Wawasmog Iodi Ulster County the rocks in

closely pursued by militiamen, they fled up the Delaware Valley, struck off into the wilderness near Vernon, and buried their spoils on Crabtree's Island, then a knoll of high ground situated in an almost inaccessible swamp.

After the war, a member of the wealthy DeWitt family, which was largely Loyalist during the Revolution, stated to authorities in Vernon that the treasure party had stopped at his house in 1776 and given him the location of the stolen money. The announcement triggered a series of attempts to recover it which went on for a hundred years. In 1813 a party of treasure-hunters dug down 20 feet on Crabtree's Island, where a workman struck an iron chest with his pick. Efforts to haul it up agitated the quicksand in which it lay, and the chest sank from sight.

Over the years many other expeditions were formed to go after the Crabtree's Island loot. The experiments of Mesmer and Madame Blavatsky brought a wave of interest in psychic phenomena to America in the nineteenth century, and as an offshoot, clairvoyants and "gold witches" with hazel dowsing rods combed the area. But all efforts were in vain. By 1877 the legend had assumed a slightly sinister supernatural character. The treasure was thought to be bewitched, and an elaborate ritual grew up: the would-be treasure-hunter had to follow a precise series of actions and observances in his quest, any deviations being considered fatal.

Since that time, of course, the countryside of northwestern New Jersey has altered completely. Swamps have been drained, and even the location of Crabtree's Island is in question. Only the legend of six mysterious Tories hiding a fortune by night in the heart of the old swamp remains.

June 6, 1877
THE LEGEND OF CRO' NEST CAVE

"Cro' Nest," the old name for a lofty scarp of the Hudson Highlands across the river from Fishkill, New York, is connected with one of the most interesting episodes of the Revolutionary War, the tale upon which Fenimore Cooper based his celebrated story, "The Spy."

Enoch Crosby was a renowned spy for the Americans during the war. In 1777 the Committee of Safety was in session at Fishkill. It was reported to them that recruits for the enemy were being gathered in the vicinity, which was a stronghold of British sympathizers. The man behind the recruiting drive was a British officer with a secret headquarters somewhere in the Hudson Highlands, then a wild, largely unpopulated region of wooded hills and crags overlooking the west bank of the river.

The Committee sent Crosby to check into the truth of the rumor. He reached a farmhouse in Cornwall, at the base of the mountains. The farmer revealed himself as a Tory, and Crosby, pleading common cause, told him he wished to reach the British lines. The farmer guided Crosby to the officer's cave on Cro' Nest Mountain. He was greeted cordially, and liberally plied with food and drink, of which the cave had a great store, supplied by Loyalist farmers of the district. During the evening Crosby learned that the British officer had already recruited 30 men. They were to gather in three days at the barn of a Tory on the west side of Butter Hill, from thence proceeding to the British Army.

Townsend's Rangers, a vigorous group of patriot irregulars, were conducting operations against the British in the vicinity. But Crosby knew he couldn't sneak away from the cave without arousing suspicion. So he warned the British recruiting officer of the presence of the patriot force in the area, and suggested that he and his recruits split into units of one and two men, and hide separately until the Rangers had left. The officer believed him, and took his advice, but confirmed that the whole band would rendezvous at the time and place already set.

Left alone, Crosby contacted a patriot farmer and sent him to the Committee of Safety with a message which outlined the British officer's operation and gave details of the rendezvous. Captain Townsend was contacted, and set up an ambush at the Butter Hill barn. The British officer and his 30 men were captured without trouble.

One item of importance was missing, however. Crosby had noticed stores of money in the cave, issued to the officer to enable him to pay his recruits an advance (taking "the King's shilling" was considered a binding contract for British Army recruits of the time), buy supplies, and bribe Whig officials in the local towns where he carried out his recruiting effort. The officer wouldn't talk, and Crosby himself had forgotten the exact whereabouts of the cave. Legend has it that the money is still there.

Spanish silver pieces of eight, accepted as legal dollars in colonial America, were split into four-bit halves (worth four *reales*) and two-bit quarters (worth two *reales*).

October 3, 1909
CHAMPLAIN FARMER FINDS BURGOYNE GOLD

A farmer named Vostburg, living near Champlian in upstate New York, turned up a quantity of ancient gold coins while plowing yesterday. Digging further, he found more coins than he could carry home at one time. Their value is several thousand dollars.

It is believed the treasure was buried by persons who stole it from the British Army which camped near Champlain during General Burgoyne's campaign against New York State. The robbers probably lost their lives subsequently, so that no one knew what they had done with their booty.

September 12, 1924
BURIED TREASURE IN SETAUKET, LONG ISLAND

A discovery in 1894, kept secret thirty years, has set Setauket gossiping about treasure trove. The find consisted of 100 Spanish coins. It was made by George W. Hawkins, a schoolteacher, who has lived here nearly half a century.

Thirty years ago, Hawkins was puttering in his garden, digging a few holes to plant some beans. About a foot and a half below the ground his spade struck something metallic. A little deeper it scooped up the coins. Hawkins managed to gather more than a hundred of them, which cleaning and examination revealed to be Spanish, of dates varying between 1770 and 1775. He put them away and said nothing about them.

Hawkins, now retired as a teacher, was surprised a few days ago when neighbors asked him questions about the treasure. How the news of it leaked out he does not know, nor will he say why he kept it a secret all these years. But today he admitted his discovery, and advanced a theory of their presence in his garden.

During the American Revolution, Hawkins said, the house in which he and his family live was occupied by a Reverend Mr. Brewster, pastor of the old Presbyterian Church on Setauket's village green. The green was captured by the British. Apparently there was further skirmishing, and the pastor buried his personal treasure, consisting of the coins in question, behind his house for safekeeping, intending to dig them up when the fighting was over. But he was probably killed in the battle.

The coins, Hawkins said, are in perfect condition. They are said to be of considerable value, and Hawkins has already disposed of several. He would not reveal the prices received, however.

The news of this discovery has planted hopes in the hearts of other Setauket residents. When the gardening season begins in the spring there will be intensive digging, judging from the interest created by the Hawkins find.

September 30, 1934

DREDGE GIVES HINT OF 1775 TREASURE

Spanish coins, as well as the currency of a dozen other countries, were the legal specie of the colonies, and the treasures of the Tories consisted largely of them.

The tale of a treasure chest dropped in the harbor at Whitehall, New York by Robert Gordon at the outbreak of the Revolution and never recovered, has been revived by dredging work now being done in the Haven by the State.

Gordon, a Scot, was born in London in 1739. After various adventures all over the world, he finally fell in with Philip Skene, original proprietor of this town near the southern end of Lake Champlain. About 1770 Gordon came to Whitehall with a stock of goods to trade with the settlers and Indians.

His place, which was known as the Red Barn Lot, was on the west side of Wood Creek near the south line of the town. He married and was rapidly becoming a man of substance when war broke out in 1775.

Gordon was a Loyalist, and things grew dangerous for him. He took his money and plate, packed it safely in a strong box, and late one night journeyed to the harbor and in a small boat started for Canada.

Somewhere in the marshes on the west shore of the Haven, he dropped the box, noting in his mind the exact location of the treasure.

He prospered in his new home near St. Johns, Canada. But he later disappeared on a hunting trip, never to return.

The tale might have remained but another of the many legends of Tory treasure common to the area, were it not for the fact that a big State dredge engaged in swamp clearance here recently brought up a metal box in its steel jaws. The box rested for a moment on a mound of muck in the scoop, but slipped and toppled back into the water.

Frequent explorations begun immediately have so far failed to locate the box. And as this search for the old treasure is renewed, new legends of Tory gold and silver on the bottom of Lake Champlain are in the process of being born.

The finding of several eighteenth century coins started a "gold rush" near Highlands, New Jersey today.

Several hundred persons armed with rakes, picks and shovels scratched and dug at the banks of the Navesink River near the place of the first discovery, until darkness and chill winds put an end to the search.

It all started with the finding, by William R. Cottrell, of a French gold coin dated 1770, at the top of the river bank. Mr. Cottrell said that he and his son returned the next day and found several more gold pieces, all dated in the 1700s. He said a collector friend estimated the worth of the coins at $200 each.

COINS OF 1770 START A GOLD RUSH IN NEW JERSEY

Far and away the costliest war in human history in terms of loss of life and destruction of property, World War II left in its wake a number of stories concerning vast amounts of Axis money, valuables and specie unrecovered by Allied Forces. Untold billions vanished into the maws of the German and Japanese war machines, but as the war in both theaters of operation began to turn against them, Axis leaders made plans to squirrel away valuables against a better day. High-ranking Japanese built up a war chest which was sunk in Tokyo Bay, to be retrieved after the war to aid in reconstruction.

The Nazi thugs at the top of Hitler's chain of command were not so altruistic in their piling-up of treasure. Hermann Goering, perhaps the greediest of Hitler's lieutenants, seemed to have regarded the war as an opportunity to amass a gigantic personal fortune. He seized priceless works of art from the French during the German occupation of Paris, and built up a mighty treasure, including a set of personal "crown jewels," from looted gold, silver and precious stones, some of which was part of the grisly spoils of the death camps. Hitler himself was rumoured to have stashed away a tidy fortune in the last years of the war, treasure which was to have sustained him in his last stand at his Alpine stronghold.

Other finds in the Phillipines, Malaysia, the south of France, and Greece were spoils left behind when Japanese and German occupation forces fled before the Allied advances, or personal fortunes hidden by local residents to keep them out of the hands of the invaders in the early years of the war. In a curious episode, no less a figure than General Douglas MacArthur was linked with a mysterious Japanese "treasure chest" during his postwar assignment as Commander of Allied Occupation Forces in Japan.

General Lucius Clay, postwar Military Governor of Germany, was responsible for recovering Nazi loot, and making reparations to, among others, the survivors of the Nazi death camps. He accounted for a majority of the German treasure, but a good deal of it is rumored to have been lost in Germany and Austria during the chaotic final weeks of the war.

Another source of World War II treasure, less lurid than the "war chests" and other caches of the Axis high command, but in the long run more reliable, is the ocean bottom. Millions of tons of shipping were sunk by both sides in the Atlantic and Pacific, and some of these ships carried great treasures in coin and bullion in their strong-rooms. Salvage attempts have raised only a fraction of this verifiable sunken treasure, estimated as valuing in the billions of dollars.

Facing page:
From left, General Ridgeway, an unidentified British liason officer, Lieutenant General George Patton, and General Eisenhower examine some art works found in an abandoned salt mine where they had been hidden by the Nazis in the closing days of World War II.

*July 13, 1935-
September 8, 1941*

TALES TOLD OF TREASURE AS WAR-CLOUDS LOOM

In Ethiopia and in Japan, as the count-down to World War II began, two widely different treasure stories were circulated. In 1935 the sabre-rattling of Mussolini and his *fascisti* was reaching a crescendo. Egged on by Hitler, Il Duce was planning the first phase of his grandiose scheme to recreate the ancient Roman Empire, by invading all–but–defenseless Ethiopia. Emperor Haile Selassie, anticipating the outcome, ordered the country's crown jewels and its priceless collection of Coptic ecclesiastical treasures hidden away for safekeeping. The latter was said to include both the Ark of the

Overleaf:
During the inventory of Nazi art spoils seized by American forces in 1945, average GIs from the Seventh Army came face to face with more Rembrandts, Cranachs and other priceless old master paintings than many art critics see in a lifetime.

Covenant and the Tables of the Law received by Moses on Mount Sinai, brought to Ethopia by Menelik, son of King Solomon and the Queen of Sheba (according to Coptic tradition), and founder of the Ethiopian Dynasty. Most of the treasure survived the war, despite the efforts of the Italian dictator's forces to find it after their victory.

In Japan, the war chest of Tokugawara Shōgunate, buried by its chief Minister, Oguri Kozukenosuke, in anticipation of the regime's downfall in 1868, was on the verge of being recovered in 1941, according to Kozukenosuke's grandson, Hidemori Kawahara. The treasure, buried 250 feet underground near Tokyo, consisted of gold ingots packed in six large cabinets. Its worth was estimated at 2.3 billion yen.

By September 8th, 1941, the dig had reached a depth of 220 feet. Bones, a sword bearing the Kozukenosuke family crest, and other evidence had been unearthed. Two months later the Japanese attacked Pearl Harbor, and further news of the treasure hunt was swallowed up in the bellow of war. If the treasure was indeed recovered, it would have multiplied Japan's gold reserve at the time by a factor of five. Kawahara, a devoté of the *bushido* warrior ethic the wartime junta of generals shared with the old Shōgun, had pledged to turn his find over to the State for the war effort. It is possible some of the 1868 gold lay behind the rumors of an enormous Japanese gold, silver and platinum cache, said, after the war, to have been hidden beneath the waters of Tokyo Bay (see below).

Diving operations are salvaging $1,000,000 in gold currency which the British tossed into the sea before the fall of Singapore, it was reported from that captured British fortress today.

"Tens of thousands of dollars are being brought to the surface by marine divers, giving the spectators on the Singapore shore a great thrill," Japanese radio reported.

Gold bullion worth £2,379,000 has been recovered from the strongroom of the Canadian-Australian liner *Niagara*, sunk by an enemy mine twenty-seven miles from the New Zealand coast in 1941.

The liner is in 438 feet of water, so it was the deepest salvage job yet undertaken. Spread around the area were 150 enemy mines, which were removed.

An Italian company salvaged £1 million from the liner *Egypt* in the Bay of Biscay (NOTE: SEE *THE SALVAGE OF THE EYGPT*) after five years of work at six times the cost of the *Niagara* salvage. The *Eygpt* lay in 400 feet of water.

All the sunken galleons of Spain never yielded such a tale of treasure-trove as the story of the war-chest of the defeated Japanese nation, reportedly hidden beneath the water of Tokyo Bay in the last years of the war, to be retrieved later and used to rebuild the shattered country.

The loot, primarily in the form of platinum and silver ingots, originally came to the attention of American occupation forces through a tip from an unnamed geisha. It was later confirmed by an obscure group of Japanese businessmen, who maintained they had long been mistrustful of the military regime which had brought the nation to ruin, and were providing information concerning the hidden treasure as a proof of their eagerness to cooperate with occupation forces.

The estimate by the businessmen of the treasure's value was initially given as a dazzling 30 billion yen ($2 billion, in 1946). It was said to have consisted of the nation's entire stock of platinum, as well as gold and silver looted from the Phillipines, the Dutch East Indies, Burma, Thailand (Siam), and China during the Japanese occupation of those countries.

Acting on information supplied by a Japanese laborer who had helped bury the ingots, the occupation forces began to dig in the mud around a Tokyo wharf used by U.S. Navy ships. Lieutenant E. V. Nielsen of Stamford, Connecticut, an officer in the Thirty-second Military Government Unit, was head of the diving team, and succeeded in locating the hidden hoard.

"I stripped and went down into about six feet of water," Lieutenant Nielsen said, "And there, in three or four feet of mud, I could feel two areas—each about twenty feet square—which seemed to be paved with (platinum) blocks."

He brought up the first ingot himself, a seventy-five pound hunk of solid platinum. Further explorations proved a disappointment to those who had believed in the original $2 billion estimate. After Lieutenant Nielsen's find, no more platinum bars were recovered, nor did the team raise any gold at all.

The U.S. Navy team with part of the cache of silver bullion they recovered from Tokyo Bay. The sunken hoard was thought to be part of the "war chest" of Imperial Japan.

Sandwiched between reports on the major events of WWII and its aftermath, the New York Times recorded off-beat tales of hidden treasure and captured loot.

Ethiopia Hides Jewels And Biblical Treasures

By The Associated Press.

ISTANBUL, Turkey, July 12.— Reports reaching here tonight from Addis Ababa, capital of Ethiopia, said Emperor Haile Selassie, anticipating an Italian invasion, had ordered _ _ _ _ country's valuable crown jew _ _ _ _ siastical treasures for saf _ _ _ mountains for saf _ _ _ _

The church tr _ _ _ to include the t _ _ _ ceived by Mose _ _ _ as well as the _ _ _ nant. Both _ _ _ brought to E _ _ _ salem by M _ _ _ ing to Ethio _ _ _ son of Kir _ _ _ Queen of S _ _ _

GREEK HUNTS TREASURE

Message in Bottle Found in Sea Says $25,000,000 Was Buried

ATHENS, Nov. 28 (Nana)—A Greek fisherman has found a bottle floating in the sea and in it a treasure-trove message written by four German officers at the time of the German retreat from Gre _ _ _ message, sealed with _ _ _ ty one-ounce bottle, _ _ _ yptic language how _ _ _ rs buried 2,500,000 _ _ _ (worth about $25,- _ _ e headquarters of _ _ e-Lovers Soviety. _ _ re was a rough _ _ pointing to the _ _ ake the position _ _ re the words _ _ s from door—

M'ARTHUR AIDE DENIES TREASURE CHEST TALE

TOKYO, May 25 (AP)—Gen. Douglas MacArthur's Chief of Staff denied today that his boss had an oriental treasure chest.

Maj. Gen. E. M. Almond declared after studying Washington reports that General MacArthur held a key to a chest full of gold and jewels that there was no similarity between Occupation headquarters' holdings of impounded property and the reported chest. General Almond did not report how much headquarters held. No other source ever has announced it.

Earlier, lacking official comment, it was assumed the "chest" report had been based on impounded property in the Bank of Japan. Its vaults hold precious gems and metals put there by the Occupation.

Former Secretary of War Robert P. Patterson may have had that in mind when he told a House Interstate and Foreign Commerce subcommittee of a fabulous treasure chest to which General MacArthur had the key. A Washington dispatch yesterday said the House group had assigned an investigator to get to the bottom of the mys _ _ _

John F. Conslin, Gen- _ _ _ Civil Property _ _ _

_ _ _ _ nd the build- _ _ e door. Ove _ _ "light, sur _ _ motto. No _ _ stry has _ _ the fishe _ _ treasu _ _ iern tre _ _ il belo _ _ if to _ _ 00,000 _ _ with _ _ spo _ _ m _ _ at _ _

Tokyo Says Divers Save Singapore Gold

By The United Press.

TOKYO, May 14 (From Japanese broadcast recorded in New York)—Diving operations are salvaging $1,000,000 in gold currency which the British tossed into the sea before the fall of Singapore, it was reported from _ _ _ that captured British fortress _ _ _ _ thousands of dollars _ _ _ _ brought to the _ _ _ _ _ giving _ _ _

Divers' Search of Austrian Lake Deflates Wild Tales of Nazi Gold

Special to The New York Times

VIENNA, Dec. 7—It has cost the Austrian Government 2 million schillings (about $80,000) to put at rest the melodramatic tales of a Nazi wartime treasure cached on the bottom of Toplitzsee, a remote Alpine lake in the Dead Mountains of Styria Province.

The Ministry of Interior, which announced the figure at the close of its search, listed the results. Among these was the recovery of the body of a 19-year-old amateur diver from Munich, who had perished in a secret attempt to bring up the rumored treasure chests.

Since Oct. 23, well-equipped divers using a sounding device and underwater television, then diving after any sightings, have covered the entire bottom of the small, deep lake and produced the following:

Twelve chests of Nazi-counterfeited English pound notes. Two chests containing counterfeiting plates unboxed

stamps for insertion of dates and serial numbers.

This discard was from a Nazi concentration camp project called "Operation Bernhard," believed to have been intended as some kind of economic attack on the British wartime economy—perhaps the destruction of foreign confidence in British currency.

The collapse of the Hitlerian war effort evidently overtook the project, but it has not been fully explained why the Nazis jettisoned the evidence in the Austrian lake.

One suggestion is that they were ashamed of it. Another is that the counterfeiters themselves intended to put some of their product into postwar circulation, but considered it necessary to avoid flooding the greater part destroy the "mark

The recoveries turned over Engl

The remainder of the cache consisted of ingots of 99.95 per cent pure silver, valued at the time at $600 each. Fifty-three of these silver bars had been recovered by April 20, 1946. The final estimate of the worth of the treasure cache, which proved far less extensive than originally believed, came to something under $35,000.

But Colonel R. Carleton, who was in overall command of the salvage effort, stated that more ingots might have sunk deeper into the mud of the harbor. It is possible that some of them remain to this day, overlooked by the Navy divers of the 1946 search.

The hoard of Tokyo Bay was not the first hidden treasure found by U.S. troops in Japan after the war. $250 million was seized from Japanese banks. Other caches of precious metals and jewelry, including eleven crates of platinum and 8,000 carats of diamonds, were also among the spoils which fell to the Americans after the Japanese surrender. Most of this treasure was paid out in reparations, or returned to the Japanese Government at the end of the Occupation.

May 25-26, 1950
GENERAL MacARTHUR'S TREASURE CHEST

An Oriental treasure chest filled with gold and precious gems, said to be in the custody of General Douglas MacArthur, aroused the curiosity of Congress in 1950.

A Congressional subcommittee heard about the fabulous chest from former Secretary of War Robert P. Patterson, during secret hearings on legislation dealing with alien property and war claims. General MacArthur, Mr. Patterson testified, had the key to the chest and was awaiting orders as to disposition of the treasure, said to consist of "jewelry, precious items, gold and foreign currency." It was seized from the Japanese at the end of the war, but the committee did not know where the Japanese got it.

Mr. Patterson said the treasure chest was in Tokyo. He did not estimate its value, but committee members said it was sufficient to "pay a potentate's ransom several times over."

But in further developments, Brigadier General John F. Conslin, General MacArthur's Civil Property Custodian, declared: "I know of no chest at all, no key." MacArthur's Chief of Staff, Major General E. M. Almond, backed up the denial by stating that there was nothing in the records of the Occupation Army's holdings of impounded material which resembled the treasure chest.

It is possible that Mr. Patterson had confused a report concerning the impounded property found in the vaults of the bank of Japan, which consisted of precious gems and metals, with an actual "treasure chest" in the possession of General MacArthur.

MacArthur was soon swept up in the Korean campaign, which eventually led to his recall by President Truman and his subsequent retirement. No further mention was made of the treasure chest, and it must be added to the other mysteries which surrounded the career of MacArthur, one of America's most brilliant and enigmatic military leaders.

An American officer examines part of a store of bullion found hidden in the barn of the Japanese farmer shown here. The farmer said he thought the silver was lead, and he planned to make kitchen utensils out of it.

First Cavalry Division troops found 32 tons of pure silver, drawn into strands and looped, with a value of $2 million, in a deserted air raid shelter outside Tokyo.

THE LOOT OF NAZI GERMANY

American soldiers and an art historian from the Metropolitan Museum in New York carry three paintings (including a priceless Chardin) from one of Goering's hiding places, a Bavarian castle near the Swiss border.

When First Army troops cleared the Ruhr communications center of Siegen in April, 1945, they came upon a cave full of art treasures hidden by the Germans. Shown here is an American private admiring the crown of Charlemagne, part of the treasure of Siegen.

General Lucius D. Clay, former United States Military Governor of Germany, testified before the House Interstate and Foreign Commerce Committee in 1950, and provided information on war loot taken from the Nazis.

He stated that the invading Americans had seized between $250 million and $300 million in Nazi gold, which was split up among sixteen nations claiming war reparations from Germany. Russia was not one of them.

The General estimated at "many millions of dollars" the value of property that had belonged to the Reich Marshall Hermann Goering. Goering's holdings included corporation stocks, land, paintings and other art objects, and real estate. It also included what a member of the Committee called "the crown jewels of Hermann Goering, a large piece crowned with very large precious stones, perhaps diamonds." Goering's loot was turned over to his widow, and later seized by the German Government when the lady was held to be a Nazi.

Jewelry, gold teeth, watches and other valuables taken from concentration camp victims, according to General Clay, originally had been turned over to Storm Troopers and deposited in German banks. The American Occupation Army turned them over to relief organizations, which sold them for an estimated $30 million and used the money to help the survivors.

Heuschwarstein Castle at Füssen in Bavaria, with the Alps in the background. Huge stores of looted art were secreted here at the orders of the Reichsmarschall.

Two suitcases containing gold coins and gems estimated to be worth $3 million were reported found near Pont-Saint Esprit, in Provence, by a treasure-hunting expert.

The local police gave the following account of the burial and recovery of the treasure:

In 1941 a certain Joseph Pozzi, then residing in jail, was told he was dying of cancer. He then told his cellmate that while at liberty he had seen two men bury the suitcases. Pozzi was arrested the day after the incident, and kept his secret until the news of his fatal disease made him want to share it with someone.

When the cellmate got out of jail he had forgotten some of Pozzi's details about the loot, so he went to Louis Begasset, the treasure expert. M. Begasset said he believed that the treasure was a collection of valuables belonging to several families who wished to hide them from the Germans.

May 25, 1948
FRENCH REPORT DISCOVERY OF TREASURE WORTH $3 MILLION

As the war veered against the Nazis, the high command hid most of the crumbling Reich's gold reserves in disused salt mines near Merkers. They were recovered by Occupation troops at war's end.

Also found in the salt caves at Merkers was this Manet painting, "Wintergarden," part of art treasures hidden with the gold.

Not measurable in dollars and cents, the art works the Nazis looted from museums and collectors all over Europe stands as one of the grandest "pirate" treasures on record. A GI inspects part of an art cache liberated by the U.S. Army in Königsee in 1945.

As the Allies swept over the German border, Goering was frantically trying to move his stolen art to a safe location. The boxcar carrying this statue and other works was found abandoned on a siding near Berchtesgaden.

November 29, 1953

MESSAGE IN BOTTLE CLUE TO GERMAN TREASURE IN GREECE

A Greek fisherman found the proverbial message in a bottle floating at sea in 1953. But this message led him, not to a castaway on an island, but into a hunt for treasure-trove supposedly left behind by four German officers at the time of the German retreat from Greece.

The message, sealed with wax in a dirty one-ounce bottle, described in cryptic language how the four officers buried $25 million worth of gold sovereigns near the Athens headquarters of the Greek Nature-Lovers Society. With the message was a rough map with arrows pointing to the burial spot. To make the position clearer there were the words: "location: 12 meters from door- light, water."

The fisherman found the building mentioned, and sure enough, over the door was written the Society's motto: "light, sun, water." He obtained a license from the Greek Finance Ministry and started digging, anticipating half the treasure as his share. No mention is made whether or not he unearthed the treasure, so painstakingly concealed by the German officers during the war.

November, 1954-December 1961

WAR TREASURES STILL BEING RECOVERED

In Manila, a Filipino named Salvador Mosquera, digging in Iloilo City in the central Phillipines, announced that he had uncovered an $800,000 treasure buried by the Japanese occupation forces during World War II. Human skeletons, possibly of slave laborers used to bury the hoard of gold and jewelry, were scattered about the area.

Two French chimneysweeps discovered about $300,000 in notes and bonds, in a small suitcase stuffed into a hole in the chimney they were cleaning in Cholet, France. The police, commenting on the find in 1961, said they believed the treasure was hidden there by Felix Levy, a wealthy Jewish cattle trader, shortly before he and his family were taken off by the Nazis in July, 1942.

And in Malaysia, a combined salvage attempt by the British Royal Navy and the Royal Malayan Navy in 1957 was broken off inconclusively, in the waters off the west coast of Penang Island. The object of the marine quest, gold bullion and precious ornaments supposedly lying in a Japanese submarine sunk during World War II, may still be there.

August 28, 1955-December 8, 1963

THE MYSTERY OF TOPLITZ LAKE

The bizarre rumor of a German fighter plane bound for Hitler's Alpine fortress crammed with treasure for the Fuehrer's last stand, turned into the even more bizarre revelation of a secret Nazi plot to undermine the economy of Britain with a flood of counterfeit banknotes, as investigators plumbed the bottom of Austria's Toplitz Lake, where the fighter was supposed to have crashed.

The legend of the "treasure plane" maintains that on April 17, 1945, during the last days of Germany's collapse, the twin-engined plane carrying gold, platinum and official documents to Hitler's redoubt, was shot down by pursuing Allied fighters and crashed in the Austrian lake. Karl Kaltenberger, cap-

tain of a steamer that plied the lake, rescued two of the plane's three crewmen, but they vanished into the ruins of the Third Reich, and were never traced.

The first fruits of the Austrian Government's postwar search for the plane were tragic. In 1963 the body of a young diver, wearing a weighted diving suit, was spotted by the salvage team's remote-control television camera. Raised to the surface, the youth was identified as a German, Alfred Egner, a 19-year-old Munich draftsman, who had vanished underwater on a private hunt for the Nazi gold, on the night of October 6th, 1963.

Apparently the unfortunate Egner had not been following reports in a German illustrated magazine, which three years earlier had sponsored a salvage effort in Toplitz Lake. The magazine's 1960 search brought up part of a sealed cache of what proved to be Nazi-counterfeited British paper money. Further searching by the Austrians in 1963 yielded a case of printing equipment. The mystery of the Nazi gold was replaced by an even more intriguing puzzle.

More notes and more counterfeiting gear continued to be brought up from the bottom, and by December, 1963, the pieces of the puzzle had been assembled. Twelve chests of counterfeit British pound notes, two chests containing 32 counterfeiting plates and various unboxed stamps for the insertion of dates and serial numbers, led the Austrians to a search of wartime Nazi records.

In the last years of the war the Germans, using concentration camp labor, began a project known as "Operation Bernhard." The scheme was apparently intended as some kind of economic attack on the British wartime economy. The Nazis, by introducing a flood of counterfeit notes ground out by their concentration camp "factories," intended to destroy Allied confidence in British currency.

The collapse of the Reich and the German war effort evidently overtook the odd project, but it has not been fully explained why the Nazis jettisoned the evidence in an Austrian lake. One suggestion is that they were ashamed of it. Another, more probable, is that the officers in charge of the counterfeiting project intended to put some of their product into the postwar circulation, but considered it necessary to destroy the greater part of it to avoid flooding the market.

The recoveries were turned over to the Bank of England. As for the legendary plane, no trace of it has ever been found. Since Hitler himself never reached his Alpine hideout, the odds are that the treasure plane scheme, like so many other wild ideas hatched in the desperate minds of the Nazi inner circle during their weeks of *Götterdammerung*, died a-borning.

"Tobacco Road" is a place in everyone's imaginary geography of the South. Although roadsigns for it still exist, like this one outside Augusta, Georgia, "Tobacco Road" isn't so much a place as a state of mind associated with Erskine Caldwell's down-and-out dirt-farmers of the Great Depression.

September 14, 1890

A TALE OF BURIED TREASURE

Facing Page: Lee Spence, discoverer of five wrecked Confederate blockade runners off Charleston, displays some of the china from the cabin of a sunken vessel.

Although most tales of buried pots of gold in the American south seem to be the stuff of musical comedies like *Finian's Rainbow*, or the bitter-funny fantasies of Depression-era dirt farmers like Erskine Caldwell's Jeeter Lester, there have been enough authentic finds over the years to justify the survival of the legend of lost Confederate treasure.

The great plantations of the Old South, self-sufficient as medieval baronies, and as remote from one another and the towns, kept a portion of their surplus cash in banks. But the conversion to Confederate notes which followed the secession of the southern states rendered many a paper fortune worthless as the war turned against the C. S. A. As is always the case in times of economic upheaval, the well-to-do fell back on gold and silver. Hard money and other valuables were hidden by plantation owners and smaller independent farmers, as the Union armies began to march into the south.

The dreams of latter-day treasure-hunters as usual exagerrated the amount of buried money to be found. As *Gone With the Wind* fans will remember, even the proudest of the plantation owners was reduced to beggary as the long war wore on. Surplus hard money was never in great supply in the agriculturally-based Confederacy, and most of what there was went to the war effort.

Still, individuals here and there did manage to keep aside a nest-egg, to be hidden against a better day. And there is at least one sizeable fortune, a massive British loan to the C. S. A. in gold and silver, rumored still to be lying in Virginia soil.

Another source of lost Civil War treasure is the sea. Early in the conflict the superior Union navy set up a tight blockade of southern ports. The hard-pressed Confederacy, in order to bring in vital goods, munitions and specie, had to run the gauntlet of Union naval guns with fast blockade runners operating out of Bermuda and the Bahamas, or trade through Canada. Northern shipping, which went on almost normally throughout the war, was less vulnerable to the weak southern navy. But the sea and the weather did not stop taking their toll simply because there was a war on, and off the Pacific coast a major storm disaster led to a search for sunken treasure.

During the days when the famous Confederate raider John Morgan was slashing into southern Ohio with his troop of irregular cavalry, attacking the fat farms of the Union's breadbasket, there lived in Summit County a wealthy farmer named William Huddleston. War prices made farming profitable, and Huddleston, wary of any sort of paper money in unsettled times, put his savings into gold, which was then at a high premium. He had accumulated $6,000 in gold (Note: worth well over $100,000 in 1978), when Morgan's Raiders began to pillage farms in his region.

Sensibly mistrusting banks or bonds or other ventures based on conventional commerce, Huddleston buried his treasure somewhere on his land.

The war ended, leaving the resourceful Huddleston still farming his property. Content that he had buried enough gold to fall back on in case of misfortune, he never bothered to dig up the hidden hoard. He shared the secret

Tobacco being transported from a Richmond plantation to the seaport along a real "tobacco road" in 1845.

of the gold's location only with his wife. His children scattered as soon as they grew up, and one of them, Elizabeth, wound up in Cleveland, where she managed to earn a good living.

The elder Huddlestons died, and the farm passed into other hands. A Clevelander, Charles F. Brush, acquired the property, but he immediately rented it out to a series of tenant farmers.

One of these, a man named Wilkinson, unearthed the gold while plowing his rented acres in the 1880s. He spread the news of his windfall widely, and it came to the attention of Elizabeth Huddleston, who was still living in Cleveland.

She could not remember the location of the hoard, but she clearly remembered that her father had asked her to gather a number of empty oyster cans, in which he buried the coins. She immediately took steps to recover the treasure.

Discovering that Judge Timballs of Akron had been retained by Wilkinson, to help him clear his title to his find, Elizabeth Huddleston consulted another Judge named Marvin, and asked him to investigate the Wilkinson claim and her own rights in the treasure matter.

To Miss Huddleston's chagrin, Marvin returned from his conference with Timballs and informed his client that he could tell her nothing without violating the confidence which obtains between lawyers and those who retain them. Said Judge Marvin, "All lawyers have secrets which they must keep, and Timballs could not tell me what he knew. All that I know positively is that a large amount of money was found."

The canny Wilkinson, when questioned, would say nothing about the matter except that he had found "a few bogus dollars." Defeated by the legal confraternity, which almost certainly shared in the Wilkinson windfall, Miss

The Depression sent many a broken-down Southern share-cropper into wistful dreams of hidden Confederate gold. With agricultural prices at rock-bottom and bank loans out of the question, there wasn't much the Southern small farmer could do but dream.

Huddleston made a last effort, going the rounds of the banks to try and find out if Wilkinson had made any large deposit recently. In this attempt she ran square into the protocol of the banking community, which guards its secrets as carefully as do the lawyers. The bankers smugly told her nothing. Presumably Wilkinson died rich. As for Miss Huddleston, deponent sayeth not.

Aided by old papers his father left him, Gayus Whitfield of Middleboro, Kentucky, unearthed more than $200,000 in buried gold on the Whitfield farm near Demopolis, Alabama. Directions for locating the gold were contained in papers left to his son by C. Boaz Whitfield, a member of one of the oldest and most aristocratic families of Alabama, and descendant of the pioneer general, Nathan Bryan Whitfield.

When Gayus Whitfield began his search, thirty-five men were employed to uncover an old boundary stake on the Shady Grove farm, eighteen miles from Demopolis, near Jefferson. For a week the large force worked without results, but today a large cache of gold coins was discovered. They consist of twenty-dollar gold pieces, minted in 1850 and before, which were buried by Boaz Whitfield during the Civil War.

There are eight heirs who may put in claims for the gold, all of them sons and daughters of the four Whitfield brothers, born in Civil War days, themselves sons of General Nathan Whitfield.

Other gold pieces had been found on the old Whitfield place prior to the present discovery, but the matter of instituting an active treasure-hunt was never given much attention by the Whitfield family until an ancient key left by Boaz Whitfield was found in Kentucky. Apparently he buried his gold to prevent its seizure by Union forces during the Civil War. Similar instances were recalled by older inhabitants of the region, but in no case has so large an amount been involved.

Buried gold has interfered with tobacco planting on the edge of Stewart County, Tennessee, a few miles from the Kentucky town of Hopkinsville. Two youths told the story when they came to Hopkinsville to buy an automobile with part of the treasure they had found buried.

Ernest Roberts, 20, and his brother Austin, 18, made the find. The boys were setting out tobacco on the farm of their uncle, William Thweatt, when one picked up a five dollar gold piece. When they made another row of tobacco, they found a twenty dollar coin. Thereafter the tobacco planting languished while the youths searched for treasure. Before long they had uncovered $675 (note: 1926 valuation) in gold of a coinage antedating the Civil War. They took their treasure home, where they told their mother about the finds.

Coin collectors are offering premium prices for some of the gold pieces. Several of the five dollar gold pieces, dated 1834, are worth $15 each, it is said.

The finders say the gold was scattered about with the remains of a glass jug which had been buried just under the surface and had been broken, letting

the coins fall out. It is believed that the money was buried during the war to hide it from one side or the other of the fighting forces.

No steps have been taken by anyone else to claim the money, so the boys will get their auto.

April 3, 1942
CHILDREN FIND $5,885 IN POT

Four youngsters of Florence, Alabama, have uncovered a pot containing almost six thousand dollars in gold coins. Lynn Scandlin, a taxi-driver, reported the discovery made by his two sons and two other children. The gold, probably hidden by local planters during the Civil War under the threat of Sherman's southern campaign, became the object of a dispute between representatives of the children, and a person who claimed he owned the property where the find was made.

October 31, 1947
BRITISH LOAN TO CONFEDERACY THOUGHT BURIED IN VIRGINIA

A tale of buried treasure valued at between $10 million and $11 million in gold and silver bullion, and belonging to the Confederate States of America, came out of the office of the Governor of Virginia.

Governor William M. Tuck said that he had received a letter from F. L. Weathers of Greenville, South Carolina, telling of his grandfather's part as a Confederate soldier in helping to put the bullion, a loan to the C. S. A. from the British Government, in a "strong iron box," and burying it.

"I know the exact location in Virginia where the money is buried," Mr. Weathers wrote. "Some time ago I talked with a resident of that area, who said that the place I have mentioned has remained undisturbed since the close of the Civil War."

The bullion, Mr. Weathers stated, came from England at the end of the Civil War, but arrived too late to avert the fall of the Confederacy. "There is no known record of its having been spent," he added.

Governor Tuck, faced with budget requests for more than $500,000 in state funds, told reporters he would be glad to help anyone who "thinks he can dig up another $11 million anywhere in Virginia." He invited Mr. Weathers to come to Richmond to discuss the treasure, but the record shows no evidence of a subsequent hunt for the British gold.

August, 1890-
November, 1934
TWO SEA STORIES

In 1865 a small boat carrying sixteen persons landed on the beach at Crescent City, California. They stated that they were the only survivors of the United States steamer *Brother Jonathan*, which had been wrecked in a storm, breaking up on rocks ten or twelve miles south of the town.

The boat held Third Mate Patterson, 2 passengers (a woman and her son), and 13 deck hands. A lifeboat was manned and sent to the scene of the wreck, but the *Brother Jonathan* had already disappeared beneath the water.

She had been bound from San Francisco to Victoria, British Columbia, with a cargo including $850,000 in gold (note: 1890 valuation), when she went down on July 20th, 1865. Over 200 passengers and sailors were lost.

The rescue boat herself was caught in a squall off Point St. George, and foundered on the rocks. No further attempt at salvage was made until 1890,

Occasionally the outclassed Confederate Navy overturned the odds. Here a Confederate warship burns a Union merchantman intercepted en route to the northern ports.

when a Crescent City sailmaker named Wood tried to locate the hulk by making soundings in the waters where she was thought to have gone down. A local "old salt," one Captain Gee, outfitted a schooner and hired divers. But his efforts, like Wood's, were in vain.

In 1927 Frank L. Moorman, described as a "Pacific coast capitalist," picked up half the costs of a joint salvage venture of private industry and the United States Government. The Government, which provided Navy divers and equipment, was interested in Civil War pay records carried in the *Brother Jonathan's* strongroom, which could aid in clearing up many pension cases brought before Congress in the years since the end of the war. Moorman, of course, was interested in the gold. Submarine salvage equipment was to be used, but the venture broke down in squabbles between Moorman's private investors and the Government, over title to the treasure.

The *Brother Jonathan* floundered in a terrific gale, and her heavy cargo carried her to the bottom before too great a break-up could ensue. Over the years since the disaster, the strong-box may have settled into the sea bottom, but it is probably still lying close to its original position a few miles south of the northern California town, off what is now part of Redwoods National Park.

In 1934 a report appeared from the Bahamas which calls up memories of the derring-do of bold Confederate blockade runners and their Union Navy foes. During the Civil War the Confederacy, with the support of their nominal allies the British, outfitted a great number of low, stripped-down steam yachts to run the Union blockade of southern ports. Operating from safe har-

bors in the British Bahamas and Bermuda, these fast, rakish craft, built low to the waterline to minimize their silhouettes against the horizon, succeeded in outstripping slower Union men-of-war and bringing in vital cargo to the beleaguered C. S. A.

Not all of them escaped, of course. The expedition in 1934, outfitted by the Bahamian Government, was out for an iron chest full of gold bullion, once the property of the Union government, which was thrown overboard by the crew of a Confederate blockade runner hotly pursued by Federal navy ships.

The venture involved diving equipment carried on the two-masted

schooner *Mayflower*, a Bahamian vessel. Native supporters of the scheme included a woman, Kataline Sweeting, who lost a relative when the Confederate craft was later shot to pieces by pursuing Federals.

There is no record as to whether this particular hunt for Civil War gold was successful. But the waters between the Bahamas and the U. S. Coast, as well as the more northerly passage between Bermuda and the mainland, are littered with the bones of unsuccessful blockade runners. Rumor has it that millions in British gold, intended as loans to the C. S. A., may lie on the continental shelf beneath these waters.

The famous *Lutine* Bell, which signals the recovery or loss of missing ships to waiting underwriters, hangs atop the Rostrum at Lloyd's of London.

Facing Page: An American design, in 1909, of a device to be used in the projected salvage of the *Lutine's* gold.

Lloyd's of London was already 29 years old when the wreck of the British man-of-war *Lutine* occurred in 1799. The insurance group had been doing well, but its association with the *Lutine* disaster, according to the principle that it's an ill wind that blows no one good, was to secure Lloyd's the position of premier maritime underwriting firm which it holds to this day.

There was never anyone named Lloyd involved in the company. In the middle of the eighteenth century, shippers and underwriters used to meet informally to read the broadsheets describing marine casualties, sailings and arrivals which a Welsh coffee–house owner named Lloyd used to print for his clients.

The group at Lloyd's coffee–house gradually joined forces on a more formal basis. War has always boomed maritime insurance: first the American Revolution and then the Napoleonic Wars boosted the enterprises of the Lloyd's group to major proportions.

But the loss of the *Lutine*, and the gigantic payment Lloyd's underwriters made on it, provided the capstone to the company's reputation worldwide. John Julius Angerstein, called "the father of Lloyd's," led the group of underwriters in paying the British government the total loss on the ship, some $4.5 million. Angerstein was one of Britain's earliest serious art collectors, and he left his collection to the nation when he died. It formed the foundation of what later became the British National Gallery.

The massive insurance payment on the *Lutine* was due to the fact that she was carrying no ordinary cargo when she went down. Estimates of the gold and silver bullion aboard the vessel have ranged between $5 million and $10 million over the years. Lloyd's itself, in 1938, set a value of £1 million on the *Lutine* treasure, a sum which would convert close to the higher amount mentioned above.

Having sustained the loss, Lloyd's then had to stand by helplessly while the Dutch, who claimed the wreck in their waters according to maritime law, initiated a series of salvage attempts beginning the year after the disaster. Some treasure was recovered in the early years, but the Dutch eventually abandoned their efforts, and returned title to the wreck to England's King George IV. The King handed the wreck over to Lloyd's, and finally, in 1857, the insurance firm was free to try recouping some of its multi-million-dollar pay-out by bringing up the vessel's treasure.

Gold coins and bars were salvaged in the 1857 work, but the object which has become part of the Lloyd's legend was the *Lutine's* bell. Salvaged in that year, it was placed in the firm's Committee Room, together with a table and chair made from the vessel's rudder. The bell, a symbol of the company and the wreck which brought it into prominence, was used to signal news of missing ships to waiting investors and underwriters. Two strokes signified that a long overdue vessel had turned up. But three meant that hope had gone for its return. So accurate were the announcements of the *Lutine* bell over the years that its three strokes were automatically taken by marine and legal circles as meaning that underwriters must settle. Money owing to crews was paid over to the heirs and wills were probated when the *Lutine* bell tolled thrice.

*Various dates,
1911-1938*

THE WRECK OF THE LUTINE

H. M. S. *Lutine*, outward bound for Amsterdam with a cargo of bullion for British troops and German bankers, went down off the Zuider Zee in a 1799 storm.

The *Lutine*, a 900-ton man-of-war originally built by the French, was captured by the British admiral Lord Hood, in naval combat at Toulon in 1793. Reconditioned and fitted with more cannon to bring her up to ship-of-the-line status, the *Lutine* had a brilliant combat career in the French wars under Nelson and Hotham.

In 1799, with Napoleon's armies running roughshod over most of Europe, two urgent messages reached London. The first was from the commander of British Armies operating against the French in northern Holland: supplies and troop morale were low, and an immediate shipment of money was requested. The second message came from Hamburg, where German bankers and their British backers feared a collapse of confidence in the sterling standard, which would bring about economic disaster to add to the war-related troubles of England's German ally. A heavy shipment of gold and silver bullion was put together in England to shore up the faltering network of Hamburg banks.

With naval warfare raging in the Channel and the North Sea, the British could not entrust their golden cargo to a merchantman. Instead, the doughty *Lutine* was selected, as she was considered more than a match for any French warships she might encounter en route to the Netherlands.

Under the command of Captain Lancelot Skynner, the *Lutine*, with a crew of 300, sailed from Yarmouth Roads for Amsterdam at midnight on October 8th, 1799. Her treasure, estimated at about $10 million, consisted of £140,000 in gold and silver coins for the British Armies in Holland, the rest being made up of ingots of the precious metals for the Hamburg banks.

By four o'clock on the afternoon of October 9th, the warship had reached the West Frisian Islands, the chain which guards the entrance to the Netherlands' Wadden Zee and Zuider Zee. A violent storm blew up, and the *Lutine's* crew shortened sail and tried to ride it out. The winds increased, and the ship was unable to find sea-room, being trapped by angry seas too close to the rocks of Vlieland and Terschelling Islands. Finally, at ten p.m., the vessel's sails were blown away. Helpless, she wallowed onto the rocks between the two islands and foundered. All but one of her 300 men were drowned, and the survivor reached land only to die of his injuries the following day.

The Dutch Government claimed salvage rights to the wreck, and by 1800 it was engaged in the first salvage attempt. Many were to follow, but although some treasure was recovered over the 180 years since the disaster, by far the greater portion of the *Lutine's* fabulous cargo still litters the bottom of the sea, off the Westergruende of Terschelling Island.

*October 8, 1911-
September 22, 1912*

BRITISH SALVAGE FIRM DIVES ON LUTINE

170

In 1911 the National Salvage Association sent a powerful salvage steamer to the waters off Terschelling Island, to remove the thirty-six feet of sand which then covered the vessel, which had gone down in fifty feet of water in 1799. The company's sand-removal efforts were initially successful, and the hulk was reached by divers, who were able to walk along her lower hold forward and amidships.

But a more formidable obstacle was encountered. Over 150 tons of ballast,

consisting of iron bars and cannonballs, had fallen into the treasure hold from the munitions room when the ship broke up. This layer of iron, five to six feet deep, buried the treasure of gold coins and ingots, and its removal proceeded slowly. Dynamite was used to remove two tiers of cannon balls, and some coins were recovered. Even more promising was the recovery of a piece of rusty iron with a cavity in it showing an impression exactly the size of a gold bar.

The storms of October cancelled the 1911 effort, and the company returned the following year. Again the bullion was reached by divers, but the work of removing the barrier of cannonballs and ballast proceeded too slowly. When heavy weather once again closed off the work, the company had not succeeded in raising a single ingot.

In 1929 the Consolidated Drosin, Texel and Doaksen Company, a Dutch salvage firm operating out of Terschelling, took over the rights to the sunken *Lutine*'s cargo, under the terms of an agreement with Lloyd's of London, which has owned the wreck since the Dutch gave it back to the British Crown in the early nineteenth century. The Dutch group began serious salvage work on the *Lutine* hulk in 1933. Their effort was the seventh try at the vessel's cargo of treasure, since the attempt of 1800, also Dutch, which netted $330,000 in coins and ingots.

In 1821, with title to the wreck back in British hands, a second attempt was made, but drifting sand defeated the divers. Lloyd's of London financed the third try, in 1857: along with the famous *Lutine* bell, the salvors brought up 46 gold bars and 64 bars of silver, worth approximately $225,000 at the time. A French attempt in 1867 yielded nothing of value. The Germans had a go in 1886, and gathered $11,000 in coins and bars. Finally, in 1911-1912, Britain's National Salvage Association spent two frustrating seasons over the wreck, actually reaching the gold with divers, before being turned back by heavy weather (see above).

The 1933 treasure hunt was distinguished by the use of a gigantic suction device, invented by a German, E. Becker, who saw service with the Kaiser's submarine fleet during the First World War. The apparatus, carried out to the wreck site on its own barge, consisted of a 51-foot metal shaft with a diameter of 12 feet, connected to a huge cone whose mouth flared to a width of 120 feet. Powered by a 320-horsepower Junkers aircraft engine, the shaft and cone were lowered onto the wreck to suck up the layers of sand which had buried it many feet deep over the years. A new type of diving bell was also used in the salvage work. But the shaft and cone proved hard to manage in the rough seas off Terschelling Island, and despite the high hopes of Lloyd's and its Dutch contractors, the salvage attempt yielded little.

During the summer of 1938 Lloyd's once again contracted with a Dutch firm to go after the *Lutine* gold. This time a huge Dutch dredge, the *Karimata*, was used, and by the end of July a number of coins of Spanish mintage, known to have been among the contents of the *Lutine*'s strongroom, were

August 6-
November 9, 1933
LUTINE GOLD LURES THE SALVAGER ANEW

A Dutch attempt to raise the *Lutine* treasure in 1934 involved the use of a specially-designed diving bell, but the search was in vain.

May 15-August 15,
1938
THE KARIMATA

raised. The *Karimata* had little difficulty digging through the layers of sand which covered the hulk, and when iron ballast bars and cannonballs began to turn up in the scoop, the salvors knew they were close to the treasure. On the 29th of July a gold bar weighing seven pounds was raised.

The find was greeted by frenzied cheering from the villagers of Terschelling Island, where the salvors had made their headquarters. The ingot was brought ashore and taken in a procession to the burgomeister's house under the direction of a Lloyd's representative.

Lloyd's itself, which claimed 30 per cent of all salvage under the terms of the 1938 arrangement, signaled the news of the find in the time-honored manner, by ringing two strokes of the *Lutine's* bell in their London offices. Members crowding the floor of the underwriting room fell silent while a caller solemnly announced that a bar of gold had been recovered from the long-lost frigate.

After the initial excitement over the ingot, valued at $4,200, had died down, the crew of the *Karimata* went back to work. Three cannon were raised in August, but no more gold. As the end of the summer approached tension heightened aboard the dredge. The *Kárimata* was built in the East Indies, for work in the relatively calm waters of the Karimata Strait. She was by no means equipped to cope with the vicious autumn storms of the North Sea, and in any case was pre-contracted to return to her native waters by the first of September.

Two sand-sucking tugs were assigned to speed up the clearance effort and give the *Karimata's* scoops room to work. But alarming news reached the Lloyd's representative. Close study of objects salvaged from the wreck, com-

The fragile superstructure of the dredge *Karimata*, designed for the calm waters of the Dutch East Indies, resembled something made from a giant Erector Set. It proved no match for the vicious seas off Terschelling Island.

pared with the 1857 map of its location, which had been the expedition's principal guide, resulted in the conclusion that the map was inaccurate. The cannon and the gold bar, decided the dredgers, had been recovered from a fragment of the wreck, which had broken apart over the centuries. The main part of the *Lutine*, including the stern section which housed the treasure-room, was located elsewhere.

The *Karimata* and her tugs scouted a few other spots off Terschelling Island, but failed to find the vessel's stern compartment. Finally the weather and the *Karimata*'s committments in the East Indies called a halt to the work. World War II swallowed up the Netherlands subsequently, and sunken treasure was the last thing on anyone's mind. According to the record, there were no more salvage attempts made on the sunken *Lutine*.

The frigate and her treasure are among the best-documented in history. Her approximate location is known, and although her parts are scattered over the bottom, salvors in the past have come tantalizingly close to her main treasure–room. Efforts over the years have netted some $570,000 in gold and silver coins and bullion. If the rough estimate of the treasure's total value, $10 million, is correct, there is still $9,430,000 in precious metal waiting off Terschelling Island for the next set of hardy salvors. Lloyd's of London, which is still nearly four million dollars short of recouping its 1799 pay- out on the lost ship, will no doubt welcome any sensible scheme.

On the night of May 21, 1922, the Peninsular & Orient liner *Egypt* was groping through the fog off the coast of Brittany. She was bound for England with passengers and a cargo of gold and silver bullion amounting to more than $5 million, sent by Egyptian bankers to the Bank of England, when the fog closed in, cutting visibility to nil. Suddenly out of the dense gray roil the outline of a French tramp steamer, the *Seine,* loomed fatally close. Unable to turn in time, the *Seine* ploughed into the helpless *Egypt.* The British vessel immediately began to settle, going down so quickly that only a few of her lifeboats could be launched.

Sixteen passengers and eighty-six crew members lost their lives. Among the passengers was a Roman Catholic nun, Sister Rhoda (in private life Miss E. R. McNellie), who was returning from missionary work in Egypt. Adding a note of quiet heroism to the night of catastrophe, when she was offered a place in one of the lifeboats, she said "Give it to another." As the survivors pulled away from the stricken liner, they could see Sister Rhoda kneeling on deck, peacefully praying. Then the ship swirled under, bearing her victims and her cargo of treasure to the bottom.

The area where the Egypt sank, 25 miles southwest of the island of Ushant and 30 miles off Point du Raz on the Breton coast, is a nasty patch of sea. Strong tides and currents prevail, and the weather is unrelentingly mean. Only in the short summer season do the seas and winds calm sufficiently to permit salvage vessels to operate, and even the summer months are plagued with fogs. To add to the would-be salvor's problems, the *Egypt* went down in 400 feet of water, a depth never before reached by divers in conventional diving suits.

Nevertheless, salvage work began immediately, and by 1923 experts felt they had at least pin-pointed the position of the wreck. But the *Egypt* was not to give up her treasure without a long struggle. Numerous salvage attempts failed, until an Italian firm began work in 1930. For five years the Italians toiled over the sunken hulk, losing fifteen men and one salvage vessel in the process, until they finally achieved a stunning success.

The salvage of the *Egypt,* though outstripped in terms of cargo value by efforts during and after World War II (NOTE: SEE *WORLD WAR II: NAZI LOOT AND JAPANESE SPOILS*), remains one of the most startling feats in the history of treasure-hunting. It was hardly the work of amateurs. Heavily capitalized, the Italians settled in for a long job, bringing to bear on the formidable problems presented by the *Egypt's* location a battery of equipment, including devices never before used in salvage work. The gruelling, dangerous work of the divers, and the Italian professionals' calculated readiness to take chances based on their solid engineering skills, combined with an endless store of patience and optimism to haul the *Egypt's* treasure from the deep. There is romance in the story, but it is shown in the everyday heroism and cheerfulness of the young divers, and in the passionate enthusiasm of the salvage captain, who turned the long years of work into a personal battle between himself and the sunken gold.

Facing Page:
Italian diver Fortunato Sodini peers cockily from the turret-hatch of the observation shell during a pause in the *Artiglio II's* salvage operations on the sunken *Egypt* in 1931.

Underwriters in England, who had had to bear the cost of the loss of the *Egypt* and her treasure, were understandably eager to salvage the wreck as soon as possible. The first order of business, of course, was to locate the sunken ship, and in 1923 a Swedish captain, by the name of Hedbach, announced that he had found her 400 feet down, off the French lighthouse at Armen, Brittany, in a spot where currents are particularly violent and work is possible only in calm weather.

The first serious salvage operation was mounted by a group of German divers, who had perfected their trade and their new-design diving suits working over the wartime wrecks of Scapa Flow, scene of a famous naval battle during World War I. One of the crucial questions the German divers hoped to answer was how the vessel lay on the bottom. If, as is often the case with a ship sinking quickly, she had turned turtle and was lying upside down, the work would be immeasurably more difficult, since to reach the bullion room the divers would have to cut through the hull and many layers of decking.

But before the question could be answered, the vessel had to be found, and it turned out the Swedish captain's information was inaccurate. A French salvage ship, the *Iroise*, which was working with the German diving team, sent down grapples at the spot indicated by Hedbach. There was initial excitement when a mass of cables was brought up in the claws of the great hooks. But to the chagrin of the *Iroise* crew, the cables turned out to be part of the Brest-Dakar submarine telegraph line. Salvage work was broken off in the fall of 1926.

The Italian firm obtained permission from the *Egypt's* under- writers to begin salvage work in the late spring of 1930. After six months of unrelenting work, in which divers spent up to eight hours a day in the water, the team announced, on September 1st, that they had definitely found the sunken ship. A reporter from *The New York Times*, David Scott, was dispatched to the Italian salvage vessel *Artiglio*, and provided daily coverage of the story for the rest of the season.

"Lying on gray sand 400 feet beneath the surface of the Atlantic the wreck of the P. & O. liner *Egypt* with $5 million of gold and silver in her hull was identified today (1 September) by Italian divers.

"A waving jungle of seaweed blurred the outline of the sunken treasure ship, and a cloak of brown vegetation covered the hull; the external fittings were gone and a tangle of splintered wood and broken cables covered the decks. After months of search, however, there could be no doubt that the wreck on the ocean floor was the liner . . .

"'The sunken vessel is lying upright on her keel among scattered rocks at Lat. 48 degrees 7 minutes N., Long. 5 degrees 30 minutes W., about twenty-five miles southwest of the island of Ushant, one mile from the point fixed bycoe Swedish captain Hedbach, who searched for it in 1923.

"It is almost impossible to see on the bottom, perhaps because the strong tides of the last few days have troubled the waters. At first the divers could not tell whether they were seeing the fore or after part of the ship. In the end

it was seven hydraulic cranes of a type which the *Egypt* was known to carry, which gave up the ocean's secret.

"It was a week ago that the wreck was first located, but not until today were the divers certain it was the *Egypt*. The first descent was made by Alberto Bargellini, youngest of the *Artiglio's* divers, after a night of thick fog with the fog horns moaning incessantly on a gray-green ocean.

"When the salvage ship arrived at the buoys (note: buoys attached to the grappling-hooks which first struck the submerged vessel provided the salvors with the exact location of the hulk) the tide was slack and there was no time to lose. In less than half an hour the ship was moored and Signor Bargellini plunged 400 feet to the ocean floor in his steel shell.

"On deck his mates crowded around the telephone and watched anxiously as Alberto Gianni, chief diver, put on the headphones to talk to him.

"' How far can you see?' asked Signor Gianni.

"' About two yards,' was the answer from the ocean floor.

"'Can you see anything?'

"'No, not yet.'

"At that moment Signor Bargellini could see nothing but a dim green light all around him. Five minutes before it had been blackness, but now his eyes were getting used to the underwater light.

"'Lower a little,' said Signor Gianni to the winchman on deck. 'Let him touch the bottom.'

"'Touched bottom!' exclaimed the diver far below.

"'Can you see the bottom?' asked Signor Gianni.

"'No,' replied Bargellini, explaining that he could not see downwards as far as his own feet.

"He was hoisted a little and the *Artiglio* moved to port. A yell came from the telephone.

"'What can you see?' asked Signor Gianni.

"'I can see the end of a ship's hull,' the diver replied. ' I can see the taffrail.'

"'How many rails has it?'

"'Three: it's a big ship!'

"On deck there was pandemonium. So this was no rusty green tramp or Spanish orange boat. This was the treasure ship which had been sought for eight years, and which experts claimed was carrying a cargo of gold and silver worth $5 million . . . "

by Arthur Warner

The *Egypt* sank in 400 feet of water, about twice as far down as a man can work under compressed air in an ordinary diving suit. The important new device adopted for work on the *Egypt* is a kind of robot, a mechanical shell with jointed arms and legs, in which the diver is lowered. The shell is made of steel, with massive glass windows, and has sufficient resistance to withstand the pressure of the water about it without compressed air. The diver breathes air at normal pressure from oxygen reservoirs, and so can stay down as long as

August 9, 1931, The New York Times Magazine

ROBOT DIVING SUITS USED BY ARTIGLIO DIVERS

(top): The articulated "robot" suit, one of two types used by the divers of the *Artiglio*, is shown here with its accessories, emergency air tanks and tools. It was lowered from the surface on a thick cable which contained its main air supply, pumped down by compressors aboard the ship. Though the rigid structure of the suit, built to withstand pressure at the *Egypt*'s 400-foot depth, constricted movement, the diver was able to walk in a limited way and handle objects underwater with his mechanically-operated manipulator-hands.

(bottom): The grippers of the diving suit used on the *Egypt* salvage effort were simple tongs manipulated by the diver's hands operating mechanical controls inside the round metal cuffs. The Italians' manipulator principle served as the foundation for the "hands" of modern submersibles, which are capable of intricate movement surpassing the abilities of the hands of a diver at extreme depths. Modern submersibles' "hands" are true robots, operating by electronic remote control keyed by divers within the craft or technicians in the surface tender ships.

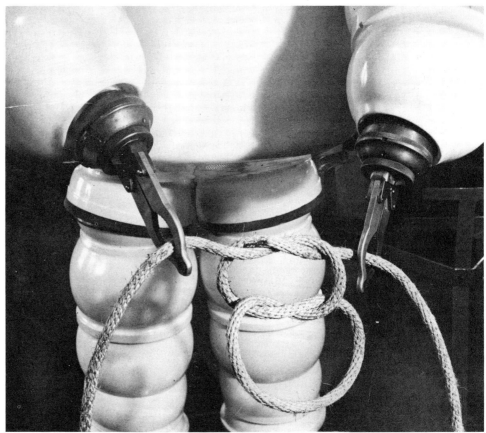

178

Diver Lowered on One Cable Directs by Telephone Surface Crew Operating Hooks, "Grabs" or Explosive Charges on Second Cable

Hurricane Deck

Boat Deck

Upper Deck

Diver in Shell Bossing Operations

Main Deck

Mail Room

Bullion Room

Hold

A diagram of the salvage plan of operations used on the *Egypt*. The divers had to blast through four of the sunken liner's decks to reach the bullion room and the *Egypt's* treasure, positioning their "scissors grab" (shown here) or their explosive charges according to directions telephoned above by a diver in the limbless observation shell (below the grab). The observation shell, whose suspension cable contained the telephone wire as well as the diver's air supply, was the second type of rigid-structured diving suit used during the operation.

the supply lasts and come up immediately when he wishes to without suffering a case of "the bends."

The mechanical shell has telephone connection with the salvage ship above it, and in the lower part of the robot are tanks into which the diver lets water by means of a valve when he wants to go down, and from which he expels the water by compressed air when he wishes to rise. But undoubtedly the unique part of the robot, that upon which its ultimate success or failure rests, is a set of moveable arms. These end in a kind of pincers, like a giant lobster's claws, and are equipped with hammers and other mechanical facilities operated from within through water-tight connections, as one would move the hand-puppets in a Punch and Judy show.

September 2, 1930
DAVID SCOTT'S NARRATIVE

"Three explosive charges were fired today, detaching one of the hydraulic cranes on the sunken liner. They were the first charges ever fired at such a depth during salvage operations, and soon after a great crane weighing several tons was brought to the surface. It was a remarkable feat which promises well for the recovery of the *Egypt's* sunken treasure, demonstrating that it will be possible to clear away the top hamper amidships, the first step in penetrating to the gold-laden strong-room below.

"Today the divers worked like slaves for ten hours. From now on all their efforts will be directed toward the bullion room in front of the hulk's forward funnel. Above it are the boat decks, hurricane deck, spar deck and main deck, counting downward.

"All these decks are of steel, varying in thickness from a quarter to three-quarters of an inch. The grabs of the shovels must come at the treasure vertically from above. If the ship were lying on her side only the hull and one partition would have to be pierced. As she is upright four decks must be cut through, but this is really preferable, because the work is easier to follow on the ship's plan.

"The floor and the walls and ceiling of the treasure room are thicker than the surrounding structure. Around it again are four mail rooms for Egyptian, Indian, Australian and Chinese mails, which may contain unexpected prizes.

"It is unlikely that the divers will reach the gold before autumn storms close down the salvage season. They then will face the problem of marking the *Egypt* through the winter. The solution will probably be one large service buoy and a quadrilateral of smaller buoys suspended ninety feet below the surface, safe from storms. Already divers have had much occasion to reflect on the perverse and impish nature of marine buoys. A buoy in the hold is just a tiresome half ton of iron painted red, which bangs about when you hoist it and will smash your hand or shinbone if you let it. Drop it into the sea and it becomes a living, illusive thing which bobs sarcastically at you while you are in sight, spinning and tugging and working itself free of its five-ton anchor as soon as you turn your back."

FIND CAUSES BIG STIR IN LONDON

The discovery of the treasure-laden wreck of the *Egypt* has created a first-class sensation among London marine underwriters. The position of the wreck agrees with that officially recorded by Lloyd's. The *Egypt* sank in 1922 and the precious metal she carried consisted of $4,195,000 in gold and $1,075,000 in silver, a total of $5,270,000. Since then, however, the price of silver has depreciated heavily, but the value of gold has held up. If the salvaging efforts are successful there ought to be a good reward for the Italian divers, and a pleasant return for the marine underwriters who paid the claims after the liner sank. There have been numerous cases of successful salvage of reasure-carrying liners in recent times, of which perhaps the richest was the steamer *Alonso XII*, wrecked off the Canary Islands in 1885, which yielded about $450,000 in gold. But it is recognized everywhere that if the *Egypt's* hoard is recovered it will be the greatest achievement of its kind.

DAVID SCOTT'S NARRATIVE, CONTINUED:

"Having triumphantly hauled up the hydraulic crane, the divers turned their attention to more valuable booty. Access to the bullion room is not yet possible, but the Captain's cabin is in an accessible position on the boat deck. It contains a safe, possibly bearing money and valuable papers, and the divers made this safe the immediate object of their quest.

"To reach it they had to get into the cabin, and the only way in was through the roof of the deck house, which is not very robust, especially after eight years under water. The *Artiglio* removed it by the simple, but hazardous, process of tearing it off with a grapnel.

"A three-pronged hook, painted white to make it visible, was lowered and directed by divers under the edge of the cabin roof. The *Artiglio* took the strain on her derrick, heeled twenty-five degrees, and suddenly rolled back heavily as the structure pulled loose.

"The audacious young diver Bargellini went down with the grapnel, trying to hook it onto the safe, which he found fixed to the wall of the uncovered

captain's cabin . . . . In the process, the Atlantic saw fit to remind the impudent explorer that it is not to be played with.

"The diver's turret-shaped observation shell has in its hollow base a plate anchor fastened to a light cable on a drum. With this the diver can anchor himself to the bottom, float up to the end of the cable, and work undisturbed by the rise and fall of swells, currents and tides. If he lets go of the anchor altogether, he will float to the surface—his only hope if the main cable breaks.

"Bargellini's anchor came adrift from its cable and dropped clear. The diving shell began to rise at once. The diver saw a loop of the cable fall past his window, and thought the ship had let down too much. He shouted up to haul it taut. The winch heaved, but the cable came up twisted, since Bargellini was already rising.

"Gianni, on deck, snatched the telephone. Recognizing that panic was the greatest enemy to the diver in trouble, he attempted to soothe Bargellini with a rather labored joke.

"'Oh, Bargellini,' Gianni laughed into the trumpet, 'your cable is broken, but no matter! Let your anchor go and come up yourself. You are quite safe.'

"Bargellini knew very well he was anything but safe. He tugged at the anchor gear, but the anchor had already gone, and the unweighted cable was fouled in the wreck. He gave himself up for lost, and called desperately over the telephone while the men above waited helplessly for his shell to free itself somehow and bob up. Finally the diver managed to slip his cable free. The world of water turned from green to gold, and he knew at last he was rising.

"He glanced at the depth gauge and remarked calmly through the telephone, 'A lot of fuss about nothing.' He broke the surface thirty yards ahead of the *Artiglio* and was hauled in gingerly with the tangled cable. He emerged from the shell laughing rather shakily, looking quite pale beneath his tan."

The Italian crew, continuing to dive through the open roof of the captain's cabin, succeeded in bringing up a quantity of silverware from dining rooms and closets nearby. Working nearer and nearer to the captain's safe, they also succeeded in raising sixteen bags of mail.

Using dynamite to blast through the steel decking of the sunken liner, the Italians then lowered electromagnets to bring up the debris, clearing a passage large enough to permit divers to descend within the wreck. They hope to reach the treasure room by the end of the week, but tonight the barometer began falling. A westerly breeze was freshening and beginning to whip the sea into nasty waves.

"Today divers succeeded in raising the captain's safe from the wreck. Five million dollars' worth of gold and silver in the hull is still untouched, but each day the divers are coming closer.

"After a day in the harbor at Brest, spent repairing the observation shell and coaling, the *Artiglio* returned to the wreck site yesterday morning. Again young Bargellini was called upon to descend, bearing a specialized grapnel

Septemeber 4, 1930
SILVERWARE AND MAIL SALVAGED FROM LINER

September 6, 1930
DAVID SCOTT'S NARRATIVE, CONTINUED:

181

A high point in the salvage of the *Egypt* occurred on September 6th, 1930, when the divers succeeded in bringing up the captain's safe from the sunken liner's mailroom.

September 8, 1930

DAVID SCOTT'S NARRATIVE, CONTINUED:

Facing Page: The divers of the *Artiglio* and their leader, Alberto Gianni, pose proudly with the recovered safe. It proved to contain foreign mail bags and the key to the bullion room.

with flat jaws which open wide but are not more than two or three inches thick, so that they work well in a confined space.

"After several attempts Bargellini gave word that the safe was held by the grapnel. Inch by inch the safe, held precariously in the jaws of the device, was pulled up until it cleared the surface. It was seen that the jaws were not closed around the bulk of the safe at all, but bit into its surface not far from the edge. Fearing that the precious safe would slip and fall back into the sea, the crew pushed the *Artiglio's* motorboat under the safe to catch it if it fell. The safe would probably have crashed through the bottom of the little boat, but the iron did not loose its grip, and the safe was deposited on the *Artiglio's* deck with sea water pouring from inside it. It is a little rusty and has on it patches of sea anemones. The back and sides, thinner than the door, have been forced inward by water pressure, and present concave surfaces.

"Five charges of explosives, meanwhile, were lowered on a spar to the boat deck. They fired simultaneously, and a few minutes later two boats from the mother ship raced to pick up fish killed by the explosion, among them a twenty-pound eel."

"The captain's safe was opened today, while the *Artiglio* was waiting out a storm in port. It contained a key to the bullion room, a separate, unmarked bunch of keys, and a diplomatic mail bag containing British Foreign Office correspondence. There was nothing else. The ship's money and the valuables belonging to passengers are presumably in the purser's safe in another part of the wreck.

"The safe was opened publicly on the *Artiglio's* cargo hatch while a crowd of 200 to 300 looked on. An oxyacetylene blowtorch was played on its bolts and hinges, and in a short time the door of the safe was pried open with a crowbar.

"A musty odor of rotting canvas and wet iron rose from the dark interior. Someone seized the neck of a mailbag to pull it out, and the bag fell to pieces. The papers, sodden and stuck together, were carefully lifted out and placed in a wooden box. From their muddy black, white and brown a patch of vivid color stood out from time to time: the vermilion seal of the British Foreign Office.

"The papers were of interest chiefly for their dates, all headed April or May, 1922, which corresponded with the sinking of the *Egypt* and gave underwriters legal grounds upon which to base their identification of the wreck.

"The storm which drove the *Artiglio* off the work yesterday is an example of the hazards facing the salvors in this inhospitable patch of the Atlantic. The fine weather of last week changed with striking suddenness. At one moment the men were working in hot sunshine on deck: at the next the sky was darkened as if a giant's hand had thrown a veil over the sea.

"A gray curtain of rain swept the horizon, and out of it came a deep, vibrating note of warning. Then the easterly breeze stopped and a squall from the west sent foaming waves crashing against the *Artiglio's* sides. In an hour an angry sea was running full, and it was clear the *Artiglio* could not stay at her moorings.

"The engine of the motor launch chose this moment to break down. In a small open boat a crew of three rowed out to cast loose from the buoys, going to each in turn and untying the lashings which bound them to the 200-foot cables.

"They went first to the stern buoy and reached it in quick time, running with a strong tide. But the return trip involved a battle with the sea. Sometimes their boat was lost in a trough. Then it leaped upward, standing almost on its stern, and hung for a moment before plunging again. Soaked to the skin, the three sailors panted at the oars, fighting vainly against the current. At last a lifebuoy with a line attached was thrown overboard. It floated down to them, and their boat was hauled in.

"The chief objective was to save the expensive manila hawsers which still bound the *Artiglio* to several buoys. The intrepid young diver Bargellini again proved his worth, spelling the exhausted sailors in the rowboat, and leading the struggle from buoy to buoy, until finally the *Artiglio* was free to haul in her cables and make for port."

September 10, 1930
DAVID SCOTT'S NARRATIVE, CONCLUDED

"While the *Artiglio* lay inactive at sea all day in the rain, Alberto Gianni and his divers devised a scheme for raising the *Egypt's* treasure which should rank as one of the most remarkable operations ever performed in the history of marine salvage, if it succeeds.

"The divers intend, if possible, to cut into the *Egypt's* hull as a surgeon cuts into a patient's body, to remove the entire bullion room and bring it to the surface without opening it, and carry it bodily to land.

"The reasons for attempting this are two. In the first place there is the question of time. A whole season of work will be needed to lay the bullion room bare. If the room were opened in place and its contents scooped out bit by bit, the work would run into a third year.

"The second reason is that piecemeal salvage would involve inevitable and perhaps heavy loss. Scoops and grappling irons cannot go into the corners and crannies of a rectangular chamber to pick up every scrap of its contents. They can only get a hold on the more exposed material, and must leave behind as much as thirty percent. But if the whole bullion room can be raised, whatever is inside will be saved.

"The method proposed is as follows: first, the whole of the ship's structure above the room must be cleared away some distance fore and aft. This would have to be done in any case, as it would be far too dangerous to drop a diver into the narrow hold with overhanging edges to trap him or cut his cable.

"When the clearance has been finished, the chamber, 24 feet long, 6 feet wide and 9 feet high, will be left isolated, perched on a bulkhead which runs along its length below, and supported laterally by the deck on which it stands. Next, decking will be blown away to expose the ends of the bullion room, and two slings or stirrups of heavy steel crossbars will be lowered and slipped over the exposed ends. A cylindrical caisson, through which supporting chains will pass, will next be lowered to within a few feet of the bullion room, where it will automatically be locked by a ratchet gear on the chains. Enough air will be pumped into the caissons to take the weight of the bullion

room, and the remaining deck bulkhead will then be cut away. Finally the caisson and bullion room together will be gradually raised to the surface, to be further secured and towed to land.

"The divers estimate they will need 300 working hours to clear away the bullion room, which is roughly equivalent to three months under favorable conditions. Therefore the audacious operation is scheduled for next season. For the present the divers will content themselves with removing the *Egypt's* boat deck and making preparations for next year."

The *Artiglio* was forced off the wreck site by bad weather in October of 1930. Though her crew were preoccupied with plans for the next salvage season, she was still an all-purpose working ship, and her backers had as yet seen no profit whatsoever from the sunken treasure ship. Accordingly, she was assigned the task of blowing up a cargo ship, the *Florence*, also located in the Bay of Biscay. The *Florence* had gone down during World War I in shallow water near the major shipping lanes, and had long been considered a menace to navigation.

The *Artiglio* and her crew began work in December, 1930, using dynamite to break up the hulk of the *Florence*. The winter seas were very rough, and a combination of extreme cold and limited daylight may have forced the Italians into working carelessly. In any case, an accidental explosion occurred aboard the salvage ship. Her dynamite stocks were touched off, and the *Artiglio*, with fourteen crew members, was sent to the bottom.

The disaster did not daunt the remainder of the Italian crew. The treasure of the *Egypt* had been located, and all hands were convinced it was only a matter of time and the working out of proven salvage techniques before the gold and silver would be raised. In May, 1931, aboard a new ship, *Artiglio II*, they commenced work on the bullion room again. David Scott of *The New York Times* once more accompanied the divers.

David Scott's Narrative

"The new Italian salvage ship, *Artiglio II*, sailed from Brest Tuesday and made for the wreck via the Armen buoy. The crew found the *Egypt's* marker buoys without any trouble, three weather-beaten cones with green frills of weed grown during the winter. The first job was to get the buoys aboard and put new ones in their places. This year their iron anchors are being replaced with concrete ones fitted with steel rails on their bottoms to stick in the bottom and prevent them from dragging.

"The new ship is livelier than the old one, but she is bigger, and handled the big concrete blocks with ease, by means of her derrick. The derricks are equipped with a balance weight that automatically unhooks itself as soon as the anchor touches bottom.

"The divers also tested the deep diving shells. The *Artiglio II* has four divers, Raffaelli and Mancini, who are old hands, and two new men, Lenci and Sodini, who replace men lost in the destruction of the first *Artiglio*.

"Lenci went down first in the observation shell, which with a second shell

The salvage of the EGYPT'S gold was major news to a Depression weary world. The New York Times put a correspondent aboard the salvage ship to follow the breaking story.

DIVERS ENTER CABIN OF TREASURE SHIP

One Nearly Loses Life in the Egypt, 400 Feet Below the Surface, Near France.

CABLE BECOMES ENTANGLED

Line Fouls After His Anchor Slips Loose, but He Floats Up 30 Yards From Ship.

CAPTAIN'S SAFE IS EXPOSED

But Grapnel Fails to Move It From Wall After Tearing Roof From His Quarters.

By DAVID SCOTT.

FIND TREASURE SHIP WRECK

Salvagers Hope to Recover £10,000,000 In Gold Lost on the Egypt

LONDON, ... Salvage experts have at last ... in locating the whereabouts of the P. and O. liner ... went down on May 21, ... sion with ... Seine off Ushant ... miles ... a dep ...

DIVERS WORK APACE ON TREASURE LINER

Three Explosive Blasts Detach Hydraulic Crane on Egypt, 400 Feet Below Sea.

WEATHER FAVORS EFFORT

But $5,000,000 In Gold and Silver Is Deep in Ship—London Underwriters Greatly Stirred by Feat.

By DAVID SCOTT.

BREST, France, Sept. 1.—Three ex-

Egypt had aroused nothing but doubt in the minds of underwriters that the feat could be accomplished. Now, however, the first stage of the job has been completed, and there is confidence that the second stage—the actual recovery of the bullion—will be equally successful.

The position of the wreck agrees with that officially recorded by Lloyds. The Egypt sank in May, 1922, and the precious metal she carried consisted of $4,195,000 in gold and $1,075,000 in silver, a total of $5,270,000. Since then, however, the price of silver has depreciated heavily, but the value of the gold has held up, and if the salvaging efforts are successful there ought to be a good reward for Italian divers and a pleasant return for the marine underwriters who paid the claims after the liner sank. At the time a number of reinsurances were effected.

One of the most famous salvage cases known to the London market was the recovery of gold in the steamer Alfonso XII, wrecked off the Canary Islands in February, 1885. Aboard were ten boxes, each weighing about 200 pounds and containing 10,000 Spanish gold coins, each worth nearly $5. The gold was insured in the London market for about $525,000. It was stowed in the lazarette, and

186

...ve.
(AP).—... getting ... gold and ... sunken liner

...ers penetrated ... ship, 400 feet ... and prepared to ... ich lies under the ... below. They said ... hat, should the pres... r continue, they may ... ace explosives around ... room before the end of ... nd blow it apart to gain ... he precious metal. ... ypt, a Peninsular and Ori... er, went down in 1922. The ... salvage experts striving to re... the gold are trying to comple... task before the Septem...

...ns. ...arly this morning the Italian ... ffio stood alongside the s... vessel Artiglio bringing dynam... powerful electric magnets t... through the steamship's ste... that divers might penetr... ...'s strong room. ... ret ... peration of ... is expe... ...sure ... one ...

SAFE RAISED FROM SHIP TO BE OPENED AT BREST

British Consul to Be Present at Examination of Strong Box Taken From the Egypt.

Special Cable to THE NEW YORK TIMES.

PARIS, Sept. 6.—The office safe, raised from the sunken British liner Egypt, lying sixty fathoms below the waves off the French coast, will be opened in the presence of the British Consul and other officials at Brest Monday.

The Italian salvage expedition which raised it after painstaking operations are confident it belongs to the Egypt, which sank in 1922 with 102 persons and a treasure in gold and silver bars worth more than $5,000,000.

Some idea of the difficulties being met by these expert divers working

$450,000 GOLD LANDED BY SALVAGE VESSEL

Artiglio's Crew Has Recovered $3,250,000 of $5,000,000 of Liner Egypt's Treasure.

PLYMOUTH, England, Sept. 21 (AP).—The Italian salvage ship Artiglio today deposited at this port a fourth cargo of gold retrieved from the sunken liner Egypt. The latest haul was the equivalent of $450,000, making the total salvaged $3,250,000 out of the $5,000,000 in bullion in the Egypt's strong-room when she sank in 1922.

Divers Find Liner's $5,000,000 Bu... Intact; Reach Egypt's Cargo After Thre...

Wireless to THE NEW YORK TIM...

BREST, France, Nov. 1. — The Italian divers of the salvage ship Artiglio II finally succeeded yesterday in ripping the stubborn steel roof clean off the sunken liner Egypt's bullion room, and as far as can be seen the boxes of bullion are intact and some should be raised without difficulty as soon as the weather clears.

The divers, therefore, have at last reached the goal toward which they and their predecessors have fought their way with such patience and determination for nearly three years.

Work on the Egypt was begun in the Spring of 1929 with a search for the sunken wreck which proceede... unsuccessfully all Summer. Last ye... the old Artiglio and the salvage sh... Raffio resumed the search, using ... proved gear. They located the E... and identified her Aug. 30.

Both those salvage ships no...

sunk by th... munitions ... was worl... Guernsey ... working...

It is ... hopes ... bullio... even ... vage... and ... by ... ce... v...

...s ...d ...ac- ...een ...k so ...of un- ...perils and it ...parable

...ntal liner ... gold and ... as rammed ... Ushant in

SUNKEN LINER YIELDS $200,000 MORE GOLD

Salvage Ship Artiglio II Lands Precious Metal in England From the Egypt.

Wireless to THE NEW YORK TIMES.

LONDON, June 3.—The Italian salvage steamer Artiglio II landed £50,000 [about $200,000] worth of gold from the wrecked liner Egypt at Plymouth today. It is believed that bullion worth another £400,000 remains in the hold of the sunken vessel.

The liner Egypt went down in a collision in 1922 off Ushant, France, and in her hold was more than $5,000,000 in gold and silver bullion. Although salvage operations on the sunken vessel have gone on for nearly four years and have claimed fifteen lives, the first haul in reclaimed treasure came to the surface last June when the crew of the Artiglio brought up about $875,000 worth.

The old ship lies in extremely deep and dangerous waters, which are affected by severe tides. For years the task of reclamation was held in many quarters to be impossible. But when the crew of the Artiglio II retired last October for the Winter about $3,750,... bullion had been recov... The first ship... a large par... to the...

fitted with mechanical manipulators, makes up the complement of the salvors' advanced diving gear. Being smaller than Gianni and Francesci, for whom the shell was designed, he needed an iron weight to keep him down. Even so, the shell was inclined to stand on its head. The jointed shell lay on its face first, while the ballast tank filled, and then slowly sank. Both shells leaked a little, the observation shell through one window and the jointed shell through its left ankle. Otherwise all went well, and by the end of the week the leaks had stopped and all the new buoys had been placed."

June 8, 1931

David Scott's Narrative, Continued

"The capricious Atlantic weather again has driven the *Artiglio II* from her quest. We sailed from Brest early Thursday morning under fair skies, but immediately encountered variable west and southwesterly winds and seas choppy to rough.

"The new ship has a peculiar jerky motion in heavy seas which is very bad for unaccustomed stomachs, so much so that even one or two of the experienced crew suffered from sea-sickness. The rolling pumps suspended divers up and down underwater and makes it difficult and dangerous for them to get near the wreck.

"Faffaello Mancini, second diver, descended first. The light was very poor and the water was thick with sand from the strong currents of the last few days. At his first dive the observation shell proved too light, and had to be hauled up again and weighted with chains. At his second dive one of the windows leaked and had to be fixed. When Mancini finally reached bottom the shell was snatching at its cable, banging him hard against the sea floor. Conditions were so difficult that operations were suspended for the day.

"On Friday the sea was calmer, but a pouring rain with heavy, low clouds made the light bad. Mancini, Lenci and Sodini all went down for various periods of time. None of them saw anything but dim green water outside their shells. Finally, on Saturday morning, the sun emerged and, although the sea and tide were troublesome, the wreck was found.

"Mancini went down in the morning and stayed at the bottom until he had used up all his oxygen, without seeing anything. In the afternoon he descended again. As the *Artiglio II* swung in the current he made out two dim shapes to either side of him, and for a moment he thought he was between two wrecks.

"Actually, he was swinging in the middle of the crater that Gianni and his mates blew last year in the upper works of the *Egypt*. Twisted walls of wreckage were all around him. He probably had dropped blindly into this jagged-edged pit more than once before, a dangerous business.

"But with contact remade, the first part of the job was done. As soon as weather improves, the demolition of the hull over the bullion room will begin."

June 17, 1931

David Scott's Narrative, Continued

"Blasting a way to the bullion room began in earnest this week. Last year

in the old *Artiglio* divers Gianni and Bargellini demolished the captain's cabin and salvaged his safe, but they left the boat deck and three more decks below it, intact over the bullion room. The boat deck is an affair of wooden planks laid on thin angle-irons, and hardly counts as an obstruction. The hurricane deck and the upper deck are of iron, however, and the main deck is steel. All have a covering of wood. Between them is a maze of partitions and bulkheads, and all this mass of metal must be cleared away for a good distance fore and aft above the bullion room.

"Fortunately, there is a good deal of spare space just over the bullion room: the dining saloon on the main deck, above it, the main staircase, and over that, the skylight.

"Last Saturday divers with explosives began to clear away the boat deck and deckhouse containing the officers' cabins, just forward of the captain's cabin. They used shaped charges made of iron, bored and filled with the waxy yellow explosive, which are electrically detonated from the surface.

"Although the sea was by no means smooth, the divers succeeded in firing three charges of two tubes each, shattering the structures of the boat deck and deckhouse. On Sunday grapnels and cables were lowered from the *Artiglio II*'s derrick, and the loosened wreckage was hauled up. Most of the boat deck came up whole, but the deckhouse resisted. The derrick chain broke, and it was necessary to fire another charge below, before the structure came free.

"But as darkness fell on Sunday the west wind came up in gale force, and the *Artiglio II* was forced to flee."

David Scott's Narrative, Continued

August 10, 1931

"The divers of the *Artiglio II* are within sight of their gold. In the last four days they cleared away the hurricane deck of the sunken liner and, working quickly in difficult conditions, they cleared the upper deck and made a large hole in the saloon below it.

"The bullion room is under the floor of the saloon. Through an opening not yet big enough to admit the observation diving shell, divers can see the roof of the bullion room laying exposed.

" 'Now the gold is afraid,' said Mario Rafaelli, chief diver.

"New gear and new methods enabled the crew of the *Artiglio II* to moor to the buoys attached to the sunken liner in record time. Using light steel cables in place of the heavy manila hawsers, the mother ship steamed slowly around the interior of the circle of buoys, while her motorboat buzzed back and forth like a busy shuttle, making her fast. The ship and the boat kept moving all the time. It looks easy, but it needs smart work from everyone.

"The first diver went down at midday Tuesday and began clearing partitions and deck plating from the wreck. The sun shone and our spirits rose. But now a new enemy descended on us: fog.

"*Artiglio II* lay in the white mist, sounding her whistle at three-minute intervals. Divers can still see a couple of yards underwater even with fog above, but if there is a collision between the mother ship and other shipping in the area, they have no chance of escape. When fog comes, there is noth-

The original *Artiglio* sank because of an accidental explosion which occurred during an off-season salvage venture unrelated to the *Egypt,* in December, 1930. The Italians outfitted and crewed a bigger, more sophisticated vessel, which they named *Artiglio II,* and returned to the *Egypt* business in 1931. Here they man the winches powering the second vessel's grab, which has brought up sections of the *Egypt's* deck plate. At center is the observation shell.

ing to do but haul up divers and wait it out. For two days the *Artiglio II* lay idle, her whistle going day and night. Remembering the fate of the wreck beneath us, which sank after a collision during just such a fog, was not good for the nerves.

"Finally, on Thursday, the fog lifted, and the divers worked for twelve hours that day and Friday, making up for lost time. As fast as the wreckage was cleared, more decking was loosened with explosives, until the wound in the *Egypt's* hull was bored close to the treasure. The upper deck is now loose from the bulwarks all along the port side, and half cut across forward of the bullion room. A big piece of the deck has already collapsed into the saloon, and with smooth water it may be possible to clear it in a day.

"But in these waters, as soon as fog lifts the winds come up. Strong northerlies made the sea too rough for diving by Saturday morning, so we put in to Brest for stores, having come down to the ship's biscuits of our provisions, and being in great need of tobacco, Chianti and good fresh bread."

October 8, 1931

David Scott's Narrative, Continued

"Once again bad weather has snatched the prize from us at the last moment. Divers have been engaged in cutting through the last barrier above the bullion room with explosives. If high winds had not interrupted the work yesterday, one or two more days would have seen the treasure laid bare at last.

"The last stage of demolition is infinitely more delicate than the earlier work, and new obstacles are encountered nearly every day. To begin with, the divers are now working at the bottom of a crater thirty feet deep cut in

the *Egypt's* hull. The divers sometimes go down quite blind, seeing nothing at all either outside or inside their shells as they sink into the darkness of the wreck.

"But the poor visibility does not explain all the slowness in the last stage of the work. The explosion of a line of charges at the bottom of the crater blows the water outward and upward through holes in the decking and between the decks. When the gas of the explosion has escaped, water rushes back again, bringing with it all the debris in the nearer parts of the wreck. The edges of the broken decks above the bullion room are all sagging outward in such a way that the rubbish easily slides down into the crater. The result is that every time a charge is fired, the roof of the bullion room, which has been laboriously cleared of wreckage a dozen times, is again buried under two feet of timber, piping, bits of plating and other odds and ends.

"But despite the difficulty, the divers cut around three sides of a section of the main deck on which they have lifts. Best of all, they have torn one complete deckplate, 25 feet by 6 feet, from one side of the main deck, leaving a rent through which the closed door of the bullion room shows enticingly below."

October 23, 1931
BULLION ROOM OF SUNKEN LINER TORN WIDE OPEN

Tuesday morning, after a great many explosions, the *Artiglio II* made a final effort to tear the roof bodily from the treasure room. She heeled well over, exerting a pull of from fifteen to twenty tons on the cable.

The idea of tearing the roof off the vessel's treasure room replaced the original scheme of raising the entire room intact, when conditions on the wreck made the latter scheme appear impossible.

The roof was lifted somewhat, and then the divers placed three bombs across it and cut it in two. By the time they had cleared the wreckage, however, it was dark. And with dawn Wednesday gale-force winds arose and drove the salvors back into port.

November 2, 1931
BULLION INTACT

Divers have at last succeeded in reaching the goal toward which they and their predecessors have fought their way with such patience and determination for nearly three years.

Succeeding yesterday in ripping the last fragments of the steel roof of the bullion room clear, they descended into the chamber. As far as can be seen, the wooden boxes of bullion are intact, and some should be raised without difficulty as soon as the weather clears.

It is now so late in the season that hopes of raising any large part of the treasure this year cannot be high. But even if only a few boxes can be salvaged now the tenacity of the divers and their shipmates will be rewarded by the sure promise of ultimate success, and their methods will have been vindicated.

No piece of underwater work so difficult, so strange and so full of unsolved problems and unknown perils has ever been accomplished, and it is unlikely that anything comparable will be done soon again.

With the roof of the treasure room removed, divers descended to try and salvage at least a box or two of the bullion before the end of the season. But the weather was foul. Visibility was almost zero, and the plunging *Artiglio II* yanked the suspended divers around on the ends of their cables like so many marionettes, dangling them perilously close to the jagged edges of the explosion-torn deck plates. The worst fear of the salvors had been dispelled, however, when the bullion room was finally breached. The team had worried that the room might have been compressed into a shapeless mass, like a crushed toothpaste tube, by water pressure. However, the room was intact, and the divers knew they would be able to use their scoops and grapnels easily within its rectangle, as soon as the weather gave them a chance.

But the obdurate Atlantic continued to slam the salvage ship with heavy autumn seas and storms. A final attempt was made on December 3rd. The ship steamed out from Brest, only to find that one of the wreck's marking buoys had been carried away. It was back to square one for the team: far from spending their last day raising some of the elusive gold, they were faced with the prospect of finding the hulk all over again, and marking it with a new buoy.

In a wildly pitching sea diver Lenci descended along the line of the cable from one of the remaining marker buoys. Banging up and down against what he thought must be part of the *Egypt's* intact decking, he was unable to see a thing except his "palla", or white-painted balance weight, "shining like a Chinese lantern." Unable to ascertain for sure whether he was anywhere near the crater in the wreck which led to the treasure room, and not entirely sure he was even on the wreck itself, he made three more recklessly courageous dives over the afternoon and the next morning. But his efforts were in vain, and with great reluctance the *Artiglio II's* diving master called off the expedition until the following season.

After the immense labors, hairbreadth escapes and general derring-do through which the crew of the *Artiglio II* had gone to cut through the hulk and reach the treasure room during the past three years, the actual salvage of the bullion came almost as an anticlimax.

Working smoothly in fine weather in the summer of 1932, the divers quickly cleared the winter's debris from the hulk and widened the gap into the bullion room. The fact that the wooden boxes which held the ingots had survived intact simplified their work enormously. They easily deployed their grapnels and "crabs," and began methodically hauling up the treasure.

By August they had succeeded in raising some £550,000 worth of gold and silver bars, nearly half the *Egypt's* original consignment of $5 million. In September a further strike netted an additional $450,000, bringing the 1932 total haul to $3,250,000. Weather continued to be a problem, but the divers were old hands by now, and felt almost at home working in pitch blackness and heavy swells, 400 feet down. The last haul was made in the short span of five hours, and was duly sent to London for appraisal.

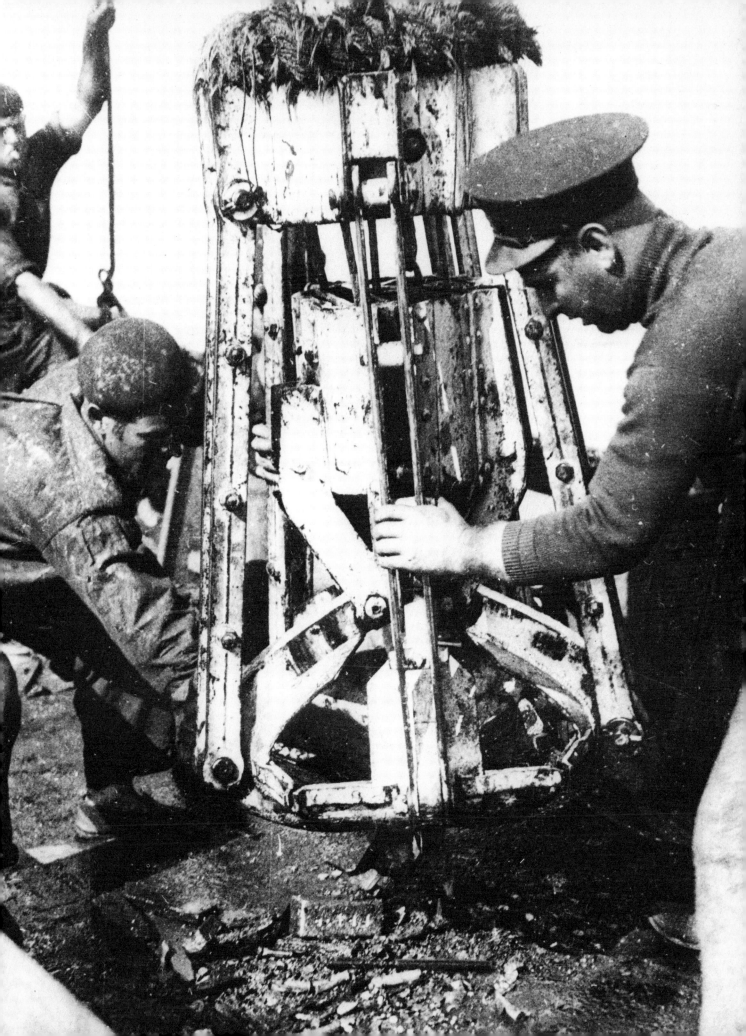

Setting back to work again in 1933, the *Artiglio II*'s divers resumed the businesslike routine of bringing up bullion. $200,000 came up in June. In July 610 silver bars and five of gold were raised, bringing the total of recovered ingots to 797. The *Egypt*'s manifest listed 1,229 bars of both metals, and the divers continued work.

True to the Italians' continually inventive approach to their long task, a new technique for raising loose coins and ingots was brought to bear on the wreck in the 1933 season. Mario Raffaelli, head diver, devised a metal tube with a glass cover on its bottom end. It was lowered over the boxes and coins in the bullion room and pumped to near vacuum. At a diver's signal, the glass was mechanically broken from the surface. In rushed the water, equalizing pressure, carrying with it the precious litter of the treasure chamber. At the first try Raffaelli recovered 6,000 gold sovereigns and several bars of gold and silver weighing more than 10,000 ounces.

By such methods the team succeeded in adding another half million dollars' worth of treasure to the total salvage by the end of the season.

Patiently working through the 1934 and 1935 salvage seasons, the *Artiglio II* continued to bring up treasure. August, 1934 saw a haul of gold bars amounting to 20,000 ounces, plus five bars of silver and 14,856 gold sovereigns. Nineteen gold bars and 5,400 sovereigns came up in September.

The last haul was made in July, 1935. £45,000 in gold bars and sovereigns were raised by the vacuum method. Only bits and pieces of the treasure remained, mostly loose coins in insufficient quantity to justify the expense of continued work.

The extraordinary salvage work on the *Egypt*, which took nearly seven years from the first scouting of the wreck site to the recovery of the last bar of gold, resulted in nearly total success. When operations were finally suspended in 1935, 90.9 per cent of the *Egypt*'s consignment of gold sovereigns, 97.4 per cent of her silver bars and 98.25 per cent of her gold bars had been recovered. Of the treasure of $5 million, only a few thousand dollars' worth of loose change remains scattered about the sunken bullion room. Since conditions over the wreck rule out amateur expeditions, and the amount of gold remaining does not justify another *Artiglio*-style professional effort, it is doubtful if the treasure remnants will ever see the light of day.

The work of the two *Artiglios* and their divers was a landmark in treasure salvage. The robot-like diving shells and other equipment developed for the salvage of the *Egypt* remained the state of the salvor's art for years, clearing the way for even greater treasure recoveries made during and after the great slaughter of ships in World War II.

Today salvage techniques are different, innovations in pressure systems having made it possible for divers in flexible wet suits to do without the cumbersome "robots" the Italians used for deep diving. But the robot suits themselves led the way to modern deepwater diving modules which are essentially

mini-submarines. These are self-propelled and equipped with mechanical manipulators, jointed arms with grippers capable of delicate underwater work, more sophisticated, certainly, than the Italians' pincers, but no more than an extension of the idea the *Artiglio* divers pioneered under field conditions.

Without the Italian forerunners' willingness to take risk and adapt their techniques and equipment to seemingly impossible conditions at depths where salvage divers had never ventured before, it is probable that the whole concept of deepwater salvage would have remained undeveloped for years.

In 1936 the *Artiglio II*, its work on the *Egypt* brought to a triumphant close, set off on another quest for treasure. This time the target was the rumored hoard of a Spanish vessel, the *Polluce*, which went down off the island of Elba in the early nineteenth century. The Italians made little fuss about the adventure. After the *Egypt*, they knew that if there was treasure to be found aboard the *Polluce*, they would find it eventually.

21

The great Cunard liner *Lusitania* was en route to England from the United States when she was sunk by German torpedoes. She carried 1,257, of which 1,198 were drowned, the ship going down so fast that the shocked crew had no time to launch lifeboats. The terrible loss of life, and the fact that the *Lusitania* was believed to be an unarmed civilian vessel in no way connected with the British war effort, was luridly played up in the American and English press. The Germans were portrayed as conscienceless monsters, and the loss of the *Lusitania* became a rallying-point for the faction in the United States which favored America's entry into World War I.

The *Lusitania* was off the Irish coast when she was hit. 18-year-old Leslie Morton, a crewman posted as an extra lookout on the vessel's forecastle, spotted "torpedoes coming on the starboard side" at about 2:10 P. M. on May 7, 1915. He managed to warn the bridge of the calamitous approach of the twin torpedoes, which had been fired by a German submarine, one of many known to be operating off the south coast of Ireland. Then the torpedoes struck, knocking Morton off his feet, and dooming the vessel before her officers had time to do anything.

The *Lusitania*, out of control, her main steam pipe shattered, continued to plough forward for fifteen minutes. A starboard list became acute. Many passengers and crew members jumped into the sea, but most remained huddled numbly on the deck, paralyzed by the suddenness of the disaster.

At 2:26 the liner sank, bearing most of her human cargo to the bottom with her. The lookout, Morton, survived, as did the *Lusitania's* captain, her navigator, her purser, and a few other crew members and passengers. The survivors rendered an account of the catastrophe, and it is upon their word that the location of the wreck and the nature of her cargo rests.

A difficulty which was to plague post-war salvors concerned the hulk's location. The *Lusitania's* navigator, Mr. Besteg, had been having trouble pinpointing the vessel's position during the morning of the 7th of May, due to fog. Lookouts were posted to spot landmarks on the Irish coast, and in the meanwhile navigator Besteg began working on a four–point bearing on his charts.

At 12:10 P. M., having missed Fastnet, the first of their landmarks, in the fog, the lookouts spotted what they thought was Brow Head. It was a guess, but on the strength of it Captain Turner made his planned course correction, hauling in thirty degress to the northward, his intention being to get a fix at the Old Head of Kinsale, a promontory between Clonakilty Bay and Cork Harbor midway along Ireland's southern coast. German submarines in the vicinity were reported by the Admiralty, some of which were spotted heading toward the *Lusitania's* position. She increased her speed to eighteen knots, six and a half under her maximum. At 1:40 the course altered back to S. 87 E., and Mr. Besteg, taking the course and speed changes into account, began plotting the isosceles triangle which would fix the ship's position.

He never finished it. The explosion of the torpedoes not only destroyed the *Lusitania's* steering mechanism, it also blew up her steam line, making it impossible to slow the vessel down or regulate her speed in the fifteen minutes of life that remained to her.

Facing Page:
The *Lusitania*, pride of the Cunard Line, was one of the fastest and most luxurious passenger liners of her time.

198

A detail of Schweiger's chart shows the course of the U-139 off the south coast of Ireland (heavy line). Circled and marked with a sketch of the sinking liner is the spot where Schweiger estimated he had encountered and sunk the *Lusitania*.

(inset): A rare photograph of the German submarine U-139, which, under the command of Lieutenant-Captain Schweiger, sank the *Lusitania* in 1915.

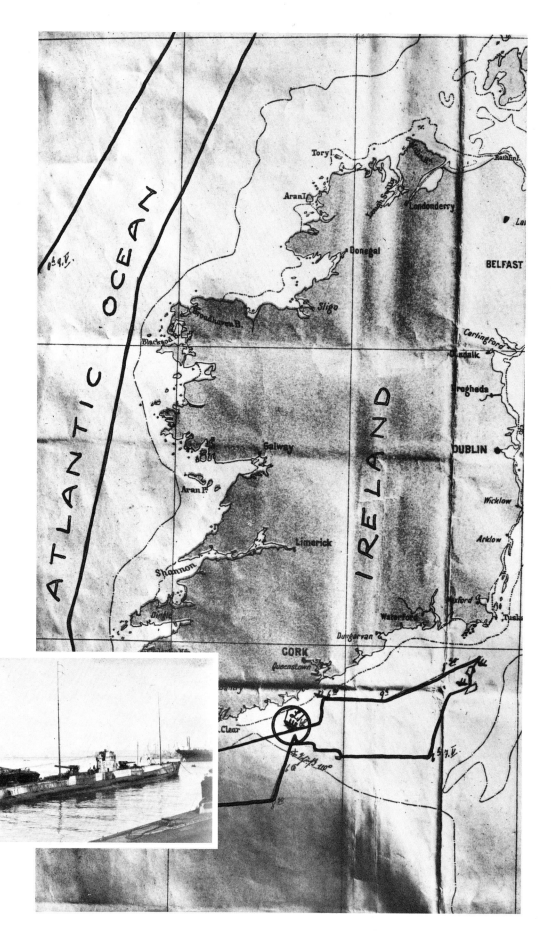

Translation

7.15
2,0 p.m.   Right front appears a steamboat with 4 chimneys and
2 masts coming vertically on us (coming from xxxxxx
xxxxx South South North to Galley Head) The ship is
a big passenger steamboat.

2,5 pm   We change our course to 11 and with high speed and
converging course to the other ship hoping that it
would change its course to St.B. along the Irish
coast. The ship turns St.B., takes course to
Queenstown and makes therefore an approach for
shooting possible. Accelerated speed to 3 h pm in
order to get a good position.

3,10 pm   Side shot on 700 Meter (G-Torpedo put to 3 Meter
depth), angle 90 , estimated run 22 sn. The shot
hits the ship's side immediately aft of the bridge
behind.

Then happens an extraordinary big detonation with a very big cloud
(much higher than the chimney in front). There must have been
a second explosion besides the torpedo (boiler or coal or powder?)
The buildings above the hit area and the bridge explode, fire
starts, smoke covers the whole bridge, the ship stops immediately
and leans rapidly to starboard, at the same time sinking more in
front. It seems to sink in a short time. Big confusion on the
ship; the boats were readied and partly lowered to the sea. There
must have reigned confusion on board; some boats are full, quickly
lowered they touch the water with their front or rear and get
immediately full of water. On the back board side the boats cannot
be lowered because of the ship's oblique position, only a few. The
ship sinks; in front you can see the name "Lusitania" in gold letters.
The chimneys are black, no flag at the rear. It ran 20 knots.
It seems that the ship will sink any moment, it makes 24 knots and
heads for the sea. I could not have fired a second torpedo in
this crowd of people trying to save themselves.

4,15 pm
   Gone on 11 knots and looked around. Far away on backboard are drifting some salvation boats; nothing more
to see from the "Lusitania". Th
The light house Old Head of Kinsale is in a d
on 90 n water. (in a distance of 27 sn of Que
6 N and λ = 8° 31' N.
The land and the light house were very distin

4,20 pm.
   While looking around backboard a
heading for Eastnet Rock. With
position to shoot. Shoot 90° fr
estimated angle 90°, shoot condi
favorable, missing by normal sho
impossible. Torpedo does not hi
for some time after the shot is
not be established why the torpe

5,08 pm.   left allright, but it did not r
angle. It is impossible that tl
wrong angle because the torpedo
The ship, a freighter of the Cu

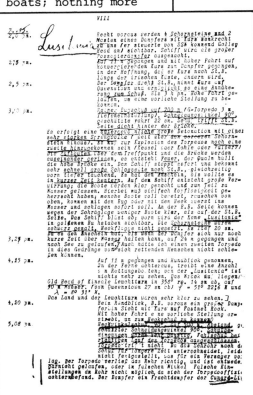

201

Captain Turner was closely questioned by the Admiralty Board after the disaster, and confessed that he himself was unsure about the vessel's exact position when she went down. The Old Head of Kinsale had been sighted, but the navigator had not finished his fix on the chart. In any case, it was impossible to tell how far the stricken ship had wallowed on after the explosion. At one point Captain Turner stated that the *Lusitania* was at Lat. 51.25 degrees N. and Long. 8.35 degrees W. when torpedoed, "more than fifteen miles south of the Old Head of Kinsale in 51 fathoms." But later he qualifed: "I thought it was about fifteen. The officers marked it off and made it ten."

The five-mile discrepancy was to bedevil seekers for the wreck after the war.

The Italian salvage team which raised the treasure of the liner *Eygpt* (NOTE: SEE *THE SALVAGE OF THE EYGPT*), with more precise data to hand than was the case with the *Lusitania* seekers, still took two years before they located their wreck.

Regardless of ambiguities concerning the *Lusitania's* position, salvage attempts began in earnest in the 1920s. Salvors were lured after the sunken liner by rumors that she had been carrying a stunning $20 million to $25 million (by today's valuation) in gold bullion and passenger jewelry when the Germans sank her. But the question of the *Lusitania's* cargo is as ambiguous as her position, and the history of the attempts to penetrate her mysteries is distinguished principally by the figure of the submariner-showman Simon Lake, who formulated his most audacious engineering scheme for use on the wreck of the great liner.

*July 6, 1923-
September 10,
1930*

THE EARLY EFFORTS: RAISE THE "LUSITANIA"?

The first try after the *Lusitania's* rumored gold was mounted by a British firm headed by one Count Landi. Landi commissioned a steamship, the *Semper Paratus*, which set sail in the summer of 1923 from Dover. But the expedition failed to locate the sunken liner. It did, however, generate considerable interest when it was reported in the papers, and an engineer named J. Edward Cassidy wrote a letter to *The New York Times* describing his experiments with raising scale models of sunken ships by means of caissons.

Cassidy built an accurate model of his apparatus, which apparently operated along the lines of an old method of raising sunken ships which involved submerging huge, hollow steel compartments, or caissons, attaching them to the hulk, and then pumping the water out of them from the surface. Cassidy maintained that his improvement on the principle, which he had tested 150 times on a scale model of the *Lusitania*, in the muddy waters with a scale depth of 500 feet, had raised his model boat intact on all but two tries. He maintained that his salvage method, which eliminated the tedious and dangerous work of cutting through the hulls of sunken ships, often destroying them and their cargoes in the process, should be used to raise all ships lost in waters too deep for conventional diving methods.

Simon Lake, inventor, salvage expert, submariner and all-round self-publicist, was nearing the end of his glamorous career when he became involved in a scheme to salvage the *Lusitania*. Associated with just about every major salvage effort during the 1920s and 1930s (NOTE: SEE *THE GOLD OF NEW YORK HARBOR* AND *THE MYSTERY OF THE SPANISH PAYROLL*), Lake began his innovative underwater career in the 1890's, going after salvable hulks aboard his specially-equipped ship, the *Argonaut*. Active in developing diving gear and prototype submarines for the Allies during World War I, he achieved the high point in his life work, in terms of notoriety if not recovered salvage, with his expedition after the *Lusitania's* lost cargo.

He teamed up with a noted explorer and seacaptain, H.H. Railey, a man whose career rivalled Lake's own in glamour. Captain Railey had been Admiral Byrd's personal representative during the latter's Antarctic expedition, and he was accustomed to odd missions requiring clever seamanship. The pair announced their intention of attacking the *Lusitania* problem in November, 1931, and Simon Lake himself wrote a piece for *The New York Times* setting forth his objectives and methods.

by Simon Lake

By the first of the year, if the British authorities give final sanction to a project now under way, I hope to see the decks of the Cunarder *Lusitania*, which was sunk in eighteen minutes by a German torpedo in 1915, with the loss of 1,198 lives, including those of nearly 200 American citizens.

In the safe of the purser, which in a salvaging expedition we expect to be able to bring to the surface, there will undoubtedly be documents of vast importance, and as our men go into the depths of the ship they will find effects which may give posterity lasting mementos of one of the great disasters of history.

There will be photographs of the dining saloon, taken with special apparatus which has been perfected for photographic work underwater. These will show how the magnificent room of sixteen years ago, quickly deserted in the moments between the direct hit of the torpedo and the sinking of the vessel, looks today.

To the layman this project of ours may sound like another story from the pen of Jules Verne, and I am almost amused at the incredulity which laymen have evinced for the last sixteen years.

Twenty years ago I invented a tube designed to recover the treasure of the *Lutine* (NOTE: SEE *THE STORY OF THE LUTINE BELL*), a British frigate sunk off Holland's Zuider Zee with $6 million (sic) in gold bullion.

The war stopped that enterprise, for I was called back to build more submarines for the United States Government. I recently started to operate under contract, building the apparatus for the *Lusitania* venture. The underwater part of it was thoroughly developed and has been proved in recovering cargoes from a number of ships sunk at a lesser depth than the *Lusitania*.

The under water camera equipment with which inventor Simon Lake hoped to take pictures of the interior of the sunken *Lusitania.* The lamp shown here was supposed to withstand ocean pressure at a depth of 200 feet without a protective lens.

Facing Page:
The *Lusitania's* lavishly decorated lounge. Lake was bent on obtaining undersea photos of this room, with his specially designed gear. His motives for choosing such a melancholy photographic subject are unclear, but it is probable that he was exploiting the glamor surrounding the controversial sinking of the liner to gain financial support for his engineering projects during the money-tight 1930s.

It is simply a question of increasing the length of our enclosed apparatus, arranging for details above the surface, and handling the subsurface mechanics necessary for this particular job. In other words, the theory has been proven sound, and it is now only a job for the steel production plant.

Now, the *Lusitania* was not sunk in the middle of the ocean, and her keel is only 240 feet beneath the surface. The top deck, A Deck, is only 175 feet below, and the stacks are naturally higher up.

As I see it definitely, after numerous experiments and after having received many reports concerning Britain's Winter coastal conditions, we should have the (purser's) safe on board a trawler within two days after our soundings identify the sunken ship. I expect to go down to the bottom of the sea and smoke as comfortably as in my own laboratories.

It is impossible to give all technical details of our present plans, because many of them are secret, and because, too, Great Britain has not yet given its formal approval. But I will say this: from the mother ship, which is 134 feet long, with a beam of twenty-four feet, we will send below a steel tube which will rest on the A Deck of the *Lusitania.*

The hydrostatic pressure there will be 75 pounds per square inch, but no one will feel it more than they do in a submarine. All must go down the tube through a long staircase, until they reach a room twelve feet wide, eight feet long and eight feet high. The tube itself is five feet in diameter, and will be perfectly supplied with air from the pumps above. There will be no pressure for the individual.

It is only necessary to walk down this flight of stairs, inside the tube, under normal atmospheric pressure, until one enters the divers' observation chamber at the lower end. This operating chamber is outfitted with look-out windows.

Various motor-extended winches will be on the exterior, also two doors providing exit for the divers when it is necessary for them to go outside to do their work.

You might call the arrangement for preventing accidental opening of these doors foolproof, as it is impossible for them to be opened until the sea pressure is equalized by admitting the air to the compartment. When this pressure is equalized the exit door is opened downward, and no water will enter the room. Instead, the air flows outward from the compartment.

Through the glass windows, with the aid of powerful searchlights, the spectators in the observation chamber will watch the work of those on the *Lusitania.* Vision of from forty to sixty feet will be possible.

The submersible tube for the divers' operating compartment is shut off from the rest of the apparatus by means of an airlock, which permits ready passage to and from the surface vessel under normal air pressure. It is only in the divers' compartment, where the air is under pressure equal to the compartment's depth of submergence, that the exit door is opened. This arrangement eliminates the "bends," ordinarily a great danger when men are under water.

We know exactly where the safe is and we will bring it out from the side of the ship by a method which I cannot explain at this time. We wish to get

Simon Lake himself, submarine engineer, entrepreneur and large-scale dreamer. His Jules-Vernesque scheme for raising the rumored gold of the *Lusitania* gave press and public a case of treasure fever during the Depression.

everything of value, actual or sentimental, and bring it back to the world above from the sunken *Lusitania*. And considering that we shall be able to utilize about ten days in any Winter month, we expect remarkable photographic results.

Confidence was Lake's strong suit, but some practical objections were raised about his fantastic stairway to the sea-bottom before the device even began trials off Brightsea, England. The tube concept is an old one, and quite workable in shallow water. Its most recent proposal for deepwater use, before Lake, came from Captain Williams in 1911, who suggested a version of it be lowered over the treasure-laden wreck of the *Merida* off Virginia (SEE *THE QUEST FOR THE MERIDA*). But Williams, and Lake after him, underestimated the effect of pressure at depths below 200 feet. Lake apparently intended to trust the steel walls of his tube alone, to hold off the crushing pressure of 1053-8 pounds per square inch which obtains at the *Lusitania's* estimated depth of 240 feet. The half-ton pressure did not worry Lake, because his own figures were wildly short of the mark: he gave a reading of only 86.6 pounds per square inch for 200 feet, for example. As a submariner he should have known better, but it must be remembered that the submarines he helped develop had an extreme operating depth of only about 100 feet, and that only in emergencies.

Modern subs, bathyscaphes and other deepdiving vehicles operate, of course, by matching the outside water pressure by air pressure within the craft. Thus their hulls can be relatively thin, and the problem of the bends, which results when divers breathing normal air at high pressure develop bubbles of nitrogen in their bloodstream when that pressure is suddenly lowered, can be minimized by using a breathing mixture composed of pure oxygen and an inert gas such as helium.

But Lake proposed to circumvent the pressure question altogether, simply by dropping his tube, with an interior pressure of one atmosphere (14.6 pounds per square inch), to a depth where the surrounding sea would be squeezing its walls with 73.7 atmospheres of pressure. For his scheme to work, the walls of the tube toward the bottom would have had to have been so massive that the weight of the thing would have required a vessel at least the size of the *Lusitania* herself to transport it to the site and lower it. And although his plan for an airlock in which divers could equalize pressure with the surrounding water before venturing outside is sound, it is doubtful if the gaskets and other fittings of the airlock's door could have been built sturdily enough by the technology of the time to withstand the immense pressure differential involved. As an editorial comment in *The New York Times* of November 24, 1931 remarked, ". . . a cautious engineer would wish to test his invention in a less spectacular manner than Mr. Lake has in view, and on a hull which lies nearer the surface."

Nonetheless, plans went forward for the project. Lake's chief diver, Frank Crilley (NOTE: SEE *THE QUEST FOR THE MERIDA*), a much-decorated Navy veteran who had been cited for his lifesaving dive of 306 feet during the rescue of the sunken submarine F-4 in Honolulu during World War I, was enthusiastic. "This invention whereby you bring your diving chamber to your

work is what I've been looking forward to for a long time," he said in December, 1931.

But there remained the detail of the *Lusitania's* whereabouts. The British Admiralty informed the Lake team, which had already set up a base of operations at Kinsale in Ireland, that the hulk lay fifteen miles south of Old Kinsale Head in fifty fathoms (300 feet) of water. But the marine superintendent of the Cunard Company placed the wreck only ten miles south of the headland, and didn't hazard a guess as to her depth.

The question of the *Lusitania's* cargo again cropped up. Asked about the reputed $5 million in gold which the ill-starred liner had been carrying when she was sunk, Captain Railey said, "It is not true. There is no gold in the wreck of the *Lusitania*." He submitted to the press a statement of the expedition's intentions, which included recovering documents of historical and patriotic interest, but seemed chiefly concerned with vindicating Simon Lake's faith in his tube, and taking undersea still and motion-picture photographs at a depth never before attempted. Railey himself thought the *Lusitania* lay about eight miles from the Old Head of Kinsale, in 276 feet of water, "probably in an upright position," in his opinion. He went on, ". . . contrary to belief we frequently encounter, no attempt will be made to raise the vessel."

Captain Railey's denial of the existence of treasure aboard the lost liner was confirmed by W. H. Harkness in May, 1932. Harkness had served as the *Lusitania's* senior assistant purser on the fateful last voyage. Said he: "The only gold we had as freight was a tiny bar worth about $50 which was placed in the safe without any distinguishing mark upon it." Harkness's account of what *was* in the hold of the *Lusitania*, though it passed almost unnoticed at the time it appeared in *The New York Times*, was to cast rather a different complexion on the true nature of the liner's mission during her last cruise.

"There were some cases of shells in the hold, and 50,000 rounds of small arms ammunition," said Harkness.

Subsequent examination of Admiralty records confirms and elaborates on Harkness's memory. The *Lusitania*, whose torpedoing was waved like a bloody flag by the American and British press as an example of German barbarity, had in fact been a floating munitions warehouse, carrying arms from nominally neutral America to support the British cause in the early years of the First World War. If there was a villain in the piece, he was on the Allied side, for the decision to camouflage the vessel's martial cargo by sending her out with a full complement of civilian passengers, as if she were on a routine luxury passage, was cynical to say the least. Of course the Americans and British hoped the Germans would not discover the truth, but German spies abounded on both sides of the Atlantic. The U-boat which sent the liner and 1,198 souls to the bottom in 1915 was acting within the somewhat elastic rules of war, since the arms in the *Lusitania's* hold effectively cancelled her peaceful status. The drowned passengers and crew were victims of the ruthless application of *realpolitik* which increasingly governed the conduct of the Great War, and put paid forever to the nineteenth century notion of a chivalry of war.

Lake's invention involved a massive pipe lowered from a surface tender, through which divers could descend at normal air pressure to the observation chamber on the upper deck of the sunken liner. The chamber was equipped with airlocks to equalize interior and exterior pressure. Divers, donning their cumbersome suits in the chamber, would have immediate access to the wreck, without having to risk the slow and dangerous dive from the surface.

The observation chamber with the divers' sliding air-lock door, shown during construction in the early 1930s.

It may be that the discovery of the true nature of the liner's cargo dampened Simon Lake's enthusiasm for his grandiose salvage scheme. In any case, his 1932 venture was perfunctory, and he failed even to find the hulk. The great stairway to the bottom of the sea was never put to use, which is probably just as well, since it would not have worked. Lake returned to his submarine research, and came up with a baby sub, the *Explorer*, which was used successfully in the Bahamas, diving on sponge beds which lay too deeply for normal undersea harvesting work. Lake announced in September, 1933, that he intended to use the *Explorer* for a final effort to recover the *Lusitania's* treasure, which he still believed in, despite the denials of the liner's purser and his own Captain Railey. But the attempt was never made, and the flamboyant Lake's connection with the famous wreck ended on this inconclusive note.

In April, 1934, the Italian salvage vessel *Artiglio II* (NOTE: SEE *THE SALVAGE OF THE EGYPT*) was reported to have done some preliminary exploration in the Irish waters where the *Lusitania* drowned. But the *Artiglio II's* hunt never got beyond the placing of a few marker buoys, and it developed later that she was actually after other World War I wrecks, whose cargoes of copper and other valuable material were more substantial than the *Lusitania's* mythical gold.

A Glasgow firm spent some time in 1935 trying to locate the wreck, but was unsuccessful. The record shows no major salvage attempts subsequently, and the *Lusitania* lies undisturbed off Old Kinsale Head.

Facing Page:
A view down Simon Lake's diving tube, a stairway to the depths which proved more imaginative than practical.

209

22

Facing Page:
For two full years
(January, 1948-
January, 1950),
octogenarian G. B.
Mobley of Green
Cove Springs, Flor-
ida, led his fellow
townspeople on a
merry chase after
"pirate treasure"
worth $4 million,
according to the old
man. Mobley con-
vinced his neighbors
that he had located
the loot with a
homemade diving
rod (as shown).
Streets and back
yards were cratered
by steamshovels and
backhoes, but noth-
ing turned up.

*August 25-
30, 1923*
HAUSER'S HOAX

People want to believe in hidden treasure, just as they want to believe in UFO's, ghosts, psychic phenomena and magic. There is something immensely comforting in the notion that the daily grind is not all there is to life, and we humans have been providing ourselves with pleasanter realities ever since we left the trees.

Treasure stories naturally tend to proliferate most during hard times. Just as the nominal Christian gets a lot more serious about the question of his soul's immortality when he is very sick, the victim of an economic disaster takes heart from the possibility that the wherewithal to reverse his bad fortunes might just be buried after all under the old apple tree where Great-Aunt Sally always said it was. In most cases the pot of gold isn't there, of course, or if it is, it's empty. But frustration only serves to whet the appetite of the treasure-hunter, and his avidity has provided his more devious neighbors with a rich vein of psychological gold which they have worked over the years to far more profit than anything realized by actual prospectors.

Space does not permit a complete account of all the bilkers and con-men who crop up in over a century of treasure records in *The New York Times*. Stories range from hunts for treasures glimpsed in dreams, gold "found" through voodoo and other magical means, "treasure-witches" with miraculous money-seeking wands, and the usual round of doctored pirate maps and directions to the fabulous hoards gasped out in fictitious deathbed confessions. The wealthy set has naturally been the most frequently gulled, and one amusing chain of stories traces the adventures of an American socialite, delightfully named Mrs. Wally Wilde de Villareal, as she gamely squandered large sums all over the mountains of Czechoslovakia, on a treasure hunt cooked up by a group of genial gypsy con-men.

The three tales of bilkery presented here are, we hope, typical of the genre. It is useless to suppose that they will warn off prospective backers of treasure schemes, for as every trickster knows, the only bottomless treasure-chest in the world is human credulity.

In August of 1923 a 28-year-old laborer named Lee Hauser was swinging his pick on the Brownsville-Weverton Road project near Hagerstown, Maryland, when he struck a movable metal object. Picking it up, he found it was a $20 gold piece. He went on, according to his account, to unearth a tin box the size of a large cigar box full of gold coins, varying in denominations from $1 to $20.

He refused to tell reporters the sum of his treasure, but hinted that he would not have to work for a long time. The hoard, which he suggested might be as high as $10,000 (by 1923 valuation), was found in the road, on no private property, and Hauser's boss, George W. Ingram, opined that it was all Hauser's.

Later in the week the story grew more complicated. The Department of Justice suddenly became interested in Hauser's alleged find, and sent four special agents to Hagerstown, to look into the possibility that Hauser's gold might have been part of a cache amounting to some $110,000 in gold and

A power shovel tears up the main street of Green Cove Springs, as G. B. Mobley continues to egg his neighbors on in search of pirate treasure. The search left the sleepy Florida town with nothing but a lot of holes in the ground.

In 1939, Mrs. Thomas J. Middleton was troubled by a dream of buried money. She consulted a psychic, who gave her the good news: the treasure not only existed, but it was hidden in her own back yard. Mrs. Middleton hired a steam shovel and removed most of her yard. No treasure.

The Hollywood Bowl parking lot would seem an unlikely spot for buried treasure, but not to Henry Jones. In 1939 the mining expert used a mysterious electrochemical device he called a "doodlebug" to pinpoint what he insisted was a cache of Mexican gold valued at $200,000.

Erecting a picket fence around the spot, square in the middle of the Bowl's parking lot, he began to dig. His efforts netted him a lot of attention, but no loot. So much for the "doodlebug."

bills which was believed to have been buried in the region by a World War I draft evader and German sympathizer named Grover Cleveland Bergdoll.

The Bergdoll case was notorious in the Hagerstown-Harper's Ferry area. In 1921 Bergdoll was on the run from Federal authorities, who were trying to catch him for draft-dodging during the First World War. His activities seem to have involved even shadier business: while staying in a hotel in Hagerstown, Grover and his brother Erwin allegedly received about $150,000 from person or persons unknown. According to the hotel keeper, Owen B. Sherley, Bergdoll hauled the hoard off in an automobile and buried most of it in five new valises "as heavy as lead." Sherley went on to state that Bergdoll used some of the money to make his escape to Germany, and later sent the hotel-keeper several post-cards from the German town of Eberbach, near Baden. According to Sherley, Bergdoll had heard of the Hauser find, and insisted that it was part of his hidden treasure.

The money had been mentioned before. When Bergdoll's mother was testifying before a House of Representatives committee investigating the Bergdoll escape, she had brought the subject up, but had refused to reveal the hiding place of the hoard. Federal authorities believed the story, and had already made some inquiries in the Hagerstown area at the time Hauser reported his discovery.

However, on August 28th, 1923, Miss Esther Hauser announced firmly that her brother Lee had made the whole story up. The Federals were not convinced. Hauser's fellow-workers stoutly maintained that they had been nearby when the gold had been dug up, and that Hauser was too sober and serious a fellow to play practical jokes.

The farce continued for several days. Finally Hauser himself, alarmed at the proportions his joke was assuming, came clean. The Bergdoll money was famous in the area, he said, and he and his fellow-laborers had decided to use the story as a way of making a worker in the road gang, who was known as a tightwad, feel envious. The only thing which he dug up, Hauser said, was a rusty can. And the only money left on the site was a dime which had dropped from the pocket of a small boy watching the road work.

The search for the Bergdoll gold went on, even so. But it is probable that Bergdoll was a better hoaxer even than Hauser and his friends. Federal authorities and local police spent a goodly sum of public money in the search, and as far as the records show, never even found the little boy's dime.

The "silly season" in the summer of 1929 was enlivened by a series of reports from the trial of Edward Emile Jochen, swindler *par excellence*, whose complicated scheme for bilking a British bullion merchant had finally caught up with him. Jochen, an American citizen, had apparently gone to England with the express purpose of finding a likely mark for his scheme, which was a pretty one as such things go. It involved that perennial favorite of treasure-hunters, the proverbial Spanish plate galleon. Jochen's mythical ship had supposedly been bound from Mexico with a cargo of Aztec silver worth $25 million, when she went down "somewhere off Bermuda." The wily trickster

chose his ground well, as the Bermuda reefs are a famous graveyard for shipping. Teddy Tucker, the well-known Bermuda diver and salvage expert, has recently prepared a map which shows the location of 38 wrecks he has investigated himself, and a good portion of them are Spanish treasure ships.

Jochen quickly found a victim, in the person of A. J. Pennelier. Having set himself up in a good London hotel, Jochen obtained an introduction to the wealthy British bullion merchant, and told him that he had the rights to sell some 50 million ounces of silver which he claimed he knew to be buried under a dummy cargo of sulphur in the hull of the old Spanish hulk.

Pennelier's greed seems to have gotten the better of him. The Englishman knew that anyone who could get hold of so large an amount of silver would be able to control the price of the metal all over Europe, and would make a fortune far in excess of Jochen's estimate of the treasure's worth. He advanced the swindler $5,000 toward salvage expenses.

Jochen then travelled to Paris, where he contacted another bullion expert and sold him the same tale. The French mark bit even harder than Pennelier, and Jochen returned to England $12,500 richer.

Pennelier in the meantime had grown anxious for at least partial delivery of his silver, and Jochen obliged, handing over two pieces which he had cut from a metal skillet and doctored to resemble old Mexican ingots.

By now the tale of the treasure galleon had given way to a version in which the silver had already been raised, and was the property of the heirs of the late President Obregon of Mexico, Jochen maintaining that he had been appointed their agent in disposing of the hoard. But Jochen had gone too far with the bogus "ingots." Pennelier informed British authorities that he had been bilked of the $5,000, and Jochen was charged with fraud.

Lieutenant Colonel W. Grant Morden, Conservative Member of Parliament, was the chief witness against Jochen during the trial. He testified that he had been introduced to the American in New York.

"I entered into a guarantee (with Jochen) to get a man to find a purchaser (for the silver). Later I saw Jochen in England. He said that he had made other arrangements for disposing of the silver and remarked that he had a contract with Pennelier. He added he would arrange to set aside $500,000 for those who had assisted him last year, to reimburse them for expenses they had incurred."

Jochen, conducting his own defense, denied the charges of fraud. He stated that he had offered to return Pennelier's $5,000 and that in addition he had offered the merchant 2 per cent interest on the net sale of the silver for breaking the contract. He maintained that the only reason he had not delivered the silver to Pennelier was because he had received a higher bid from the Paris merchant.

On cross-examination Jochen said that the treasure ship had been raised, and was on the sea up to the day of his arrest. But he refused to disclose its name. He said the vessel had been afloat eighteen months, with the wages of the captain and crew manning it amounting to $4,000 monthly. The wages, he insisted, were paid by the owners of the silver, who lived in Texas, Mexico and California.

Flim-flams and foolery concerning hidden treasure provide the press with an endless source of "silly season" articles.

GOVERNMENT SEEKS BERGDOLL GOLD FIND

Four Secret Service Men Go
Investigate $110,000
Up Near Ha

PREPARED TO

Miller Cites Law for
Treasure if Buried
Draft Evader.

Special to The New York Ti
WASHINGTON, Aug. 27
cial agents of the Depart
versed in the intrica
case were today
Maryland to
box cont
matel
of

TALE OF HIDDEN GOLD SETS GREENWICH AGOG

Ex-Convict, Arrested While Digging, Says Thief Buried $150,000 in Park.

Special to The New York Times.
GREENWICH, Conn., Jan. 10.—Mystery surrounds the detention here of an Austrian who has just ended a term in Sing Sing Prison and who came to Greenwich recently and asked for a permit to dig a hole in Bruce Park. He was arrested while Sing Sing prisoner. Rumor it that another Sing Sing and who tenced for life in 1916 and who died, told the Austrian that stolen and buried $160,000 sou upper bridge near a rock in Br He had a chart, the story ing the exact location, and now said to be in possession thorities.

Another version is that who supposed to he money received it for con der in New York City. as grown-ups, have b ging an search stopp but have been It is alleged it was in Kol Many per day, and guarded Park an been g tho nown p d in tance oney

All Baba's Cave Located.

Special Correspondence. THE NEW YORK TIMES.
MADRID, April 2.—Ali Baba's cave really does exist in the south of Spain. Police found a cache of stolen goods there among a labyrinth of caves near Alicante. Valuable religious articles were among the plunder. Whether there were one or forty thieves, however, no one knows, as the police made no arrests.

Ha
Harper
that while G
doll were in Ha
50,000 was taken to
Hotel Vivian, and later had
an automobile by Grover to a po
the mountains near the Potomac R
where it is alleged to have been bur
for temporary safekeeping. Owen
Sherley, the hotel proprietor, is now
credited with having stated that the
Bergdolls d five new valises "as
heavy as lead," which they guarded
with revolvers until they took them

JOCHEN GETS YEAR IN JAIL.

He Is Found Guilty in Bullion Case
of $5,000 Check Fraud.

Wireless to THE NEW YORK TIMES.
LONDON, July 25.—Edward Emile Jochen was sentenced by Judge Greg ory at the Old Bailey today to twelve months' imprisonment with hard labor at the conclusion of the four days' hearing of the bullion ship case.

Jochen was found "guilty" of a charge of obtaining from a bullion merchant a check for $5,000 with fraudulent intent. and "not guilt of a charge of stealing the check Jochen said in court today he alleged the ship he go of silver was the Tropic be somewhere d fou

TOIL THREE MONTHS FOR 'DREAM' MONEY

Four Hawaiians Have Dug Shaft 80 Feet Deep, but Have Found No Wealth.

Special Correspondence of The New York Times.

HONOLULU, July 11.—For more than 100 years the uplifting force of civilization has been felt in these islands. The first missionaries reached Hawaii in 1820 and their example and their teaching placed an early curb upon superstition and "kahunalism," as the witchcraft of the old natives was known. Through the influence of these church workers and through the school system of the territory, men and women of Polynesian ancestry mounted to high places, gauged even by the white man's standard of measurement.

But in spite of all the progress made in the century those of native blood living here today occasionally sink back into the mental night which enveloped the peoples ruled by the kings of old. The latest example of this primitive ignorance is embodied in a treasure hunt which a group of Hawaiians have undertaken in the eastern section of the city.

...ho authority of a 99-year-old woman, ... appeared the fire goddess ... a pillar of flame, standing ... rtain spot in the yard that ... the ancient's home. "Be- ... ty spoke, pointing to the ... body of a man, buried ... and his money. Dig ... find it."

...them to labor for the last three months, digging a shaft twenty feet in circumference and eighty feet deep in the calm conviction that eventually they will come upon the "treasure," said to amount to $25,000 in "five-cornered coins of the old monarchy."

So well had they kept their secret to themselves, working after dark, that their quest came to light only this week. In the daytime the quartet is employed during the day. In the late evening they adorn themselves with turbans of blue cloth and drape a sash about their hips to warn away the "evil spirits." Two and two they then descend their shaft and take 'urns with the digging, the pair on the surface hauling up the material excavated by their confederates and dumping it. Ukulele music and incantations, mouthed by the daughter of the aged woman of the dream, accompany their efforts.

The seekers have removed tons of debris, but so far have found nothing out of the ordinary with the exception of a smooth, spherically shaped stone which they devoutly believed to be an omen of good fortune. The canoe and the money, they confided to newspaper men this week, can be but a little further down, and that this rock has been uncovered added ramification was closed in the district court this week with the trial of another yesterday the owner of the land upon which the shaft is being sunk, disclosed, after her arrest by the Moanalua police officer, and there are involved pleading ...

Among the alleged owners, he mentioned Adolf Rosas, secretary of the late President Obregon of Mexico; the Mexican Minister to Spain; and one Colonel Gomez and his family.

"Could you produce anyone who has seen the cargo of silver?" the prosecuting attorney asked.

"If I had the money and was allowed to cable, I could get any number of men," Jochen answered.

But the Court was not impressed. Jochen then announced that the name of the treasure ship was the *Tropical Sea*, and that she was even now standing by somewhere in the North Sea. "No such ship," was the opinion of the Court, and Jochen was sentenced by Judge Gregory to twelve months at hard labor in Old Bailey on July 26, 1929.

After the jury had found Jochen guilty he was identified by fingerprints as a man who had been sent to the penitentiary back in the United States for fifteen years in 1919, on a charge of embezzlement. But Jochen, maintaining a bold front to the last, firmly denied he was that man.

November 9-20, 1934
THE GNOMES OF PALISADES PARK

The New York Times ran the following story on the front page, and according to a reader who wrote to say that he had almost forgotten to eat his breakfast because he had been so engrossed in it, it made the "most sparkling little newspaper story" in many months, during the blackest period of the Great Depression.

The tale of a hunt for long-buried treasure deep in the wilds of the Harriman section of Palisades Interstate Park, of the destruction of the side of a mountain during the search and of double-dealing and chicanery was first unfolded on the 8th of November, 1934, by Major William A. Welch, general manager and chief engineer of the Park.

For many months rangers in the Interstate Park, seven miles below Bear Mountain, had been hearing mysterious echoes like thunder in the vicinity of Letterrock Mountain in broad daylight when there were no thunderheads in the sky.

William Gee, chief ranger, and a man who knows his Washington Irving, was a bit uneasy. He recalled the legend of the gnomes in "Rip Van Winkle," the flagon-quaffing little men who make thunder with their ninepins. But he decided to leave them out of his speculations.

Finally one day his men came upon a fresh scar, huge and widespread, on the side of old Letterrock, and in a deep hole in the ground not far away, a cache of mining tools, pneumatic drills, hammers and dynamite. They confiscated the stuff.

For weeks the rangers and the Bear Mountain State police tried to fill in the puzzle. They kept a watch on the Letterrock site. On the morning of October 27th, 1934 one of the rangers saw four little men, all hunched under loads of mining tools and more dynamite, toiling up the mountain trail.

The little men put down their loads carefully, listened awhile for suspicious sounds, and, hearing nothing, set to work. One drilled a hole in the mountainside, another plugged it with dynamite, and a third lit the fuse. The little men backed off to a safe distance, the charge went off, the countryside

rocked with the detonation, and the echo rolled back like thunder.

Chief Ranger Gee and his men, who had been concealed nearby, emerged at this point and surrounded the little men, ordering them to drop their tools. The strangers, not gnomes after all, but human, if diminutive, and furious at having been interrupted, obeyed reluctantly.

As the rangers marched their prisoners down Lake Tiorati Brook Road they came upon a large truck hidden in the trees. It carried more dynamite and tools.

The amateur miners were eventually persuaded to talk, after lengthy interrogation by rangers and police. They gave up copies of a contract which each of them held. It bound them to turn over to a fifth individual whatever treasure they found on Letterrock Mountain.

The men admitted they had been hired to hunt for a great hoard of silver bars and barrels of silver coins hidden somewhere in a cave on the mountain. The secret of the spot, and how to reach it, they insisted, came out of a faded map in the Morgan Library in New York City. They had been sent into the park, a few at a time, to blast away the mountainside in search of the cave. They tried, whenever possible, to time their blasts with the blasts of a team of CWA (a Government relief agency which provided work for the unemployed during the Depression) laborers who were putting a road through the park, so as not to arouse suspicion.

The men would not reveal the "master mind" behind the treasure hunt, but examination of the names on their contracts turned up a mysterious Bronx syndicate of silver hunters.

The four "little men" said they were Bernard Lantt, E. Gothberg, Fred Johnson, and Albert K. Carlson. But the addresses they gave, in Manhattan and the Bronx, were spurious, one of them turning out to be the location of a bakers' supply plant, J. Grob & Co., where none of the men had been heard of.

At this point manager Welch remembered that some time ago he had received a letter from a man named Charles W. Wenk asking him for permission to search for a cave in the Harriman section of Palisades Park, which Wenk believed contained treasure. Major Welch had agreed, promising to send some rangers into the woods with Wenk, but adding that he himself did not believe there were any caves of extensive size in the territory. No answer ever came from Wenk, and the matter was dropped.

The rangers looked up Wenk, who was surprised by the story of the four treasure-hunters and their arrest. He maintained that he knew nothing about their search, and that he himself had not been ready to start his own hunt for the treasure. Wenk had gotten the tale of the cave from a man named George Gyra, with whom he had worked some years before in the Vanderbilt Garage on East 33rd Street near Lexington Avenue. Gyra went off for awhile to work on a CWA project in Palisades Park, related Wenk.

"He wandered away from the other CWA workers at lunch time one day," Wenk continued. "Quite by accident he found a small crevice in the mountainside. It was barely large enough to admit a man, but he crawled inside. It was dark, and he lit matches, but they made hardly a splash in that

Mrs. Ova Noss of Las Cruces, New Mexico, started the Victorio Mountain "gold rush" with a story that her late husband, Earl "Doc" Noss, had found the hoard. There was only one problem: Victorio Mountain lies in the middle of the top-secret White Sands Missile Range.

great dome of darkness. He threw stones, trying to hit the opposite wall of the cave, but they didn't hit. Then he crawled out again. There was another man with him, and they both say that when George came out of the cave they found bits of silver or gold clinging to George's breeches.

"He made a sketch of the spot and came home and told me about it, and I said: 'There's only one way to go about this, George; we must write to the Governor.'"

Which Wenk did; the letter was forwarded to Major Welch. Wenk maintained he was too ill to begin seeking for the silver or gold or whatever it was that had come off on the trousers of his friend. So Major Welch followed up the story himself.

The area around Letterrock, according to Welch, was rich in treasure lore. One story told of a lode called Spanish Silver Mine, on Black Mountain, a mile east of Letterrock, where Spaniards up from the West Indies were supposed to have buried treasure.

The Major also investigated the supposed Morgan Library map. He found a letter dated circa 1690, which said, in part, "Start at Samuel More's landing and go to Belcates, which is three miles across the mountain that leads to New Windsor. You follow marked oak trees, and when you get on the mountain, turn to the right hand. Keep on till you come to a bog meadow. Cross an old dam. Keep on until you come to old Indian fields, then Stony Brook. Keep up that brook half a mile, then turn to the right hand to a brook that leads between two mountains. Keep down that brook one mile until you come to some large rocks. Then you are close to the mine. In the mine is bars of silver and two barrels of dollars, hid in a crack of the rock near the brook. This brook empties into the Hudson River."

These directions, said the Major, are rather vague, but if the writer meant the stream now known as Stony Brook, its highest waters rise two miles west of Letterrock Mountain, but anyone going up the brook and crossing to a stream flowing into the Hudson might possibly reach Stillwater Brook, south of Letterrock.

The four "little men" were released, after paying a fine of $25 each for defacing State property and possessing explosives without a permit. Park officials tried to track down some of the names signed to the treasure contract, and turned up only one of the strange silver syndicate, a part-time Manhattan barber named Nick Carbonaro who lived near the old Third Avenue "L." Carbonaro said only, "I know nothing about this treasure. I do not know how my name comes on that paper." He stuck to his story, denying all knowledge of the syndicate and saying he had never heard of any of the men mentioned. Then he returned to finish his haircut.

The story did not quite stop there. A day later William H. Carr of the American Museum of Natural History, who was director of the Museum's Trailside branch in Palisades Park, came forward to state that he had seen the four treasure hunters an hour or so after they had been found out by Park rangers and State Police. They insisted, said Mr. Carr, that they had found landmarks matching an arrowhead-shaped rock on a map in their possession, which allegedly pointed to a spot where Spaniards had buried their loot,

Victorio Mountain, New Mexico, was scarred by the bulldozers of treasure hunters in March of 1977, as they searched for $350 million in gold bars supposedly hidden there.

The government gave Expeditions Unlimited, a company of treasure hunters, permission to bring in teams of diggers and a backhoe for a limited period. Except for a caveful of graffiti, tin cans and unexploded dynamite left by earlier prospectors, all the group found were some Indian artifacts.

221

Stories continue to circulate in Arkansas and Missouri about caches of booty supposedly left here and there by the notorious James Gang. Fred Emerson and Gene Wirges, shown at the bottom of the hole they dug near Paragould, Arkansas in 1953, thought they were on the verge of recovering gang loot, when their probe "hit something." But most historians agree that Frank James died broke, and Jesse used his share of the gang's booty to set up as the respectable householder known as "Mr. Howard," before he was shot in the back by ex-gang-member Bob Ford. Ford's $10,000 reward for the slaying of Jesse James was the only "treasure" reliably associated with the outlaw.

along with the bodies of 3,000 Indians whom they had been using as slaves in their silver mine. The tale sounded plausible enough to Mr. Carr, and he was even more strongly persuaded that the "little men" (whom he described, despite Major Welch's romantic identification of the treasure-hunters with Irving's gnomes, as being quite tall) were on the track of something valuable, when they broke down and wept in front of the Park rangers, offering them $5,000 of their mysterious backer's money in return for being allowed to continue blasting into Letterrock Mountain.

But the four were unceremoniously kicked out of the park. Mr. Carr could not resist having a try himself. He persuaded John T. Tamsen, superintendent of the Harriman section of the park, to allow him to make a test of the

area for possible hidden caves. He maintained that by listening for variations in the ground reverberations caused by setting off a blast of dynamite, he could tell whether or not there was a cave in the vicinity. The superintendent authorized the test, and the charge was duly detonated. No cave.

Whoever the members of the syndicate were, what they were trying to find, if anything, and the roles of Charles Wenk and the part-time barber Nick Carbonaro in the affair, are questions which were never answered. The story of the "gnomes" of Palisades Park can safely be chalked up to the prevailing desire for "something for nothing" which pervaded the atmosphere of the Depression.

In 1911 the Ward Line steamship *Merida* was en route to New York from Mexico via Havana. On the final leg up the U. S. coast she had reached a point some fifty miles off Cape Charles, Virginia by the early morning of May 12th. The sky was overcast and visibility was poor, though apparently not bad enough to justify the use of the liner's foghorn. In those pre-radar days she was steaming blind, but safely on course, when suddenly she was rammed by the United Fruit Company's steamer *Admiral Farragut*. The *Merida* filled slowly, and her telegrapher had time to send S. O. S. messages which were received by other vessels in the vicinity. All her passengers and crew were rescued before the abandoned liner went down in 240 feet of water.

Because of her Mexican port of embarcation, rumors immediately built up concerning immense treasure in the *Merida's* cargo. 1911 marked the fall of the Diaz regime in Mexico, and the liner's passenger list included many wealthy Mexicans fleeing the revolutionaries. The most romantic rumor, which inspired the first salvage expeditions, concerned the fortune of the immensely rich Madero family, and the even more fabulous crown jewels of the Empress Carlotta, wife of the hapless nineteenth-century Mexican ruler Maximilian. Early estimates of the values of the treasure ranged as high as $6 million.

But the Maximilian connection proved to be wishful thinking on the part of the treasure-hunters. An examination of the records, confirmed by a letter to *The New York Times* in the 1930s, shows that in 1867, when the Maximilian empire in Mexico crashed, the Emperor was broke. He was unable even to raise the few thousand pesos required to bribe his guards and effect his escape after his capture by the Liberals in Queretaro.

Empress Carlotta, who in 1866 had journeyed to Europe in a vain attempt to obtain political and financial aid for the tottering empire, carried her jewels with her. The imperial exchequer was then so low that Maximilian was compelled to draw for Carlotta's expenses upon the fund for the floodwater drainage system of the valley of Mexico City.

But in 1925 a report had surfaced which suggested that the *Merida's* cargo, if not as romantic as the legendary Maximilian jewels, still justified serious salvage attempts. A resident of Mexico City named M. J. Trazivuk, who had served as ship's purser during the *Merida's* last voyage, came up with details of the contents of his office on board, where valuables were stored, as well as a report on the ship's main cargo. Hemp, beans, chicle and sugar made up the brunt of the latter, Trazivuk said, but the cargo also included silver and gold bars. In addition to the precious metals in the cargo hold, several more tons of silver and a few gold bars were stored in a locker in the purser's main deck office. Trazivuk recalled that the load was so heavy that the *Merida's* skipper ordered bracing to be placed under the locker to prevent it from crushing.

The liner's passengers also made 45 deposits, in sealed envelopes, to the purser's private office. The value of the deposits was uncertain, but it was estimated at a large figure, since the passengers were some of the richest Mexicans of the era. They included a Montes banker, a controller of sisal production, the Archbishop of Yucatán, the scions of two plutocratic Yucatán families, a millionaire shoe manufacturer named Carlos Zetina, and a number of

Facing Page:
Inventor-diver Harry L. Bowdoin led a heavily-capitalized hunt for the *Merida* treasure in 1931, aboard the tug *Salvor*. Bowdoin worked on submarine designs in World War I, like his contemporary, Simon Lake. He is best known for his innovations in the design of diving suits and other divers' gear, and his pride and joy was this huge, scoop-equipped underwater "robot," built for the *Merida* expedition.

other well-heeled refugees from the Mexican Revolution.

Trazivuk believed that an additional source, perhaps the richest, of jewelry and valuables was the personal baggage of the gilded passengers, as many of them preferred to keep their cash and the best of their baubles in their own trunks.

For the benefit of treasure-hunters who were vitally interested in the "lay" of the ship and her treasure on the bottom, the ex-purser recalled that as the *Merida* went down she listed to starboard, causing the silver and gold bars in his main deck locker to shift and burst the doors. He believed the bars went over the side as the ship sank.

In addition to the precious metals and jewelry cited by Trazivuk, the ship's cargo manifest also showed a consignment of mahogany worth $500,000 at 1911 valuation. The close-grained, dense wood keeps well in sea-water, and would still be worth quite a lot if raised today. The ship also carried 4,700 tons of copper as ballast, a good part of which would be well worth salvaging.

The most sensible estimate of the *Merida's* treasure is between $2 million and $4 million, of which $500,000 consists of gold ingots, the rest being made up of silver, passengers' jewelry, ship's funds, and the copper and mahogany. The wreck has attracted salvors from 1911 to shortly before World War II, and for a time was a favorite target of wealthy New York socialites having a fling at treasure hunting. Though professionals, notably the colorful Harry Bowdoin (NOTE: SEE *THE BALLAD OF CAPTAIN KIDD*), have taken a shot at the *Merida*, no serious salvage effort along the lines of the *Egypt* job has ever been attempted.

The *Merida* still lies in the rough chop off the Virginia Capes, where the cries of gulls overhead perhaps mingle with the ghostly screams of forty crates of unlucky parrots, part of the liner's cargo, which were trapped in their cages and went down with the ship.

June 29, 1911-
October 4, 1921
THE EARLIEST EXPEDITIONS

In June of 1911, only a month after the wreck of the *Merida*, a Captain Charles Williams of Norfolk, Virginia announced that he was raising money to form a salvage expedition to recover what he believed was $2 million in silver and general merchandise aboard the lost liner. So soon after the disaster, rumor had not had time to get to work on the *Merida* story, and Captain Williams' estimate of the value of the ship's cargo is probably close to the truth.

His plan for recovering the treasure was a little more far-fetched. He intended to use a diving device of his own invention, consisting of a long tube which would be let down from the surface, with a metal turret at its bottom end. Inside the turret, divers breathing ordinary air would operate mechanical manipulator-arms to cut through the wreckage and lift out the treasure. The apparatus was constructed of steel in three-foot sections, its joints covered by waterproof canvas, and the diving turret, large enough for two men, was equipped with glass windows. The Captain's "submarine caisson" was ahead of its time, and was never used. But the concept of a hollow, airtight, semi-flexible tube leading from surface to sea-bottom anticipated

the even wilder scheme of Simon Lake (NOTE: SEE *RAISE THE LUSITA NIA!*), which involved a submarine "elevator" to take divers down to a salvage site in ease and comfort. And Williams' turret with manipulator-arms showed up later in actual use, in the form of the "robot" diving suits of the Italian crew which salvaged the *Egypt* (q.v.) twenty years later.

The summer of 1916 brought a heavily-financed salvage expedition, incorporated as the Interocean Submarine Engineering Company and backed by Wall Street investors. A Captain Stillson commanded the fleet of three steamers which sailed for the *Merida's* grave off Cape Charles. The salvors set out marker buoys around the probable location of the wreck, and were courteous enough to warn shipping in the area about them, lest they prove the cause of another *Merida* disaster. But the expedition's steamers, after dragging the bottom within the perimeter of buoys for several days, were unable even to find the sunken liner.

In the fall of 1921 another group of New York financiers outfitted the steamship *Ripple*, which sailed from Norfolk with three experienced divers. Bad weather plagued the voyage, and the *Ripple*, her divers, and her "hand-picked crew of 25" returned unrewarded.

In 1924 a fourth salvage effort was mounted. The *Merida* had become something of a favorite with New York financiers and socialites, and this venture was solidly in the tradition. It should be remembered that "treasure hunts" of the whimsical variety were a favorite party game among the aristocratic "flaming youth" of the 1920s in London and New York, and perhaps the urge to capture the attention of the social season by setting up a quest for the real thing had something to do with the 1924 attempt. It was underwritten by a glittering group from New York's innermost social circle, including such luminaries as Anthony J. Drexel Biddle, Jr., W. Heyward Drayton 3rd, Worthington Davis and other bluebloods of the "Four Hundred."

By this time the legend of Maximilian's rubies was as firmly fixed to the hulk of the *Merida* as her barnacles, and the wealthy treasure-hunters set sail with high hopes aboard two converted trawlers, the *Foam* and the *Spray*. An aura of professionalism was lent the expedition by the presence of three divers, including Frank J. Crilley and Fredelin C.C. Nellson, former United States Navy submariners who had helped raise the World War I submarine *F-4* from the bottom of Honolulu Harbor in 1914. Equipped with dragging gear and the latest in diving suits, the *Foam* and *Spray* spent October and November, 1924, reconnoitering the wreck site off Virginia.

Heavy seas rendered the diving work too hazardous for a sustained effort, and the trawlers gave up and put in to Norfolk to wait out the winter. They set off again in June, 1925. By now the treasure estimate had swollen to $4 million, "smuggled out of Mexico by revolutionists" (in emulation, no doubt, of the rum-runners who provided the aristocratic treasure-hunters with their grog at this Prohibition-bound period). But even the blue-ribbon combination of New York money and Navy divers couldn't prevail against the sea and the weather. A diver from one of the trawlers reported that he had found

October 1, 1924-
July 3, 1925
THE "SILK STOCKING" EXPEDITION

July 11, 1931-
May 21, 1933

BOWDOIN'S VENTURE

Captain Eric Sealander, commander of the *Salvor*, looks out of his depth as he poses in the hatch of Bowdoin's diving bell. The device could carry four divers below at normal air pressure, eliminating danger of the bends.

Despite the ex-purser Trazivuk's factual account of the *Merida's* cargo, the Maximilian legend lingered, and in the summer of 1931 another group of prominent New Yorkers raised money to outfit a fifth try for the sunken treasure. The Sub-Ocean Salvage Company, as the outfit was called, sent out a 500-ton ocean-going tug, the *Salvor*, under the command of the veteran diver and inventor Harry L. Bowdoin, then a hale 63 years old.

Bowdoin, like his fellow submarine inventor Simon Lake, was typical of the pioneers of underwater salvage in the years between the World Wars. Oceanography was in its infancy, and of little interest to investors. Submarine and diving innovators depended for financial support upon the romantic effect the subject of sunken treasure had upon the purse-strings of the wealthy, until the Second World War brought military attention to bear upon the technology of underwater warfare. In addition to diving skill, courage and genuine inventiveness in the field of submarine engineering, the submariner of the early years needed a good knack for self-advertisement, and this Bowdoin had in full measure. He had no trouble convincing his backers that his many underwater inventions, including a rigid metal diving suit and special deepwater diving tanks, would make the recovery of the *Merida's* treasure a simple question of engineering.

For two seasons the doughty Bowdoin guided the *Salvor* and its crew of divers in search of the elusive *Merida*. Finally, in the fall of 1932, Bowdoin announced that he had located the wreck. He planned to begin diving operations the following spring.

But in April, 1933, a rival group of salvors led by Captain John Hall and diver Klass Evarts prepared to go after the treasure. Bowdoin, racing to complete his own preparations, slapped a court injunction on the Hall-Evarts expedition to keep them from diving on what he claimed was his rightful possession by reason of prior discovery.

Captain Hall ignored the injunction, and his trawler *Theresa and Dan* sailed for the wreck site in May. Bowdoin's *Salvor* managed to beat Hall and Evarts to the marker buoys, and for several days it looked as if the two vessels were going to do battle for possession of the sunken liner. Bowdoin radioed the Coast Guard asking for help to prevent "trouble with interlopers." The Coast Guard, somewhat bemused at the prospect of naval warfare off the Virginia Capes, dispatched the destroyer *Davis* with instructions to prevent hostilities between the rival salvors, but not to interfere with either expedition. On May 10th Captain Hall gave up and returned to his normal occupation of fishing, leaving Captain Bowdoin in triumphant possession of the hulk.

But Hall's capitulation was not without a parting salvo, fired in the press if not at sea. Arriving ashore on the 11th of May, Hall told reporters that during the high-seas standoff the *Salvor* had crossed the *Theresa and Dan's* bows, cutting one of her anchor chains. "It was a deliberate act of piracy on the high seas, and we're appealing to the courts to protect our rights," the out-

The *Salvor*, outfitted with a heavy crane and winch for lowering and raising Bowdoin's ponderous diving bell (at left), had a run-in with a rival salvage ship near the *Merida* wreck site. Bowdoin and company chased off the intruder, but never pin-pointed the *Merida* on the bottom. The "robot," which performed well in tests, scarcely even got wet on the expedition.

raged Captain protested.

Bowdoin ignored him, being too busy diving on his prize in his tanklike mechanical diving suit, similar in design to those being used at the same time in the Bay of Biscay by the salvors of the *Egypt.* Bowdoin had identified his wreck as the *Merida* in his 1932 expedition, basing his belief on the placement of her stacks and the position of her masts. Using powerful lights of his own invention, Bowdoin and his first lieutenant, John McElberon, a Navy diver, announced that they had relocated the wreck, "knew every portion of her," and were heading straight for her strong-room.

But the report did not prove out. The Bowdoin expedition, which had provided the public with the prospect of a revival of piratical combat on the high seas, returned to port having gained nothing but publicity.

The next search for the *Merida* hoard was mounted by one Thomas P. Connelly, one-time warden of the Jersey City jail. By 1936 a full-time treasure-hunter, Connelly formed a joint-stock firm with the resounding title of the Empire Marine Salvage and Engineering Corporation of New York. His brief expedition was unique in that his salvage vessel was a four-masted schooner, the *Constellation,* which set out for the treasure entirely under sail. The *Constellation,* skippered by an old windjammer hand, Captain Alvan Loesche, did not even have an auxiliary engine. A large, handsome holdover from the age of sail, the 1,045-ton schooner was built with a clipper hull 204 feet long with a 40-foot beam, at Harrington, Maine in 1918.

August 20-
September 4, 1936
HUNTING
TREASURE
UNDER SAIL

The lovely vessel ghosted out of Jersey City's Toothpick Dock on the 20th of August, 1936, with a crew of thirty, including four divers. Lashed to her mizzen-mast was a diving bell and several rigid-body diving suits.

She was also equipped with a lens-fitted steel tube for underwater observation of a donkey engine for her winch, air compressors, tanks and other diving paraphernalia.

The diving bell and solid steel-and-copper deepwater suits, built to descend as low as 2,000 feet, were Connelly's own inventions. They carried a built-in air supply and were connected by telephone cable with the surface.

Ray Hansen, another Navy diver who was linked with the recovery of the F-4 submarine in 1914 (see above), was signed as the expedition's diving chief.

He expressed enthusiasm about the suits and the diving bell.

"Why, I can stay down sixteen hours in one of those suits," he exulted. "I can't see any reason why we shouldn't clean up."

His excitement was reflected in his wild estimate of the value of the *Merida*'s cargo, which he placed at a starry-eyed $26 million, of which he was promised two percent if the salvage was successful.

The *Constellation*'s diving bell was to be used to take movies of the salvage work when the wreck had been found. A large store of nitroglycerine was stowed in the vessel's forward cargo hatch, for blasting into the hulk's treasure room. So with an intriguing combination of 1930s-modern underwater equipment, and a surface transport as old as the age of sail, the Connelly group headed for the Virginia Capes.

The *Constellation* reached a point about 50 miles off Hatteras toward the end of August. The crew believed they had found the *Merida,* and Hansen went down. But the schooner, lacking an engine, was difficult to hold in one place in the heavy swells, and Hansen was banged around all over the bottom without seeing anything but sharks.

The seas continued rough for two days while the *Constellation* cast about, dragging the gravelled bottom for the wreck. Finally a full gale struck, and the ton-and-a-half of nitroglycerine up forward began shifting about ominously. Captain Loesche prudently decided to crowd on sail and race for home. With every rag aloft, the *Constellation* bowled north, hauling so fast that she overtook a passenger steamer above Hatteras.

Her radio equipment was primitive, and her only link with land was through an 18-year-old ham operator who picked up her signals on the band reserved for amateurs and relayed her messages to the Empire Company's office. When authorities in Red Bank, New Jersey, where the schooner was bound, learned she was heading in with a cargo of nitroglycerine, they ordered her to stand off until an explosives expert from E. I. du Pont de Nemours' New York offices could board her and offload the touchy stuff. The transfer was made finally, and the *Constellation*'s cruise ended safely, if not lucratively. All she won was the glory of her wild run home, in which she became one of the last of the windjammers ever to outstrip a steamer, scudding along at 16 knots under all her canvas, while the steamer's passengers lined the rails and cheered.

After yet another failure in 1937, this one outfitted directly by the marine underwriters who held title to the *Merida,* a final expedition was set up in May of 1938. A well-equipped 500-ton steamer, the *Falco,* with an Italian crew, set off for the wreck site, and by July 8th they had found the sunken liner. Their divers had managed to get aboard her, and were using dynamite to clear a way into her treasure room, in imitation of the technique which had proved successful during their compatriots' salvage of the *Egypt.*

But the *Falco* crew lacked the *Artiglio* divers' finesse and patience. In August a dynamite charge was set off which caused the *Merida's* entire upper deck to collapse, crushing the purser's locker-room beneath tons of metal, and blocking the way into the liner's cargo hold. The *Falco* was not equipped for the weary work of removing the debris, and a spokesman cited other wreckage obstructing access to the treasure, which he maintained had been caused by careless use of explosives by other expeditions. Wherever the fault lay, the *Merida's* treasure room was rendered even more inaccessible than rough seas and foul weather could make it, and the *Falco* sailed homeward empty.

She tried again in 1939. The total cost to the Italian backers of the two voyages was over $100,000, and the *Falco* netted only a single silver bar, worth $7.20 at the time. But that solitary ingot was more than all the other expeditions had recovered, and it provided tangible proof at last, that although the crown jewels of the Empress of Mexico might have been a fantasy, there was indeed something worth looking for 240 feet beneath the waters off Cape Charles.

September 21, 1937-
August 15, 1939
THE QUEST OF THE FALCO

The 150-mile-long strand of tiny coral islands between Miami and Key West has been associated with Spanish treasure since the earliest years of the *conquistadores*. Galleons bearing the loot of the Indians, and the later bullion and plate fleets of Spanish Mexico, had to pass through the Straits of Florida after embarking from Havana on the last leg of their wallowing journey home. Driven astray and destroyed by the vicious hurricanes common to the area, scores of vessels went down over the three hundred years of Spanish hegemony in the New World.

Understandably, treasure hunting has long been a major preoccupation among the "conchs," as the natives of the Florida Keys call themselves. Proud of their descent from a genetic *bouillabaisse* of pirates, privateers and Spanish captains, the conchs have a different treasure tale for every one of the myriad inlets, coves and straits of the chain of islets. And in a departure from the normal run of treasure legends, many of the stories turn out to be true.

In 1946, divers headed by Irwin Williamson succeeded in locating one of the earliest Spanish wrecks, the galleon *Santa Rosa*, which went down off Key West in 1542. Williamson's first dive on the wreck turned up a human skull in a primitive diving helmet. The drowned diver, who had no air supply other than that contained in his helmet itself, was found in more than 100 feet of water, and had probably died during an attempt by the Spanish themselves to salvage their lost treasure sometime in the seventeenth century. For it is a "Catch-22" of salvage work on Spanish wrecks off the Keys, that on the one hand modern divers would be helpless without Spanish records and charts to guide them in their search for early galleons, and on the other, the existence of the same records is proof that divers of the old Spanish Empire have in most cases salvaged the wrecks before them.

Nonetheless, the early Spanish salvors missed enough booty to justify continuing hunts. No gold was brought up during Williamson's *Santa Rosa* expedition, but the Mexican Government placed enough credence in the estimated $30 million in looted Aztec gold which the vessel was reputed to have been carrying, to put in its claim for a share of the treasure.

Mexico's grabby reaction presaged that of the State of Florida twenty years later, when Kip Wagner and his Real Eight/Treasure Salvors companies brought up a rich haul of galleon treasure off the state's east coast (NOTE: SEE *THE TREASURE COAST OF FLORIDA*). Florida's Antiquities Act of 1965 was a draconian measure designed to regulate treasure hunting in state waters, and to establish Florida's right to all valuable marine salvage. It required salvors to sign a contract with the state which stipulated that all expeditions after sunken treasure be accompanied by a representative from the State Board of Antiquities. Further stipulations established state control over all artifacts of historical or scientific value discovered, and firmly set the state's share of salvaged treasure at 25 per cent. Its real thrust was to discourage wildcat treasure hunters and to set up stringent controls for the issuing of treasure hunting permits.

Wagner's post-1965 discoveries resulted in some court fights, but the pioneer of Florida treasure salvage emerged with the lion's share of the gold

Facing Page: Contemporary treasure salvors, substitute flexible wetsuits and light scuba gear for the heavy diving suits of earlier days. The cannon in the foreground is an obvious clue to an ancient wreck in the vicinity. In most cases coral growth and the changing topography of the sea floor make identification of sunken ships far more difficult.

Martin Meylach jubilantly holds up a coral-encrusted Spanish musket from the *Tres Puentes*, a sunken galleon the weekend treasure buff found in 1962. He kept the musket and other salvaged artifacts from the wreck submerged in his swimming pool, to prevent their deterioration on contact with the air.

he found. Florida was determined, evidently, to do better in the future, and a series of major discoveries off the Keys, beginning in 1969, offered the state a chance to test the teeth of the Antiquities Act.

The Keys treasure story begins earlier, with a diving expedition in 1962, headed by a boat carpenter and weekend treasure hunter named Martin Meylach. Meylach and his associates succeeded in hauling up artifacts, including pottery, timbers, religious medallions and muskets, from a wreck off Islamorada. Meylach believed his ship, which he identified by a cigar-shaped mound of ballast stones 65 feet by 12 feet on the sandy bottom (all that was visible of the hulk), was a galleon known in Spanish records as the *Tres Puentes*. His research revealed that the *Tres Puentes* had been one of a fleet of 17 plate ships commanded by Don Rodrigo de Torres y Moralles, which was carrying twenty million pesos' worth of silver from Vera Cruz when a hurricane struck it on July 15th, 1733. Early Spanish salvage efforts provided Meylach's key to the treasure, in the form of an eighteenth-century chart upon which were marked the graves of the hurricane-shattered galleons. A copy of the chart, which is in the British Museum, guided Meylach and his associates to what he identified as the *Tres Puentes*. Working in scuba gear with a vacuum hose for clearing away the sand which buried the wreck, Meylach brought up a variety of eighteenth-century artifacts, but no silver. It is probable that the Spanish themselves recovered most of this particular vessel's precious cargo back in the 1700s.

But the 1733 wreck continued to excite salvors in the Keys. In 1971 a mysterious crate was raised from a vessel identified by marine archaeologist Carl Claussen as the *San Fernando*, another of the unlucky Don Rodrigo's fleet. Claussen was careful to point out that he did not expect the chest to contain treasure, during the time when painstaking preparations were being made for opening the ancient, sea-changed wooden chest without destroying it. He was right. It held nothing but 15,000 sailmakers' needles.

As a member of Florida's Board of Archives and History, Claussen took a dim view of treasure-hunters in general. In a statement made in September, 1971, he spelled out the state's position succinctly.

"We look at shipwrecks," he said, "not in terms of treasure, but for their historical and archaeological value, and take the position that everything on the bottom belongs to the state."

He labelled treasure hunting, at least in Florida, as a losing proposition, and reminded would-be salvors that the state required a $600 permit fee and a security bond of $5,000, for the right to search an area no larger than 18 square miles, for a period of no more than a year. The most important part of Claussen's statement, and Florida's position, in light of later developments, was his assertion that the salvor had no guarantee of keeping anything that he found.

Claussen's views reflected those of the scientists and marine archaeologists who made up the majority of the opposition to treasure salvors in Florida, and who had been largely responsible for the passage of the Antiquities Act. According to them, treasure divers were no better than pirates who destroyed priceless historical artifacts in their search for marketable gold, silver and

jewels. The famous Parke Bernet auction of art objects and coins from Wagner's mid 1960s finds (NOTE: SEE *THE TREASURE COAST OF FLORIDA*) did little to reassure Florida's scientific and historical community, which maintained that even if Wagner's divers had taken pains to salvage artifacts of historical value intact, they had piratically proceeded to sell their art treasures to the highest bidder, instead of donating them to the state of Florida.

Claussen finished his statement by advancing his opinion that the 1733 treasure ships had already been stripped of most of their plate, bullion and coins by Spanish salvage expeditions mounted shortly after the galleons went down.

But treasure hunters remembered another wreck from the 1733 fleet, which was found in 1968. A diver named Thomas Gurr discovered the wreck of the galleon *San Jose* off Alligator Reef in the Keys, hunting, as it turned out, without benefit of a permit. Gurr and his associates removed about $150,000 worth of artifacts, coins and jewelry from the wreck before the state caught up with them. Charging him with violation of the Antiquities Act of 1965, the state took him to court.

The court found against Gurr in the *San Jose* affair. But Florida agreed to let the diver continue to "mine" his wreck, after Gurr agreed to hand over the state's requisite 25 per cent of all profits. Florida also assigned to Gurr exclusive rights to the Alligator Reef site, and Gurr believed he was on the track of even bigger game than the *San Jose*.

Thomas Gurr's greatest enthusiasm was reserved for the fabled wreck of the Spanish galleon *Nuestra Señora de Atocha*, which with her sister ship, the *Margarita*, formed part of an 18-ship convoy that left Havana September 5th, 1622, bound for Spain with gold and silver plundered from the Indians of Central and South America. A hurricane struck the fleet on the 6th of September, and nine of the ships went down, 550 passengers and sailors being lost. According to ships' manifests on record in the Spanish National Archives, the *Atocha*, numbered among the nine victims of the storm, was carrying 27 tons of silver and several tons of gold when she sank. The *Margarita*, also lost, bore about half that amount.

"The *Atocha* is the single richest ship ever lost," Gurr said in an interview given to Jon Nordheimer of *The New York Times*, at the same time that Carl Claussen was playing down the whole idea of treasure salvage in Florida waters (September, 1971). "The lowest figure (associated with her) is $2 million, but after looking at the documents in the archives in Spain, which detail her cargo, everyone knows there had to be from $15 million to $75 million in gold aboard her when she went down.

"There's so much that if you find her you don't bother to count it, man, you just go to the bank and stop worrying.

"She's going to be found, this year or the next. The technology is just getting too good, and she can't escape any longer.

"If I should go out tomorrow and stumble across the *Atocha* I'd be the most confused person in the world. I'd . . . I'd have to hire people to spend the money for me."

Florida marine archaeologist Carl Claussen prepares to open an ancient chest from the galleon *San Fernando*. It proved to be full of sailmakers' needles made of steel.

THE ATOCHA CASE

Various dates, September 27, 1969-October 28, 1978

But Thomas Gurr never got to hire his money-spenders. He continued to work the *San Jose* for more than two years, his relations with the State of Florida growing steadily more acrimonious. Finally he accused the state of withholding from him his fair share of the treasure, and in a grandstanding display of temper, he invited CBS News cameras to record him, in 1974, as he threw what he said was treasure from the *San Jose* back into the ocean at the site of the wreck.

It made a colorful television news story, but W. A. Cockrell, then Florida State Marine Archaeologist, was not convinced. Cockrell spent four days diving on the *San Jose*, and was unable to find any of the treasure. He knew what to look for, because Gurr's salvage had already been catalogued by the State Antiquities Board. Cockrell then took a team of investigators to Gurr's house in Islamorada, but the flamboyant diver wasn't home. He and his family had moved to Merritt's Island, some 250 miles farther north.

Cockrell's team began diving in a canal behind Gurr's Islamorada house, and in a short time they brought up most of the treasure Gurr had "returned to the ocean" on the air. The pieces matched their catalogue descriptions, many of them retaining their original labels and tags. Despite Gurr's attempt to use the mass media to establish an alibi, the wily diver was rounded up, arrested and duly indicted for grand larceny in Key West in January, 1974. He never had a chance to go after the *Atocha*.

But the *Atocha* story was only beginning. In July, 1973, Melvin Fisher, president of Treasure Salvors, Inc., the company that had made treasure salvage history in the mid-1960s (NOTE: SEE *THE TREASURE COAST OF FLORIDA*), triumphantly ended a search which had cost an estimated $700,000, by locating the fabulous galleon, as well as the *Margarita*.

Aided by charts and records made by the eighteenth-century Spanish salvors, who had marked the hulks only to lose their marker buoys in a subsequent storm, Fisher had been working the Keys with an official permit from the State of Florida.

The former scuba diving instructor from California had been patiently looking for the *Atocha* for about ten years. Using metal detectors, divers from Treasure Salvors, Inc., already the most successful group of treasure hunters in history, swept the sandy bottom off the Keys, hoping to repeat the late Kip Wagner's coup. In addition to charts and maps, the divers used Spanish chronicle accounts of the 1622 hurricane as their guides.

In the summer of 1971 divers brought up a rusty Spanish anchor from a site west of Marquesas Island, one of the last of the Florida Keys, lying some thirty miles beyond Key West. The exact distance of the wreck site from Marquesas Island was to become a vital piece of information in the legal donnybrook which was to follow.

With the recovery of the anchor, the hunt was up for the elusive *Atocha*. Over the next few years Fisher and his divers recovered more than 3,000 silver coins, gold and silver religious objects manufactured in Mexico for the Spanish trade, muskets, cannon, ammunition and swords. In July of 1973 a 63-pound bar of silver was brought up by Fisher's 14-year-old son, a skilled diver. Its serial number linked it firmly with the lost *Atocha*, and the com-

pany knew it had found perhaps the richest treasure wreck in history.

The value of Fisher's recoveries from the Marquesas Island site was already set at some $750,000 at the time the silver bar was found. He estimated it would take several more years to complete the salvage of the *Atocha* and the *Margarita*, to say nothing of the other seven lost ships of the 1622 fleet. Estimates of the available treasure zoomed to $600 million, in light of the recovery of the ingot which established that the riches of the *Atocha* were more than a "conch's" yarn.

Present aboard Fisher's salvage ship, the *"North Wind"*, was Robert Williams, Florida's director of Archives, History and Records. The state, fearing that some of Key West's "conchs" would yield to the call of their pirate blood and start poaching on the wreck site, as had allegedly happened at the site of a similar find off Texas' Padre Island (NOTE: SEE *THE TEXAS TREASURE*), was keeping a careful eye on the salvage operation. According to Fisher's contract with Florida, the state would receive 25 per cent of the total value of the recovered treasure, and officials began taking Treasure Salvors' findings into custody to await examination and appraisal.

Relations between the treasure salvors and Williams' marine archaeologists were precarious. Certain Florida scientists levelled the old piracy accusation at Fisher and his associates, and the state upheld the archaeologists, stopping Fisher's claim to his 75 per cent pending investigations. The scene was set for a court fight as full of marches and counter-marches as a medieval battlefield.

In September, 1975, the United States Department of the Interior entered the fray. It filed suit against Fisher's company, disputing his claim to the wreck and setting up a test case to determine the jurisdiction of the Federal Government, acting under the Federal Antiquities Act, over all shipwreck sites brought up beyond the three-mile limit, but within 12 miles of United

States territory. The issue was already a familiar one to fishermen disputing with Russian trawlers over fishing rights off California and New England, but it was the first time U.S. jurisdiction had been tested in the field of treasure salvage. The fact that the Government's opponent was a U.S. citizen, rather than a foreign national poaching on American territory, raised an interesting point concerning the Federal Government's basic motives in the action.

Fisher fought back. In court he cited the $700,000 his company had spent in the salvage effort, and demonstrated that his salvage methods had preserved everything of artistic and archaeological value recovered from the site. The court found resoundingly in Fisher's favor, and issued a stinging reprimand to the Interior Department for its bald attempt to grab the treasure.

But Fisher's fight was not yet over. As he continued to bring up more treasure from the *Atocha* over the next two years, the State of Florida continued to attack his claim to it in the courts. In March, 1978, a Federal appeals court upheld the ruling of a lower court which had judged in favor of Treasure Salvors, Inc. and its companion firm, Armada Research Corporation, which Fisher had set up for marine archaeological studies to appease his scientific critics. By 1978 the cost of Fisher's search had risen to $2 million: "Tragedy had struck Mel Fisher personally in 1975, when the top-heavy *North Wind* had

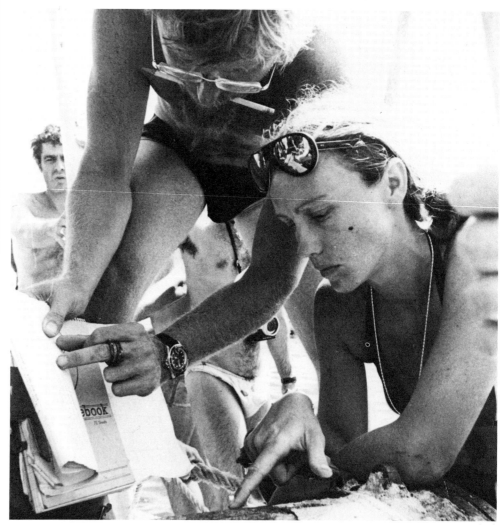

Angela Fisher, wife of Melvin Fisher's son Dirk, who was skipper of the *North Wind*, examines dates on a salvaged cannon shortly before tragedy struck the expedition.

capsized and turned turtle on July 20th, drowning his son Dirk and other divers who were trapped below decks. The appeals court took those facts into consideration when it awarded Fisher with $11 million worth of the treasure he had brought up.

The state still had Fisher's contract, however, which stipulated that it receive one quarter of his treasure, according to state law. But Fisher, emboldened by his victories, proceeded to challenge even that claim, asserting that the 1971 contract had been signed under duress, and was invalid because the wreck of the *Atocha* had been found outside Florida's territorial waters. The court of appeals agreed with him. Fisher, who believed that 95 per cent of the $400 million to $600 million treasure was still to be recovered, looked as if he might wind up keeping it all.

But Florida was not beaten yet. In April, 1978, the state won an emergency order staying the return of an additional $2.3 million to Treasure Salvors, Inc./Armada Research Corporation. Fisher countered with another appeal.

U.S. District Judge William O. Mehrtens, in a series of rulings in August and September, upheld the Fisher appeal. He discounted both the Florida and the Federal Governments' arguments of "sovereign prerogative," on the grounds that the site of the *Atocha* wreck was unequivocally in international waters.

Matters stood there as of October, 1978. But Fisher understandably feared a further appeal on Florida's part, and it is likely that the battle over the treasure of the *Atocha* and the *Margarita* will continue. The case is of obvious

Overleaf:
This crushed gold cup, part of the *Atocha's* precious cargo, shows the exquisite engraving characteristic of Spanish craftsmen of the seventeenth century.

Florida's Secretary of State Bruce Smathers is briefed on the *Atocha* treasure by State Marine Archaeologist W. A. Cockrell, during the controversy over Mel Fisher's rights to his find.

The top-heavy *North Wind* capsized and turned upside down on June 20th, 1975, drowning Melvin Fisher's son Dirk, Dirk's wife Angela, and another diver. The disaster made the grieving father even more determined to push the *Atocha* salvage through.

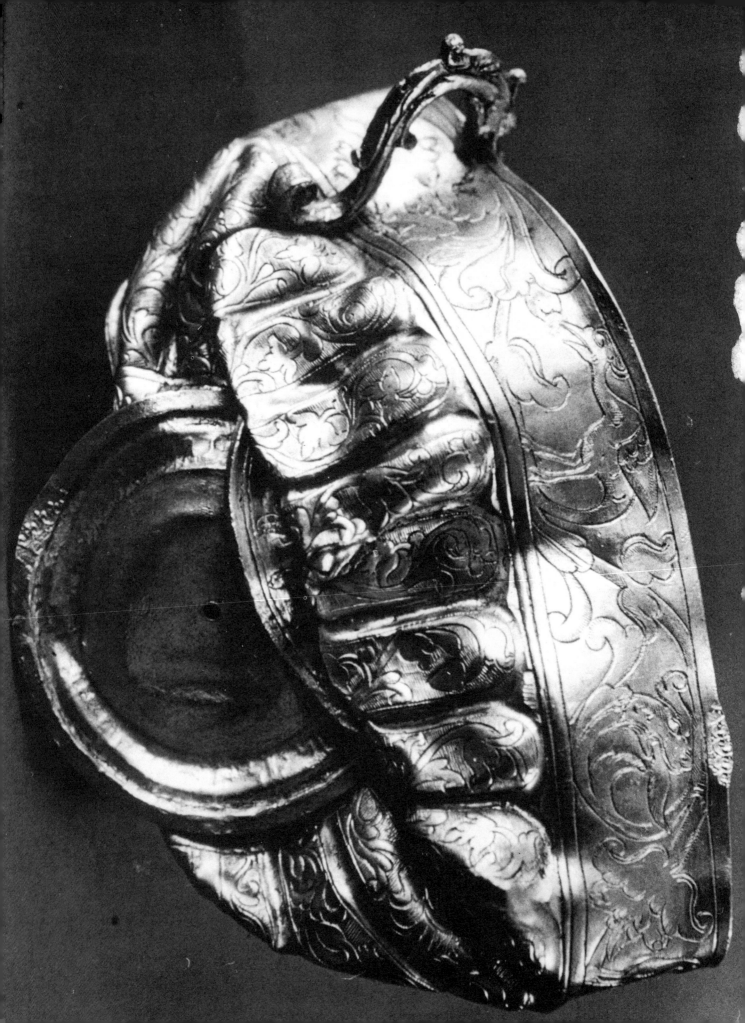

Before restoration, this fine silver pitcher, recovered by diver John Lewis of the Fisher group, could easily be mistaken on the ocean bottom for a chunk of coral growth.

importance to the future of professional treasure hunting, and to that of the salvage industry in general. The United States Government at present does not maintain the distinction established by the British Government between "treasure" and "treasure trove," the former consisting of material lost at sea by its owners due to maritime accident or act of war, and the latter involving stolen goods, as in the case of pirate hoards. "Treasure," by the British rule of thumb, is the property of its finder, whereas "treasure trove" is subject to the claim of the nation, state or individual estate which can establish itself as the original owner of the find.

The *Atocha* case was a step along the way to the establishment of a similarly clear-cut policy for American salvors. But in the meantime modern salvage teams find themselves in a quandary. Even if their expensive and dangerous work finally yields a treasure ship, there is no guarantee that the state in whose waters they are fishing will not step in and confiscate their finds. With the rise of a politically significant faction of marine archaeologists and historians concerned with the preservation of any and all antiquities, including pieces of eight, raised from American waters, it is possible that Fisher's salvage of the *Atocha* may be the swan–song of the game of treasure hunting in its purest, greediest form. Future expeditions after Spanish doubloons will no doubt be composed of scientists financed by foundations and the Federal Government, who will pay as much attention to an iron breechplate as to a *reale de oro*. The change is intellectually and culturally beneficial, to be sure. But with the passage of the plain gold-hunters another layer of romance will be sliced from an already hero-starved world.

But treasure buffs can take heart from the fact that official decisions rarely affect human nature. Whatever the outcome of the *Atocha* case turns out to be, archaeology will never entirely replace treasure hunting in human affections. As the Gurr case proves, the gold bug is irresistible, and if future salvors cannot recover golden hoards legally, they will blithely do so by other means.

Marine archaeologists commenting on the *Atocha* case may have spoken with more passion than justification in equating treasure salvors with pirates. But the divers of the Keys, and indeed all seekers after Eldorado, do share something in common with the corsairs and buccaneers of old. Given a choice between a prize bearing gold, silver and precious gems, and one with a cargo of equal value made up of more mundane materials, no self-respecting pirate would have hesitated for a moment. He'd have gone for the gold, of course. Similarly, although routine salvage work in the world's waters annually brings up cargoes whose accumulated worth far exceeds that of the *Atocha* and similar treasure ships, the finds are seldom reported except in the papers of maritime insurance concerns, underwriters' house organs and reports to investors. Fortunes are made and lost in the salvage business, but unless the cargoes involved attract a rumor of gold, the mass of men are uninterested in the hard, unglamorous industry. It is no accident that a negligible teen-aged king of Egypt, whose reign was distinguished only by its lack of historically interesting events, has become a household word. Tutankhamun was literally buried in gold and gems, and it is this connection which has se-

cured him immortality in human memory.

Similarly, it is no accident that the only marine salvage efforts which caught the popular imagination were those with a whiff of Eldorado to them. Gold, silver and gems possess a magical value far in excess of their market price at any given time. As hidden treasure, they inspire an avidity in us all which cannot be explained by the simple facts of their rarity and beauty. Treasure cannot be evaluated merely in marketplace dollars and cents. It is an object of faith and a source of glamor (a word which originally meant a magical spell) which speaks to the oldest stratum of the human unconscious, where racial memory muses over a time when human beings first fixed upon gold as the ultimate measure of material value. Melvin Fisher's wet-suited divers with their tanks and masks and the rest of their modern baggage, would have been at home aboard the *Argos*, when Jason set sail at the dawn of human dreaming in quest of a fleece of gold.

THE
CONCEPCION:
A TREASURE
DREAM COME
TRUE
Introduction

25

X marks the spot where Burt B. Webber, Jr. fulfilled a lifetime's dream and years of research and hard undersea work by finding the fabled galleon *Concepcion*.

Various dates, December 26, 1978-January 15, 1979

BURT WEBBER's DREAM

Facing Page: Henry Taylor, map and coin expert, with coins from sunken *Concepcion*, on treasure hunters' ship.

As Melvin Fisher continued to fight for his treasure in Florida (SEE *THE CONTROVERSY OF THE KEYS*), another salvor suddenly surfaced with news of a discovery off the Dominican Republic which may end by topping the value of the Fisher find.

Some 65 miles northeast of Cape Francis Viejo, Dominican Republic, lies the Silver Bank, a necklace of coral atolls with a long and grim reputation as a ships' graveyard. A fleet of sixteen Spanish treasure galleons, accompanied by two warships to protect them from pirates and English privateers, was carrying raw gold, silver, plate and coins when it foundered on the Silver Bank in a 1632 hurricane. Or so said Captain John D. Craig, a deepsea photographer and adventurer who mounted a treasure hunt for the loot in 1938, under the auspices of Bowdoin University. The 1938 team located two sunken galleons with the aid of aerial reconnaissance and underwater motion picture cameras, but the technology of the time was not up to the job of cutting through the coral which had encrusted the wrecks 75 feet below the surface.

However, the Craig expedition confirmed the Silver Bank's reputation as a treasure field. A more famous Spanish wreck had long been associated with the place. The *Nuestra Señora de la Limpia y Pura Concepcion*, flagship of the Spanish New World fleet, accompanied by several other vessels, was on a routine voyage home in 1641. She carried most of the gold and silver crown revenues extracted by the Spanish from Mexico from 1639 to 1641. Encountering a hurricane in the Bahama Channel, the *Concepion* was badly damaged and tried to run south for a safe harbor at Puerto Rico. But the coral shoals of Silver Bank intervened, and the ship went down.

The captain and most of the crew survived to tell the tale, and in 1687 it inspired an American colonial named William Phips to mount a salvage attempt. But the energetic coral had already managed to seal off large areas of the treasure wreck in the 46 years since the disaster, and Phips maintained there was much more silver to be found. Knighted for his 1687 haul, Phips was later appointed royal governor of Massachussetts. He tried to raise more *Concepcion* treasure in 1688 (coincidentally the death-date of Sir Henry Morgan, who likewise parlayed a treasure into a governorship; see THE NOBLE BUCCANEER), but was unsuccessful.

The *Concepcion* passed into legend and remained there for 290 years, until a marine historian, Goin E. Haskins, turned up the logbook of Sir William Phips' ship *Henry*.

Meanwhile an obscure Pennsylvanian named Burt B. Webber, Jr., a dyed-in-the-wool romantic and treasure buff who had been involved in one unlikely underwater scheme after another since his teenaged years, was on the verge of abandoning the fantasies of sunken galleons which had sustained him through a succession of lean years. He had read about the *Concepcion* at the age of sixteen, at a time when he was learning to use scuba equipment by diving for abandoned slot machines in water-filled quarries near his native town, Annville. His lust for the deep led him to Florida, where he took a div-

ing course and met Art McKee, one of that state's pioneer salvage experts. McKee broke Webber in on an eighteenth century wreck south of Jamaica, and Webber was hooked for good on treasure diving.

For seventeen years he divided his time between routine subsistence jobs in Pennsylvania and treasure voyages in the Caribbean. His first systematic hunt was for the *Nuestra Señora de Atocha* , a galleon wrecked in 1622. But he looked in the wrong place, misinterpreting his documents, and Mel Fisher beat him to it in 1971 (SEE *THE CONTROVERSY OF THE KEYS*). A family man with four children, Webber was caught in an economic bind between his dreams of sunken gold and the realities of earning a living until his sunken ship came in. Working in a brickyard in Pennsylvania and supplementing his income by selling encyclopedias, he continued to hanker after Spanish treasure, to the occasional amusement of his neighbors. He decided to stake everything on a last, systematic effort to make his dream turn real.

He found an interested investment broker in Chicago who helped him round up backers, and he founded a salvage company called Seaquest International, Inc., engaging an expert on documents of the Spanish Imperial period to continue his research, which now centered about the legendary *Concepcion*.

In 1977 Webber acquired a 65-foot salvage ship, with a crew of nine. He contacted the Dominican Government and arranged to split with it any treasure raised from the *Concepcion*. The gold-struck teenaged "frogman" who had dreamed of stumbling across piles of doubloons was now a serious salvage expert tracking his wreck with the aid of painstaking research and state-of-the-art underwater equipment. Through 1977 he surveyed the 42-mile-long shoals of Silver Bank, dropping buoys to mark off the most promising search quadrants.

Webber got his first break when he contacted Goin Haskins and found out about the Phips logbook, in the spring of 1978. The old salvor's notations narrowed the search area considerably, and Webber got a larger ship and crew in November, returning to Silver Bank. His second break, in the form of a $17,000 hand-held cesium magnometer, was as modern as the logbook was ancient. It operated by signalling anomalies, strong variations in the magnetic field of the ocean floor usually associated with large deposits of metal, to its operator by means of colored lights on a console and vibrations in a head-set connected to the operator's mastoids.

Although he had already plunged $350,000 into his hunt in vain, Webber remained confident that he was getting close to the *Concepcion*. On November 28th he took the magnometer on an underwater sweep around a grid sector he had already selected as a likely area. The device confirmed his suspicions, flashing its lights and pulsing its signals through his temples. Visual search revealed compact mounds of egg-shaped stones on the bottom of a coral canyon, and the divers recognized them as the water-rounded boulders from Spanish streams which were used by seventeenth century galleons as ballast. Finally, Webber and his team went down with Venturi suction hoses and began working delicately in the sand beneath the ballast stones. Suddenly, through the swirling grain, something small, weighty and

roughly rounded spun into a plastic "goody bag." It was a Spanish silver piece of eight. The hunt was over.

Back in Pennsylania Mrs. Webber, who for fifteen years had managed to carry on while her husband divided his time between home and the bottom of the sea, got the news of the end of the long search from her son.

"I was at the card club when my son called," she told Gregory Jaynes of *The New York Times*. "I thought something was wrong with the house. He said 'Daddy found the wreck.'"

Other professional underwater men, including Jacques Cousteau and Mel Fisher, who had searched in vain for the *Concepcion* themselves, began congratulating the exultant Webber. Although Fisher, perhaps acting out of a slight case of sour grapes, opined that the Phips expedition of 1687 had already recovered most of the *Concepcion's* silver treasure, Webber wasn't worried. His salvage had already yielded priceless artifacts of lasting interest to marine archaeologists: pieces of eight dated 1638, 1639 and 1640, silver candelabra, and Chinese porcelain shipped into Acapulco by the Manila fleet and trekked overland to Vera Cruz for transshipment to Spain. These, checked against ancient Spanish records, firmly identified Webber's wreck as the *Concepcion*, and her treasure had been estimated at $40 million. If the estimate was true, there was plenty left.

Webber himself became instantly famous. He figured the complete salvage of the *Concepcion* would take six months—if book deals with publishers, meetings with producers of television documentaries and appearances on the "Today" show didn't take up too much of his time. He was riding the crest of the wave, having proven that the odds don't beat the treasure hunter all the time. For the manically energetic brickyard worker from Annville, the legendary dream of doubloons had become as solid as the treasure-crammed "goody bags" he and his team are still raising on the Silver Bank.

The magnometer Webber used to locate the treasure of the *Concepcion* is a collateral, if not a lineal descendant of the "Clayton Metalphone," the Tom Swiftian metal detector that cantankerously failed to find the lost loot of Lima in the 1930s (SEE *TREASURE ISLAND*). Simon Lake's pocket submarine, the *Explorer* (SEE *RAISE THE LUSITANIA*), was the ancestor of modern deep-diving research vessels which are currently searching the ocean floor for petroleum and mineral deposits, or posing prettily for the cameras of Jacques Cousteau. Though Lake's tube to the bottom of the sea was a bit wild-eyed, his dream of establishing a safe environment at extreme depths where divers can work in comfort without cumbersome diving suits has been realized in the SEALAB experiments on the continental shelves. Research divers, "aquanauts" in the jargon of the SEALAB program, have been filmed and taped, quacking like ducks owing to the effect of the helium in their breathing mixture upon their vocal cords, entering the sea from their comfortable laboratory-homes wearing little more than breathing gear and insulated wet-suits.

Various dates, 1920s-present
FUTURE SALVAGE

The rigid diving-suits of the *Artiglio* crew (SEE *THE SALVAGE OF THE EGYPT*), with their mechanical manipulator-arms, anticipated current mini-submarines developed by General Dynamics, Lockheed and Westinghouse, among others, which combine the deep-diving capabilities of the bathyscaphe with the mobility of conventional submarines, and are further equipped with robotic arms and hands capable of surpassing the clumsy gloves of human divers in delicacy of manipulation and strength.

The "diving pollywog" invented by Hans Phillips in Germany in the 1920s, with its manipulator-pincers, electric power and 10,000 foot depth capacity, never got off the drawing board at the time. But 50 years later a version of North American Rockwell's "Beaver Mark IV" manned submersible, of virtually identical shape, similarly powered and similarly equipped with articulated remote-control arms, was in routine field use by a French salvor, André Galerne, president of International Underwater Contractors, Inc. Materials and engineering had been improved, making the German's dream a reality. But the concept was the same, and it was still based on the lure of sunken treasure.

Craft such as the Beaver Mark IV, the flying-saucerlike Westinghouse Deepstar-4000 and the Lockheed Turtle, and General Dynamics' AUTEC and ALVIN research submersibles, have been developed for uses as various as oceanographic and marine biological research, pioneering work in the establishment of undersea habitats for humans, and investigation of the mineral and energy resources of the ocean and its floor. But the sunken treasure motive which inspired their crude originals back in the 1920s has never entirely disappeared.

Of the countless billions of dollars worth of lost cargoes, ranging from the bewitching drowned bullion of the Spanish through the more prosaic but equally valuable holds-full of ores, worked metals, hardwoods, valuable chemicals and other material lost in more recent times, only a relatively small proportion has been raised. Most of the unsalvaged treasure lies at depths beyond the capabilities of Mel Fisher's and Burt Webber's wet-suited divers, in the abysses below the continental shelves. But the new breed of deep-diving submersibles are at home in such depths, and as underwater technology continues to improve, it is possible that hulks such as the *Lusitania* may give up their secrets (if any) after all.

For the moment the high-technology research submersibles remain too expensive for the average treasure hunter. Developed hand-in-glove with space technology, they are still, like spacecraft, mostly available only to nations, or to multi-national corporations with nation-sized research and development budgets. But the cost-accountancy problems of the space frontier are not shared by the world of the ocean depths. The distances involved in oceanic exploration are minor compared with those of space. Ocean water, even at immense pressure, is not as implacably hostile to human beings as hard vacuum. Support organizations, questions of fuel and guidance systems, are correspondingly less problematic—and, ultimately, less expensive.

Already a retired Navy submarine commander named George Kittredge

German Hans Phillips' electrically powered "diving pollywog," shown in a 1932 sketch, may resemble a panel from the Buck Rogers comic strip of the period. But its design principles predicted the compact submersibles of current oceanographic research.

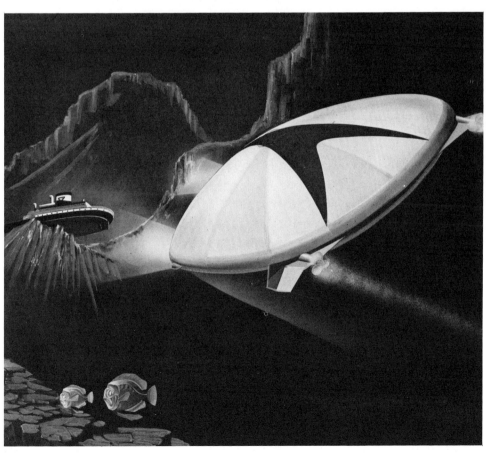

(top): In this artist's conception, the North American submersible *Beaver Mark III*, developed in the mid-1960s, aids installation of an undersea listening device at a depth of 1000 feet.

(bottom): Lockheed's *Turtle*, designed by Dr. Willy A. Fiedler, may one day see service in underwater mining and sea-farming operations on the continental shelf. This Frisbee of the deep has already been tested extensively in model form.

has come out with a line of shallow-water (250 foot limit) baby subs available to the marine explorer a $12,000, somewhat less than the price of a Cadillac Seville. And at the Maine Recreational Boat Show in 1968, an inventor displayed his Sea Kite, a diving bell equipped with moveable hydroplanes which gave it considerable maneuverability at the end of its cable. The Sea Kite cost no more than a one-design racing sailboat or a small cabin cruiser. The technology of the undersea is rapidly becoming available, if not to everyone, at least to the affluent—or fanatical—few who have always made up the majority of serious treasure salvors.

The greatest treasure the sea holds is its potential as a home for human beings, not an exploitable resource, according to the acquisitive and destructive atttitude which has governed most explorations of the depths to date, but the last (and largest) earthly frontier where people may start learning to live in harmony with their surroundings. The problems are still prodigious, but the rewards are potentially immense. And although the old lure of sunken gold will not be the primary motive impelling us to return to our primordial home, it should not be forgotten that treasure hunters initiated the technology which will make the return possible. If undersea life one day becomes as natural to future pioneers as was life on the nineteenth century's terrestrial frontier to the pioneers of the past, it is not wildly improbable to suggest that future prospectors riding mini-subs instead of burros will one day emulate their gold-seeking ancestors, setting out among the canyons and mountains of the deep in search of Eldorado.

Facing Page: Like a deep-space fighter out of *Star Wars*, Westinghouse's *Deepstar-4000* executes a graceful banking turn for the camera. But the depths here are oceanic, not interstellar. *Deepstar-4000* was already in active U.S. Navy research service ten years ago, operating out of the Navy's Electronics Laboratory in San Diego. Its descendants may form the shape of things to come, when man develops the capacity (which is not simply a matter of technology) to co-exist with the oceanic biosphere.

ACKNOWLEDGMENTS

The authors, editors, and publishers would like to thank the following for their kind permission to reproduce material which appears on the pages noted. Any omission of credit is inadvertent and will be corrected in future printings if notification is sent to the publisher.

Associated Press: 26 bottom, 28 and 29, 38, 39, 65, 73, 76, 85, 87 inset, 101, 211, 212, 213, 220, 221, 222, 225, 234, 241. British Travel Association: 54 and 55. Cunard Line: 205. Corpus Christi Chamber of Commerce: 49. Doubleday and Company: 61. Florida State News Bureau: 71. Galloway Photos: 11. John Grissim: 245. The Library of Congress: 15, 118 and 119, 165, 166, 178 top, 183, 199, 200 inset. J. B. Lippincott: 93. Lockheed Company: 249 bottom. Louisiana State Museum: 114. National Archives: 121, 162 top. National Portrait Gallery: 12, 56. North American Aviation: 249 top. Nova Scotia Information Service: 104. New York Public Library Picture Collection: 26 top, 31, 32, 41, 44, 45, 46, 47, 57, 59, 78, 79, 80, 91, 93, 94 and 95, 109, 110, 113, 116, 117, 125, 126 and 127, 128, 129, 130, 132 and 133, 134, 137, 169, 170, 207. The New York Times Photos: 16, 33, 34, 37, 50 and 51, 86 and 87, 141, 142, 160, 168, 171, 172, 173, 175, 178 bottom, 190, 200, 201, 204, 208, 209, 228, 229, 233, 240, 242, 246, 248. Jo Pinkard: 161. Rare Book Division, New York Public Library: 41. Resettlement Administration: 162 bottom. United Press International: 52, 63, 68, 74, 75, 88, 107, 179, 182, 193, 194 and 195, 206, 235, 238, 239. United States Signal Corps Photos: 145, 146 and 147, 148, 149, 153, 154, 155, 156, 157. Westinghouse: 252. Cover photo by Richard Salas. Maps by Jo Teodorescu; 24, 30, 84, and 244.

Special thanks to Susan Willmarth, Production Manager.